Songs of Innocence

Songs of Innocence

The Story of British Childhood

FRAN ABRAMS

Atlantic Books

First published in hardback in Great Britain in 2012 by Atlantic Books
an imprint of Atlantic Books Ltd.

10 9 8 7 6 5 4 3 2 1

A CIP catalogue record for this book is available from the British Library.

Hardback ISBN: 978-1-84354-896-6
E-book ISBN: 978-1-78239-040-4

Printed in Great Britain by the MPG Books Group

Atlantic Books
An imprint of Atlantic Books Ltd
Ormond House
26–27 Boswell Street
London
WC1N 3JZ

www.atlantic-books.co.uk

Contents

Introduction

Alice Foley was a bright, lively child, born into a fractious, political, overcrowded, poor household in Lancashire towards the end of the nineteenth century. Her parents' religious beliefs were not fervent, by any means, yet the little girl often found herself conflicted and concerned about the state of her soul. She could picture it, shaped like a shoulder of lamb and tucked neatly under her rib cage. But it was not, in her mind's eye, as glistening white as it should be: 'Mortal and venial sins showed up like dark and light pencil marks on its virgin surface. These unseemly blotches caused untold anxiety and I wondered curiously why this small fraction of my anatomy should be so troublesome.'[1]

In those days, original sin still loomed large in the life of a child like Alice, not least because the elementary school she attended was run by nuns. Nor was her state of mind helped by the fact that day after day she scratched her slate beneath a picture of the Sacred Heart: 'Worst of all, below the breast the robe was pulled aside, revealing a pierced heart . . . with blood streaming down. This picture fascinated even whilst it sickened me with its gory details. I yearned so intensely for happiness and security, yet here was this daily reminder of sin, cruelty and man's betrayal.'

Alice didn't know it at the time, of course, but her childish worries went to the core of a battle of ideas about childhood which by then had raged for centuries. What is a child? The arguments go back to the Enlightenment. Is a newborn infant, as Alice tended to feel, a marked and sinful thing, born out of man's depravity and in desperate need of redemption? Until 1693, when John Locke's treatise, *Some Thoughts Concerning Education*, was published, this notion of childhood had been the accepted wisdom. Yet Locke had turned this around: had Alice consulted him on the state of her soul, he would probably have told her to erase those pencil scratches from her mental vision. A child's soul was indeed pure white, he argued – at least on the day he was born. It was, Locke said, a *tabula rasa,* a blank slate upon which man would make his own marks – for good or for evil – as the child grew.

Locke's notion of childhood would be controversial even today. Influenced by Dutch child-rearing practices, which were more benign than those common in Britain at the time, he thought children should be treated as individuals – that is, that parents should attempt to influence through reasoned argument rather than by diktat: 'Slavish discipline makes a slavish temper.'

Jean-Jacques Rousseau, entering the debate seventy years later with *Émile, Ou de l'éducation,* scandalized Europe by positing the notion that a child was, in fact, neither inherently sinful nor a blank sheet on which man would write. Children were born pure, he said, but were inevitably corrupted as they grew: 'Everything is good coming from the Creator, everything degenerates in the hands of men.' The book was considered so blasphemous that it was actually burned on the streets of Paris.

As Alice Foley would learn 100 years later, the landscape of childhood would continue to be shaped and fought over by these two opposing schools of thought. Indeed, it would be easy to characterize the story of childhood throughout the ages as the story of the epic struggle between the desire to see children as inherently flawed, even dangerous, and the desire to shape them as perfected, purified versions of our own adult selves.

Childhood, of course, inspires strong emotions. And so society's deepest, most persistent myths and tropes, its most potent fears and longings, find themselves imprinted upon its surface. If the adult world fears change, and feels uncertain about the future, then it looks askance at its children. What horrors are in store? Can they be trusted to carry the baton safely through the next generation? Or are things – as one of those persistent tropes would constantly have us believe – somehow degenerating, falling apart?

'We are born with evil in us and cruelty is part of this,' wrote William Golding after the murder of two-year-old James Bulger in 1993.[2] 'If there is no one around to guide children then they go wrong . . . And when children go wrong they can often go wrong with a vengeance. There is such energy in a child, they are more powerful than any bomb.'

Yet, conversely, if the adult world feels ready to embrace hope, and optimism, then the young are venerated and cherished:

> Sweet babe in thy face
> Holy image I can trace.
> Sweet babe once like thee
> Thy maker lay and wept for me,

wrote William Blake in the early nineteenth century.

If the writing of the story of childhood were left to the philosophers and the poets, it might look like this. It might chart the battleground between these two children: the child of Blake, innocent, vulnerable, in constant need of protection and emotional nourishment; and the child of Golding, inherently wicked and in need of adult help to drive Satan from its blemished soul. Indeed, in many respects, this book will `set out to chart the sallies and the retreats in this particular war during the twentieth century. So fundamental is this moral debate to the way in which the adult world has viewed the child through the ages that it would be impossible for an account of childhood not to touch on it in some way, even if only in a peripheral, implicit manner.

So, where did the twentieth century take the child? Did the growing notion of the child as an individual, with individual rights, bring widespread joy? Or did the loss of the old certainty – that parents were in control; that so long as they did their job adequately all would be well – simply bring with it added anxiety, added grief? Did children's gradual journey from the labour market into education empower them, or did it lead them into narrower, more restricted lives? Did girls, still destined, as ever, at the end of the nineteenth century for lives of childbearing and subservience, use their new freedoms to real advantage, or did they still struggle to throw off that yoke?

The story of childhood during the twentieth century is a story that could be sliced and told in so many different ways. It could be a story of steady – or even unsteady – progress for the child: better housing, better health services, a better understanding of diet. While the social evils identified by Joseph Rowntree in 1904 – poverty, intemperance, 'impurity' and drugs, to name a few – would certainly continue to impact on the child, the absolute poverty of the Victorian inner city, with its child workers and street urchins, its relentless diet of tea and bread, and its life-shatteringly high death rate, would become a thing of the past. The twentieth century, of course, was the century in which infant mortality dropped from around 140 early deaths per 1,000 births to around six per 1,000. And so, seen from the viewpoint of the social reformer, the century could be read as a good one.

And as the child moved, over the course of a century and more, from the workplace into the schoolroom, as families grew smaller and as children's chances of survival grew greater, the child's place in society would undergo a slow, inexorable and largely positive change. This role, of course, was one that always had contradiction and paradox at its heart: a strange mix of sentimentality and fear, of love and irritation. Perhaps the adult world was never quite sure whether to cleave its children to its breast or simply, for the most part, to ignore them. At the height of the Edwardian era – a time during which children were idolized and idealized in works such as J. M. Barrie's *Peter Pan* – Emmeline Pankhurst set sail for an American lecture tour while her son lay critically ill. She returned just before he died – and days later she was off again to a public meeting in Bradford: 'If you can arrange it I would be grateful if Bradford friends would just behave to me as if no great sorrow had come just now,' she wrote to the organizer. 'Although I am very grateful for the sympathy, I want to get through my work.' Why? Was she so broken by the death that she could not bear to speak of it? Or so driven by her adult concerns that she could not quite find the right way to handle it and them at the same time? The paradox would remain strong as the twentieth century wore on, with the adult world unsure whether to speak of the child as vulnerable, fragile, in need of protection; or dangerous, out-of-control, in need of discipline. Yet as the child's economic position in the family changed – for most children worked and contributed to the family purse in some way in Victorian times – other things surely were bound to change too. Adults would begin to befriend their children, to listen to them, to 'respect' them and to accord them 'rights'. In short, as children's value as economic assets declined, their value as emotional assets would begin to grow. 'We teach with emotional intelligence, in that we are role models and our interactions are central to our ethos of empathy, motivation and praise,' ran the blurb for a private girls' school on the south coast.[3] A Children's Commissioner for England would be charged with the responsibility of talking to the nation's children: 'We will use our powers and independence to ensure that the views of children and young people are routinely asked for, listened to, and acted upon,' its website remarked.[4]

Indeed, the twentieth century was the century in which the child took on its own identity; the century in which childhood became not just a prelude to adulthood, but a crucial, formative period during which one wrong parental move could be catastrophic. The twentieth century began with Freudian insights into the psyche of the child and into the importance of childhood experience for the formation of character; it continued with a growing awareness in schools and elsewhere of the child as an individual, and it ended with the 'rights' of the child as a citizen and as a social participant enshrined in international treaty under the United Convention on the Rights of the Child.

The family, certainly, ceded power into the hands of the state in a major way during the century. Governments took on new responsibility after new responsibility with regard to children and childhood. This was the century in which the state would take a role in every aspect of children's education and health; in which it would regulate their work and demand to know whether their play leaders were suitable or not. This was the century in which the state would extend its fingers ever further inside family homes; and the century in which the state would decide, increasingly often, to remove children from those homes to places it believed to be safer.

And yet despite this increasing regulation the story of the child in the twentieth century has often been read as the story of a terrifying downhill slide, a descent from Victorian familial decency and rigour to a dystopian, morally lax place in which the child has been left adrift on a sea of sins and dangers. Joseph Rowntree's social evils are among them, of course, but during the century they have been joined by a host of other unwelcome companions to childhood – sloth, obesity, anxiety, a sense of alienation.

There is, of course, a rich brew of myth and reality in all this, and it is virtually impossible to dig deep enough to expose the roots of the repetitive scare stories about childhood with which all of us keep constant company. During the century, some have been so persistent that it would seem they must be true – if it were not for the fact that every time they surface, the spinners of the tales hark back to a golden age, thirty or fifty years earlier, when no such evils existed. Popular culture has been destroying the child's intellect, for instance, since the time of the 'penny dreadful' novel and probably before. It was doing so when the cinema and the children's comic were invented in the early years of the twentieth century, and it was doing so when television made its way into the nation's living rooms after World War Two. It was doing so still when video gave children access to the 'nasty', and when computer games brought *Grand Theft Auto* into the home. Similarly, the youth gang has been haunting the streets of Britain's inner cities since the mid-nineteenth century, if not longer. From the Scuttlers and Hooligans of the 1890s to the Teddy Boys of the 1950s, from the Skinheads of the 1960s to the postcode gangs of the new millennium, the story has been the same: the offspring of the poor have gone bad; their antics are undermining the foundations of respectable society. What will become of us next?

And that, perhaps, is the nub of it. What, indeed, will become of us? Children are, always have been and always will be – to borrow a cliché – the future. And that fact brings with it the constant uplift of hope, along with the nagging dread of uncertainty. There is always, where children are concerned, both the intrigue and the glory of infinite possibility – what might these new lives bring to the world? Who might they become? – and yet also a concurrent fear of the unknown, a horrible sense that the new generation might fail and that all we have built might fall apart. The story of childhood can never be a simple tale, because it will always be beset by this contradiction.

A conventional question at the start of a work of modern history might be: 'How did we get to here, from there?' But the story of childhood over the past century – or indeed, over any century – does not lend itself to such simple formulae. Because we are never quite sure where 'there' was; still less where 'here' is. The story of childhood will always be the story of that central contradiction, that complex, discomforting mix of emotions. So, the questions here are different, and less simple: What have we made of our children in the past century? Who, on each step of our recent journey, has been the perfect child for our times? What do our ideals – from the sweet, innocent babe of Blake to the impish sprite of Barrie; from the solid manifestation of post-war family-building to the aspirational, over-educated, hothoused superchild of the twenty-first century – tell us about ourselves? What after all, was – and is – a child for? And what, then, *will* become of us all?

1   Victoria's Children

The Children's Charter

August 26, 1889 is not a date writ particularly large in the annals of British social history. Yet on that day an event took place which continues to have the most profound effect on the life of every child born in Britain today, as well as on countless others around the world. On that day the Prevention of Cruelty to, and Protection of, Children Act 1889 – popularly known as the Children's Charter – enshrined clearly in law for the first time the right of the state to pass through the front door of the family home and to intervene in the relationships of parents with their children.

In effect, it was an Act that recognized the child as an individual, with an existence not entirely dictated by the wishes – or whims – of his or her mother and father. Even today, this is one of the knottier terrains over which public policy has to travel repeatedly as the debate over the best way to bring up a child continues. And the Act started a process which has continued: the process by which the state gradually took over the private lives of British children, taking them to its breast as their ultimate protector.

The Children's Charter – an Act borne out of the Romantic view of the child, if ever there was one – had its roots in a series of events which had begun a quarter of a century earlier on the other side of the Atlantic. When Mary Ellen Wilson was born in Hell's Kitchen, New York, no one could have predicted that her childhood story would become one of the most notorious of its age, let alone that it would spur the launch of at least two major national charities, which still exist today, along with a raft of legislation.

In truth, the story of Mary Ellen's childhood was grimly familiar. She was born into poverty and her father, Thomas Wilson, died soon afterwards. Forced to work, her mother, Francis, boarded her out with a foster-mother – a common practice at the time. When her visits to her infant daughter – and also her payments – dwindled and stopped, the child was delivered into the care of the New York City Department of Charities. A family called the McCormacks agreed to take her in, but there was to be no stability in Mary Ellen's short childhood. Her new 'father', Thomas, soon died and his wife, Mary, married again. It was a chain of events – a series of broken homes, a child no one seemed to want – which could have featured in an abuse case a hundred years later – save for the fact that the homes were broken not by divorce or separation but by death. Indeed, there was even the suggestion that Mary Ellen was in fact the product of an affair between Francis Wilson and Thomas McCormack, and that this was the reason why he had approached the charities depart-ment offering to foster her. Small wonder, then, that with Thomas gone and with a new 'father', Francis Connolly, installed in the family home, Mary Ellen found she was no longer welcome.[1]

What happened next caught a mood of growing concern not just in America but across the world. A Methodist mission worker named Etta Angell Wheeler, alerted to Mary Ellen's plight by a neighbour, gained access to the Connolly apartment and discovered the child, now aged ten, filthy, dressed in threadbare clothing and covered in scars and bruises. Although the law forbade excessive chastise-ment of children, the authorities were reluctant to intervene. In desperation, Wheeler alerted the New York Society for the Prevention of Cruelty to Animals, which sent an inspector to investigate. The society then prepared a private action to have Mary Ellen made a ward of court – and alerted the press to what it was doing. By all accounts a strikingly self-possessed child, Mary Ellen made quite an impression with her statement to the court:

> My father and mother are both dead. I don't know how old I am. I have no recollection of a time when I did not live with the Connollys … Mamma has been in the habit of whipping and beating me almost every day. She used to whip me with a twisted whip – a raw hide. The whip always left a black and blue mark on my body. I have now the black and blue marks on my head which were made by Mamma, and also a cut on the left side of my forehead which was made by a pair of scissors. She struck me with the scissors and cut me. I have no recollection of ever having been kissed by any one – I have never been kissed by Mamma. I have never been taken on my Mamma's lap and caressed or petted. I never dared to speak to anybody, because if I did I would get whipped … I do not know for what I was whipped – Mamma never said anything to me when she whipped me. I do not want to go back to live with Mamma, because she beats me so. I have no recollection ever being on the street in my life.[2]

A photograph of Mary Ellen, barefoot in a thin dress and with the marks on her legs clearly showing, helped to ram home the message. The word went out that in New York animals were entitled to more protection than children. Mary Ellen did indeed become a ward of court and her remaining childhood was overseen by her rescuer, Etta Angell Wheeler. The case led to the founding of the New York Society for the Prevention of Cruelty to Children, and to the setting up of similar societies in Britain – first in Liverpool, then in London – and to the National Society for the Prevention of Cruelty to Children, the NSPCC.[3] It also led, through the efforts of campaigners in England, to the passing of the Children's Charter.

The Romantics knew how to manage public opinion. They had large parts of the literary world on their side, of course – Charles Dickens had already done much to promote the notion of the child's vulnerability through characters such as the sickly but perky Tiny Tim in *A Christmas Carol*, and the orphaned Oliver Twist. And Benjamin Waugh, the founder of first the London and then the national society, rarely missed an opportunity to pick up on cruelty cases which were reported in the British newspapers at the time.[4]

And while charities fought shy of relieving parents of their responsibilities, so the state often hung back in circumstances where, in later years, it would certainly not have hesitated to intervene. A case from October 1888, which cropped up as debate raged over the charter, illustrates the point. On the 3rd of that month, *The Times* reported a particularly gruelling instance from the impoverished East End in which a representative of the Board of Guardians had found a two-year-old named Daniel Tobin filthy and starving in a pitifully cold family home. One of five children of John Tobin, a 'hard-working man' who 'generally got drunk on Saturdays', he had been left alone while both parents hit the bottle. Neighbours testified that they had often been forced to throw food through a window to the Tobins' desperate children. The magistrate, a Mr Saunders, had commented that 'the prisoners no doubt neglected their children, but he could not see his way to convict them'. A few days later, the paper ran a letter from Waugh. His society had recently come across no fewer than forty-eight cases of child starvation, he said, but the law which said parents must properly nurture their children covered only forty-two of them. The relevant clause under the poor laws had never been intended to protect the individual rights of children, he said, merely to ensure they did not become an unnecessary burden on the authorities. Too often the courts were forced to bow down before the rights of parents to raise their own children as they saw fit. Echoing the debate which had recently taken place in New York, Waugh wrote: 'Had it been John Tobin's dog which was in question, no difficulty would have arisen, for the law is clear as to starving dogs. It was only his child. Our Bill proposes to raise a child to the rank of a dog, which, to our shame be it spoken, is still needed to put down child starvation.'

It is hard to overstate the significance of the new Act, or its controversial nature. Even Lord Shaftesbury, the great Victorian social reformer who had pushed through the Factory Acts which restricted children's working hours, and who had been a great promoter of working-class education, was against changing the law to protect children from their parents' excesses. 'The evils you state are enormous and indisputable, but they are of so private, internal and domestic a nature as to be beyond the reach of legislation,' he wrote to a pro-charter campaigner.

And while the NSPCC celebrated its victory and pushed on for yet more support in its crusade to stamp out child cruelty, a variety of late-Victorian child-abusing 'beasts' still loomed large in the public mind. The perceived dangers seemed to be proliferating, rather than receding. Little more than a year after the Charter became law, Waugh was again writing to *The Times* about the work of his charity, which had, he said, helped no fewer than 3,000 children in five years. 'Some forms of the cruelties, from their immorality and the kind of physical miseries they involve, cannot be named,' he wrote. 'In many cases brothers and sisters had already died of similar treatment. The children have been children of drunkards, tramp children, stolen children, acrobats and performing children, step-children, little hawkers and friendless apprentices, children in baby farms.'

The cases that Waugh would not name were, of course, sexual abuse cases – and while there was some movement on child cruelty, in this arena the state continued to avoid intervention wherever possible. One particular court case, reported a few years earlier in 1885, had sparked a national scandal. The case concerned a Mrs Jeffries, who was alleged to have been running a child sex-trafficking operation involving royalty and senior politicians. King Leopold of the Belgians was said to be her most prestigious client, purchasing as many as 100 under-age English virgins each year. Mrs Jeffries pleaded guilty and was abruptly fined and released before the evidence could be presented. But the case sparked the interest both of the social reformer Josephine Butler and of the editor of the *Pall Mall Gazette*, W. T. Stead. Enraged, also, that MPs had just 'talked out' a Bill to raise the age of consent from twelve to fifteen, the two set out together to expose the extent of child prostitution in London.

The result was one of the most famous – or possibly infamous – pieces of investigative journalism in the Victorian era. Posing as wealthy clients, they engaged a team of investigators – including Josephine herself – to visit brothels, where they spent almost £100 purchasing children. The going rate for a young virgin was between £10 and £20.[5] The *Gazette* titled its series 'The Maiden Tribute of Modern Babylon', and in it Stead recounted how he had personally bought the services of no fewer than seven girls between the ages of fourteen and eighteen, four of whom had doctors' certificates to say they were virgins. Much of the detail was made up – one article described the rape of a thirteen-year-old, 'Lily', by a stranger who entered her room while she was drugged. In fact the stranger was Stead himself – and a colleague of Butler's later took her to a doctor to check that Stead had not actually molested her. Nonetheless the public reaction was one of outrage, and queues jostled to buy copies of the *Gazette* each day, hoping Stead would carry out his threat to name the guilty men. The result was impressive and swift, on two counts. First, a Criminal Law Amendment Act was passed, raising the age of consent to sixteen. Second, Stead and three of his accomplices were charged – the first under the very same Act – with unlawful abduction of 'Lily'.

Yet while the public appetite for stories of child prostitution was great, and while there was a growing clamour for retribution against those parents who neglected or beat their children, there was still little or no acceptance of the idea that parents might actually sexually abuse their own children. A recent study on the sexual abuse of children between 1870 and 1914[6] looked at hundreds of cases, but found that in just 4 per cent were the perpetrators' family members. This was partly because until the Children's Charter became law, wives were prevented from giving evidence against their husbands. In one case, in Lambeth in 1880, a woman had brought her friends and neighbours into the house so that they could witness her husband abusing their seven-year-old daughter. Incest was known about and was widely condemned – the perpetrator often becoming a 'marked man' in his neighbourhood, the author concluded. Yet in this area, as in many others, the family still remained largely a private domain, outside the purlieu of the state.

Beyond the front door

The public perception of family life in the poorer homes of late-Victorian times was riddled with contradictions. On the one hand, there was a growing awareness of the poverty and the squalor that so many children experienced – along with an uneasy feeling that there was some uncharted sea of depravity on which few had yet dared even to set sail. On the other, there was the belief that the family was the legitimate, the most wholesome and the most righteous social unit – a contradiction which persists, of course, in the modern day. And even the most chaotic and disrupted homes often had a curious veneer of respectability about them. Alice Foley, growing up in a poor home in Bolton, had a particular job to do every Friday morning: to take the family aspidistra carefully from its place of honour on top of the sewing machine. 'The ritual was . . . first to place the giant plant pot in water in the kitchen sink. Even today I can hear the eager bubbling and gurgling of those thirsty roots sucking in the refreshing draught. Then the single leaves were carefully sponged with a wash-leather, cracked portions and faded tips nipped off to make room for younger shoots, and finally polished off with a spot of milk.'

In Alice's case, the lacquer was a very thin one. In her biography, she described 'an era of privy middens . . . each summer brought an appalling plague of house-flies. Most houses had long, sticky papers hanging from gas-brackets; these trapped unwary insects who writhed until they expired. One of our street visitors was the "fly catcher man" who wore a tall hat exhibiting a broad, sticky band, black with captive flies, and called out vigorously: "Catch'em, catch'em alive-oh."' [7]

Childhood in this era was a great deal more red in tooth and claw – perhaps more similar to adult life – than the popular imagination would have had it. Alice described her family life as often impoverished, sometimes violent, but overwhelmingly tainted by a humdrum, everyday neglect. Her mother was kindly but undemonstrative, she said; her father, a firebrand and a drinker who put his Irish political obsessions before his children – even storing ammunition in the bedroom he shared with his sons.

'He worked in fits and starts, punctuated by bouts of heavy drinking and gambling. During these years mother plodded gamely on, battling with a feckless husband whom she neither loved nor understood, and succouring her six children whom she never really wanted,' Alice explained.[8] 'Poignant memories remain of a particular afternoon with mother bent wearily over the dolly-tub with her small child at her feet in a fidgety and peevish mood. Suddenly, she said quite sternly: "Now if you're not a good girl, I shall run away with a black man" ... For days and weeks I moved around in terror and heaviness at the threat of desertion. If a coloured person came in sight I wondered dumbly if that was the man mother had in mind. Pathetically, I tried to find ways of pleasing mother in the hope that she would not leave us, and on quiet evenings by the fire when we played Ludo or Snakes and Ladders, I cheerfully manoeuvred to send my counter down a long snake so that mother's could reach "home" safely.'

Yet to the modern reader it is not her father's drinking, nor even her mother's offhand cruelty, that are thrown into the sharpest relief by her account: it is the Foleys' casually neglectful attitudes to the nurturing of their children that now strike the harshest note: 'At tea time our parents shared a savoury tit-bit from one plate, Father getting the lions share, for Mother doled out tiny morsels from her portion to the younger children. At supper time Father drank beer, Mother relished a piece of bread spread with slices of raw onion, and we youngsters went to bed on a "butty" and a drink of cold water.'

Time and again, the children of the Victorian era describe their relationships with their parents as more remote, perhaps more wary, than the children of later years would do. A typical family had more children, of course, and it was usual – particularly in poorer areas – for some of them to die without reaching adulthood. Parents simply could not – or at least did not – make the same emotional investment that they do today. 'No jubilation sounded on this occasion,' Alice wrote of her birth. 'Only the dull acceptance of another hungry mouth to feed.'

Nor was it only the impoverished working classes who took this more relaxed attitude to child-rearing. Morrice Man was born into a middle-class family from Kent – his father was a barrister in Burma and the family also lived for a time in France. He described being put on a ferry alone, aged nine, to travel to school in England. A random passenger was asked to keep an eye on him: 'Nobody spoke to me, so far as I remember; the aforesaid passenger forgot all about me. I never saw him (or her) again. It was a rough passage. I was homesick and very seasick. On reaching Newhaven I got ashore somehow – I had a through ticket to Lewes where I was to be met.'[9]

While Morrice described his family life – he was one of nine children – as warm and loving, and his mother as devoted, he spent much of his time with a nurse. From the age of nine, he was away at boarding school. Yet, despite the rather buttoned-up sensibilities of the era, the childhood he described was one into which the less respectable aspects of the adult world would quite often intrude. 'Uncle Bill ... taught me the Charge of the Light Brigade and often he would take me, when he lived at Hythe, to the White Hart, and stand me on the bar ... and make me recite to the assembled company,' he recalled.

But the great incident of his childhood, long remembered, occurred during an election while the family were living at Croydon. Morrice's father went out to support the Tory candidate: 'The excitement was terrific and the night when the result was declared we children were as a treat allowed to be present at the town hall. I shall never forget the scene that night, the raging crowds. Our house was put under police protection as some of the Liberal mob considered my father mainly responsible for their defeat. We boys knew this and went to bed armed to the teeth (we slept three in a room) with sticks and toy pistols ... The only incident that occurred that night was the temporary arrest of a great friend of father's who came to congratulate him in a state of some inebriation. We were allowed to speak our minds and father always enjoyed a joke.'

While the popular imagination, fired by the works of Dickens, saw the child as a vulnerable innocent, in need of protection from the vicissitudes of adult life, parents, it seemed, took a very different view.

Out on the streets

While most families seemed to accept a certain amount of rough-and-tumble in their own lives, such behaviour was a very different matter when it was happening elsewhere – particularly in the over-crowded alleys of Britain's industrial cities. While Morrice Man was revelling in high jinks on election night, there was growing concern about the levels of violence in other quarters.

In the first half of the nineteenth century, the abolition of stamp duties on newspapers had allowed the popular press to proliferate. And by the end of Victoria's reign, there was a plethora of publications eager to catch the mood of the times – not least, to tap into the age-old feeling that society was in a state of terminal decline. In the hot summer of 1898, the Hooligan burst on to the pages of the national press after an exceptionally rowdy August bank holiday weekend. In the following weeks and months, a fully-formed youth culture solidified in print form, wearing a uniform of bell-bottom trousers, peaked caps and neck scarves, heavily ornamented leather belts and a shaved tuft at the crown. The English fair play tradition of fighting with fists and not with feet, it was reported, was in eclipse. The issue played into the hands of those who believed there had been too much romanticism about children in recent years, and not enough time spent beating the devil out of the young.

Violent youth cultures had, in reality, been a fact of life for years in the industrial cities. In Manchester, the gangs were known as Scuttlers; in Birmingham existed the Peaky Blinders. The Chelsea

Boys and the Battersea Boys also cropped up regularly, indulging in street robberies, assaults on the police and pitched battles among themselves.

Reports of casual violence were widespread throughout the Victorian period, and it was considered quite normal to settle a dispute outside a public house with fists. But these newly discovered teenage gangs had their own distinctive styles, and a recognized hierarchy. Industrialization had brought huge numbers of people together in crowded conditions – and that led to children being on the streets together. Now the adult world began to fear the young were developing their own cultures, and that those cultures could be a threat to traditional orthodoxies.

A particularly harrowing case had taken place in Manchester in August 1890:[10] a gang of teenage Scuttlers from Harpurhey, in the north of the city, had taken on the Bengal Tigers from Ancoats. Having hunted down their prey, they took off their heavy-buckled belts and used them to beat a boy named John Connor to within inches of his life. Then they plunged their knives into his neck, shoulders and back. One of the Tigers was blinded by a blow to the right eye – he had already lost the left in an earlier fight – and three more received knife wounds. No one called the police, and they found out about the incident only from the staff at the infirmary in whichthe injured were treated. Two of the perpetrators were sentenced to five years' penal servitude.

The incident was not the first that summer, but it did lead to a growing public outcry. The recorder in the case, Henry West, called for a public debate on the introduction of flogging. A special magistrates' meeting was held, a resolution in favour of the cat-o'-nine-tails passed, and a deputation sent to the Home Secretary.

Alexander Devine, a court reporter for the *Manchester Guardian* and also a founder of the lads' club movement, had chronicled the various Scuttler gangs of Manchester, which were very territorial:

the Grey Mare Boys from Grey Mare Lane in the city's Bradford district, the Holland Street gang from Miles Platting, the Alum Street gang from Ancoats, the Little Forty from Hyde Road in Ardwick, the Buffalo Bill gang from the colliery district of Whit Lane in Salford – the list went on.

Scuttlers were very style conscious, and the belts which were their lethal weapons were also used as style statements, Devine wrote: 'These designs include figures of serpents, a heart pierced with an arrow ... Prince of Wales feathers, clogs, animals, stars, and often either the name of the wearer of the belt or that of some woman.' As well as a belt, a Scuttler would wear narrow-toed, brass-tipped clogs. The Ancoats Scuttlers wore bell-bottomed trousers measuring fourteen inches around the knee and twenty-one inches around the foot. The flaps of their coats were cut into little peaks and buttoned down, and they wore flashy silk scarves. Their hair was cut short at the back and sides, and they grew long fringes, plastered down over the left eye.

According to Devine, the gang phenomenon could be put down to a lack of parental control, poor discipline in schools, slum evenings spent in 'listless idleness' on the street, and 'penny dreadful' litera-ture, which told tales of highwaymen and brigands and which 'openly defied authority and revelled in bloodshed'.

This concern that melodramatic cheap reading material could be a cause of youth crime was a common one of the day. Samuel Smith, MP for Flintshire, told the House of Commons that he had made a study of its effects, reading for his research no fewer than forty penny papers with a circulation of more than a million each week.

'Our children feasted upon these stories, and all their moral ideas were confused and drugged by this education. Could it be wondered at that we had such a large proportion of our nation who were degraded and morally unfit for the duty of citizenship?' he asked.[11] 'The poorer classes between 12 and 16 or 17 years of age ... were laying the foundations of a wasted and ruined life. They were found by tens of thousands in gin palaces, in low music halls, and in the low theatres. They were getting the education of the streets, an education in every respect vicious and low, and that was the reason why this country, beyond any civilized country in Europe, had to contend with a degraded residuum of population which constituted a great national danger.'

There were girl gangs, too, although they tended to be ancillary to the boys' gangs, knitting coloured socks and collecting stones for the menfolk to throw. Nonetheless, in March 1893 the residents of Clopton Street in Hulme sent a petition to the Watch Committee of the city council, complaining of 'disorderly young women' who had supplied missiles from their aprons 'while lads and lasses alike had "bonneted" the terrified residents' – that is, they had knocked their hats off. In February 1890, a seventeen-year-old girl named Lizzie Gordon was accused by a John Green of an assault in Salford, in which she had allegedly threatened to knife him, 'Same as I have done Paddy Melling.' Two of Lizzie's companions were alleged to have taken off their clogs and assaulted Green with them. Several witnesses testified that Gordon was among a gang of girls who had been terrorizing the residents of Gun Street.

The London press took up the issue of youth violence with gusto, and the word 'hooligan' soon passed into common parlance. The *Daily Mail*, which first hit the streets in 1896, reported four years later[12] that 300 extra police were being drafted in to cope with the problem of gangs on the streets of the capital. 'Is the Hooligan a product of the School Board system?' the paper asked, quoting a School Board member who opined that extension classes for those who had left school at twelve or thirteen were to blame: 'Our evening continuation classes, which cost £100,000 a year, are a field for Hooligans. They are mixed classes of boys and girls, who in thousands of cases join for the novelty of the thing and degenerate into skylarkers ... There is something wrong in the system. We are producing young people in whom chivalry, gallantry and respect are non-existent.'

The following year, 1901, the President of the National Union of Teachers was firing up the debate at the union's annual conference: 'The Hooligan or street blackguard is not a sudden growth; he is the result of street education. The thoughtful student of modern life sees nothing sadder than the crowds of boys and girls in the streets late at night, exposed to many and serious dangers, acquiring evil habits, and generally laying the foundation of a life of idleness, vice, or crime. Even the little ones, who ought to be at home in the care of their parents, are found in the streets in charge of those scarcely older than themselves.'

Whether or not the education system was to blame, there seemed to be a growing sense that the state should do something about the problem. Yet the more liberal elements in the press, including many correspondents to *The Times* and a large number of MPs, still tended to see the problem of street children – 'Street Arabs', as they were known – in a different, perhaps more Dickensian, light.

'All over London girls and boys roamed the streets day after day, selling matches, flowers, newspapers,' the Chairman of the Bedford Quarter Sessions, W. Francis Higgins, wrote to *The Times* in 1893. 'And, though of school age, no one looked after them. There were thousands of them every day around the railway stations of London, and in the natural course of things they grew up to be thieves and prostitutes. Education was now free, but the Arab was the last and the least cared for, because he was difficult to teach, and the teachers could not get brilliant results out of him. It was time something was done for such neglected children.'

Indeed, there had long been concern that the children of the poor were not attending school, and were continuing to do menial work on the streets for whatever few pennies they could gather. These, of course, were often the same children who were accused of being violent gangsters, threatening passers-by. But in liberal middle-class folklore, they were quite different.

A Leeds MP, Robert Armitage, raised the issue in a parliamentary debate, describing the children not as villains but as victims – often, he felt, of their own parents' cupidity.[13] The Manchester School Board had investigated the backgrounds of a large number of these children, he said, and only one third of them were from the poorest families: 'That proved that two-thirds of the parents of these children were comparatively independent, and were, therefore, unnecessarily subjecting their children to this very great hardship ... Surrounded as they were by evil associations, they were acquiring habits which would, in all probability, bring them ultimately into the hands of the magistrate and the gaoler.'

Armitage may well have been right to blame the parents. A standard job handed out to children in poorer areas at the time was the fetching of beer from the local alehouse. Seebohm Rowntree, during the research for his famous study of poverty, which would be published in 1901,[14] asked his investigators to spend a Saturday watching a 'dingy-looking house situated in a narrow street in the heart of a slum district'. In seventeen hours, they saw 258 men, 179 women and 113 children enter the premises. Lunch and supper times were busy ones for the children, but the busiest time of all was between ten and eleven at night. Alice Foley, growing up in Bolton with a father who was often violent when drunk, dreaded the order to fetch a gill of beer from the White Hart down the street: 'I conjured up the odd idea that if I dawdled there and back, the one jug of ale might last Father until he staggered off to bed. On arriving home with a jug of flat beer, I was greeted with: "Where the hell have you been?" and a volley of oaths. Sometimes I dodged out of the back door, but more frequently mooned around sacrificially in the hope of coaxing Father to go to bed and so leave the family in peace.'

By the turn of the century, the poor little 'Street Arab' was indelibly imprinted on the public imagination, notably through the description of Tom, the chimney sweep in Charles Kingsley's *The Water Babies*. Indeed, the 'Street Arab tale' had become a popular literary genre, sparking numerous publications in the last half of the nineteenth century. Most had a Romantic edge, and ended with the protagonist being rescued by a wealthy benefactor. Typically, *Froggy's Little Brother*, by 'Brenda',[15] tells the tale of two little boys left to fend for themselves in a Shoreditch attic after their parents' deaths, and despite the efforts of the older, Froggy, his little brother, Benny, eventually dies. The story ends happily, when Froggy is helped by a philanthropic doctor. These tales leaned on an age-old theme – stretching back to Romulus and Remus – of lost children abandoned by the adult world and in desperate need of protection and salvation. In an age when infant mortality was still very high, particularly in crowded urban areas, the notion of the child as a delicate, Romantic figure remained an enticing one.

Into the schools

Perhaps it might be said that in this era – maybe in every era? – the voluntary sector tended to intervene to temper the violation and neglect of children perceived as innocent victims, while the state preferred to use its powers to stamp out evil which was perceived as innate. Certainly, the rise of universal schooling, ushered in by William Forster's 1870 Elementary Education Act, could be seen in that light.

The 'Ragged Schools' which had for some time had the task of educating the inner-city poor had done great service, the Earl of Shaftesbury had remarked during the House of Lords' debate on the Bill: 'The plan … is to catch a child as he flies rapidly by … the teachers rejoice to have the opportunity, during the short time, a few weeks, perhaps, the children are with them, of imparting to them some of the saving truths of the Gospel.' Such children could later be shipped to the colonies without the risk that they might then fall into 'evil courses', he explained.

The Act, which set up a system of school boards to ensure there was educational provision in all areas, was swiftly followed by another which made school compulsory for children aged between five and ten. Yet the desired effect was not instant. 'Opened school. Children backward, neglected, but seem to have fairly good capacities,' wrote one young schoolmaster, Atkinson Skinner, as he opened his doors for the first time at Huggate, in the East Riding of Yorkshire.[16] Daily, he was to record his fluctuating attendance figures with a sense of anxiety and an awareness that an inspector might call at any time. All 'board schools' taught the same subjects, by and large: the three Rs, along with drawing for boys and needlework for girls. Singing, recitation, English literature, geography, science, history and – for girls – domestic economy were all optional. Every morning the children would march into daily assembly to their own band and would salute the headmaster before singing a hymn, saying a prayer and repairing to their classroom for half an hour's Bible study.

'The greatest importance will be attached by the board to the moral and religious teaching and training,' ran the instructions of the York school board. 'In all departments the teachers are expected to bring up the children in habits of punctuality, of good manners and language, of cleanliness and neatness, and also to impress upon the children the importance of cheerful obedience to duty, of consideration and respect for others, and of honour and truthfulness in word and act. Teachers are expected to use the Bible for illustrations whereby to teach these duties, for sanctions by which what is taught may be practised and for instruction concerning the help given by God to lead a sober, righteous and godly life.'[17]

In the early 1890s, Morrice Man was sent to public school. By many accounts, Rugby in this period aimed to produce a class of colonial servants – yet it was also something more. Under Thomas Arnold, who had been its headmaster from 1828 until 1841, it had flourished. Immortalized in Thomas Hughes's *Tom Brown's Schooldays*, it became the model for what is today thought of as the typical public school. It typified the 'muscular Christianity' which was meant to help drive the British imperial expansion, but also to turn the sons of the new industrialist class into what Arnold described as 'gentleman scholars'.

'What shall I say of Rugby?' Man wrote later. 'The hardest-working, hardest-playing school in the world. It was pre-eminently the school to which the hard-headed businessmen of the Midlands sent their sons.' Man quoted from a book by Lord Elton about Rugby: 'The public schools had no difficulty in transferring to the new class of gentlemen (i.e. the commercial classes) the old soldiers' ideas of courage in service which the feudal aristocracy (i.e. Eton) had developed during the centuries in which they led their men into battle. "Loyalty, courage, endurance, discipline." The ideal was vindicated in 1914–18 in Ypres, Jutland, Gallipoli . . . when a whole generation of public school boys gave their lives leading the men of England through "firewater" to victory.'

Man describes the Rugby of the 1890s with affection, but reading between the lines it must still have been a hard place for the non-sporting boy, a quarter-century after *Tom Brown's Schooldays* was published. The whole house, young and old, was expected to go together on twelve-mile runs, he said. 'This was far too great a strain on the youngsters to keep up, with their elders trying to tow them. The system received a shock when a boy coming in was seen to run in a circle for a moment or two and then fall down. He was picked up dead. Even then some foolish old Rugbeans said we of that generation were getting soft . . . It was certainly in those days a hard, not to say rough, experience.'

It is not clear where Morrice Man's father was educated – his mother consulted a likely looking vicar on a journey out to join his father in Burma, which suggests the family may not have had a tradition of sending its sons to a particular public school. But it is likely his sisters, Mary, Jo and Dorothy, would have been the first girls in their family to go to school. They went to Croydon High School, which had opened as a girls' day school in 1874 and which still flourishes today in the independent sector. Its first headmistress, who retired in 1901, was an active supporter of the women's suffrage movement and was arrested in 1909, aged seventy-three, with Emmeline Pankhurst while trying to present a petition to Herbert Asquith, the Prime Minister.[18]

Many of the women who forged ahead in providing education for girls were also supporters of the suffrage movement. In fact the 1870 Education Act, piloted through Parliament by W. E. Forster, the son-in-law of the Rugby Headmaster, Thomas Arnold, provided one of the earliest opportunities for women to vote. Under its auspices, women ratepayers – who had been given the vote in local elections in 1869 – were provided with their first opportunity to stand for election. Women activists including Elizabeth Garrett Anderson, pioneer of women's medical education and sister of the suffrage movement leader, Millicent Garrett Fawcett, seized this chance with gusto and were soon represented on school boards all over the country. The teaching of children in elementary schools – which hitherto had been run on a voluntary basis but which now came under the auspices of the state – gradually came to be seen as a respectable occupation for a woman, and so the education of girls was enabled to grow.[19]

It would be wrong to suggest that all girls were instantly enabled to enter the world of education after 1870, though. In fact, only about 70 per cent went to school in the succeeding decades,[20] and those who did often found themselves in private schools designed only to instil in them the correct ladylike qualities: 'The dominant idea about girls' education is that it should be as far as possible claustral, that girls should be kept from any contamination with people who drop their H's or earn their salt. It is thought that careful seclusion is absolutely necessary for the development of that refinement which should characterise a lady,' reported a correspondent from Devon to a commission on secondary education in the mid-1890s.[21]

Indeed, there was a view at the time – presented to the Association of University Teachers in 1908 by a medical adviser, Janet Campbell, that girls' brains could be damaged if they were expected to think too much after puberty: 'As regards mental work, great care should be taken to avoid any undue strain,' she said. 'Lessons requiring much concentration and therefore using up a great deal of brain energy, mathematics for instance, should not be pushed. Such subjects as cookery, embroidery, or the handicrafts may well be introduced into the curriculum as they cause comparatively little mental strain.'[22]

In general, though, the line of thinking on elementary education was similar to that which had driven the growth of public schools such as Rugby during the early nineteenth century. If Britain was to retain its technological and colonial edge, the reasoning ran, then its workers needed to be educated, and educated in a particular way: a way which would promote morality, upstanding virtues, a deep sense of Britishness which could be exported around the globe.

The reality, of course, was somewhat different. In Bolton, Alice Foley, who started school aged five in 1896, described scenes of chaotic, childish joy: 'The lessons were as dull as the surroundings, marked in memory only by some strange visits from a young priest or novice, who came most mornings to test our knowledge of the Catechism. After this devotional exercise he invariably invited our class to "come out and fight the teacher". Immediately a mad rush of young savages were whooping, shoving and kicking the feet and shins off a pale, apprehensive teacher ... just as suddenly the skirmishing would be called off; the priest departed, laughing heartily, leaving a distraught young person to regain order and to pick up the threads of an interrupted lesson.'[23]

For the majority of youngsters, schooling at the end of the nineteenth century was a hit-and-miss affair, attendance punctuated by periods of absence necessitated by children's roles as contributors to the family purse. For many, school was little more than an irrelevance – something they had to do until they were thirteen and could go to work full-time.

A dangerous world for a child

And while both the state and the voluntary sector had intervened repeatedly to make children's lives safer during the nineteenth century, the life of the child in England was still a perilously fragile thing. As the New Year dawned over St John's Church in Wortley, Leeds, in 1891, the mood was one of celebration. A working group of the church ladies' committee had planned an entertainment: the girl members of the local Band of Hope had prepared a performance entitled 'Snowflakes', symbolizing winter. Parents had been pressed into service to make pure white costumes from cotton wool, and each girl was to carry a Chinese lantern with a candle inside.

Minutes before the performance was due to begin, with an audience of about 100 gathered in the church hall, the fourteen little performers were flitting about excitedly in their dressing room. Suddenly, a waft of air from an open door flung a spark on to the dress of nine-year-old Emily Sanderson. Within seconds she was on fire. As the other girls rushed to escape, they too were engulfed by the flames. The audience watched in sheer horror as the leader of the Band of Hope, Eli Auty, and the school Caretaker, George Brookes, tried in vain to save the terrified, screaming girls.

By the end of the evening four were dead and a further dozen were in a critical condition. Over the following days, the newspapers grimly recorded the rising death toll: Caroline Steel, aged nine; Clarissa Roberts, aged eleven; Emily Lister, aged thirteen; Ethel Fieldhouse, aged fourteen; Maggie Kitchen, aged twelve; Ada Whitteron, aged eleven; Florence Brookes (sister of George), aged nine; Elizabeth Tingle, aged twelve; Harriet Riley, aged eleven; Julia Anderson, aged nine; Emily Sanderson, aged nine. With eleven dead, the 'Wortley Calamity' became a major national event. Queen Victoria, a mother of nine herself, sent a telegram inquiring about the condition of the survivors.

Death hung heavy over the Victorian era, and many of the households struck down by this disaster would have experienced the loss of a child already. Even with the death rate starting to drop, thanks to improvements in public health and a cleaner water supply, one child in six still died before the age of one year.[24] Huge numbers of adults were carried off by infectious disease or childbirth, leaving many youngsters orphaned. To the modern eye, the response to the deaths in Wortley was a strange mix of grief and pragmatism. Local parishioners collected money to place a memorial cross in the churchyard where many of the children were buried, and the newspapers, both local and national, followed the harrowing slow decline of the burned girls in some detail.

Yet the account of the catastrophe by the Vicar, William Brameld, in the parish magazine a few weeks later would strike the modern reader as nothing short of extraordinary. In their understandable distress, too many parishioners had failed to see the bright side, he wrote. Many people had worked hard to set up the 'sale of work' which the entertainment was designed to support: 'It seems to me that there is a real danger of forgetting in the presence of the terrible calamity, the loving labour, the hard work, the helpful and self-denying goodwill of all our parochial workers, which was making our sale so bright and prosperous.'

The sale had opened a couple of days earlier and had raised an impressive seventy-four pounds, three shillings and seven pence before being brought to a premature end, he reported. An earlier performance of 'Snowflakes' had gone well: 'There was a brightness and a "go" about the proceedings . . . There can be no doubt that the theatricals were an immense success.' The parish magazine did not even feature a separate list of the dead, including them instead in the list of burials for the month.

Parents in those days had to harden their hearts – a family of eight or nine children in a poor area might expect to lose two or three in infancy. The Wortley Calamity was never even mentioned in Parliament, while surely in the modern age it would have led to a change in the law. The Coroner in the case was very critical of the organizers, and pointed out that the 1889 Children's Charter required the licensing of children's entertainments. But because the Wortley children had not been paid, the clause did not cover them. Had it applied, he said, the district factory inspector would have been obliged to attend to ensure that nothing dangerous was being planned.

The public were well aware that children were vulnerable – on an almost daily basis, the papers carried a series of tiny items detailing the latest accidental deaths. From the *Bury and Norwich Post*, for example: five-year-old Emma Copsey, her father in jail and her mother forced to work, died when she went too close to the fire and her clothes caught fire; the little son of George Malyon tried to drink from a boiling kettle while his mother was at work in another room; two-year-old John Adams choked to death on a plum given to him as a treat by a neighbour.

Infectious disease, too, lurked around every corner. Once it struck, it could go through a household within days. Atkinson Skinner, the Headmaster of Huggate school in North Yorkshire, recorded in his diary the progress of his wife's young sister through typhoid:

30 September 1887: 'Ada was very bad. We despaired of her life three times. Today she seems to be mending but in her case appearances are treacherous and we are anxiously awaiting the subsidence of her fever before feeling she is safe.'

15 October: 'Various people all took turns at sitting up – the fever abated and Ada at times seemed to us to be recovering. She wandered at intervals, but at other times she seemed perfectly conscious of everything passing around her. Bronchitis and ulcerated throat set in after the fever. These she could not overcome, and she gradually sank. She died at 2.40 p.m.'

A week later, Skinner's little daughter May was taken ill: 'May was so poorly and fretful after her mother left that I sent for her to return at night.'

25 October: 'As May was getting worse we had the doctor up today. He said he feared she was starting in the fever.'

On 26 October, he recorded simply: 'May very bad.'

Another week, and ulceration of the bowels had set in. For the Skinners, there was a happy ending and May did finally recover. But for countless other families – many of whom could not afford the doctor – there was none.

Alice Foley, born in 1891 in Bolton, remembered death as something that had always hung around her childhood 'at a distance . . . something awful and mysterious': 'Occasionally a school play-mate fell sick and died . . . The day before the funeral we trooped into the house of mourning to gaze our last on the dead face of our companion and after the burial we vulgarly pressed round the door in eager expectation of a piece of funeral currant bread.' Then one day, her brother, who was sixteen and working, came home in terrible pain. The doctor diagnosed appendicitis and advised an operation. 'But when father came home he stubbornly refused to accept the medical opinion, saying in his bigotry that "if the boy had to die he should remain with his family"'.[25]

The poorest were always the most vulnerable, and many a parent must have agonized about the cost before calling a doctor. Seebohm Rowntree reported[26] that in one impoverished York parish a third of all children died before they were a year old. Across the city, a quarter of the poor failed to make their first birthday, compared with fewer than one in ten among the 'servant keeping class'. Rowntree also measured the children he studied, and found that a thirteen-year-old boy from a poor household was shorter than the average by three and a half inches. He weighed just 73 pounds – eleven pounds less than a boy from a well-off family.[27] It was hardly surprising – Rowntree's examples of the diets of poor families were striking. A carter's family, living on a pound a week, had no fewer than seven meals during a week consisting solely of tea and bread, and a further seven at which there was also butter and bacon – though if Alice's experience was typical, the bacon might well have been solely for the breadwinner of the family. On better days, the family might have potatoes, eggs, onions, Yorkshire pudding or kippers to add to their diet. In another family, where the wife was a casual cleaner earning an average of 11 shillings a week, there were a total of six out of twenty-eight mealtimes when the family had anything at all to add to its staple diet of bread or potatoes with dripping – butter on a good day – and tea or coffee.[28]

The child mortality statistics for the end of the nineteenth century reveal that the overall death rate was falling: a child aged four was now substantially more likely to survive than in the mid-century. Yet, intriguingly, the danger for a child under one year was just as high as it had been fifty years before. Why? In his book *The Massacre of the Innocents*,[29] Lionel Rose suggests a likely explanation for this:

infanticide. Tiny children have always been vulnerable, of course – even today, the recorded homicide rate is twice as high among infants under one year as among the population as a whole. Yet, in 1900, the infant murder rate was a shocking fifteen times the expected level.

Rose quotes an exchange during an inquest in Lambeth in 1895, presided over by the first medically qualified coroner, Athelstan Braxton Hicks. Hicks – son of the doctor who gave his name to shadow contractions in pregnancy – would later go on to publish a study on infanticide. The parents of the dead child in this case, a Mr and Mrs Wigden, had appeared before Hicks not twelve months earlier following the death of an earlier child, and had received a caution. This time, the jury returned a verdict of accidental death.

HICKS: Accidental death, gentlemen? Nothing else?
FOREMAN: No, sir.
HICKS: You are perfectly satisfied it was a pure accident?
FOREMAN: Yes, sir.
HICKS: Very well, Mrs Wigden, you can go on smothering your children as much as you like, the jury say. The foreman says it was a pure accident, and the jury says, after all these warnings, it doesn't matter. Well, gentlemen, if you think that is a proper thing to do, by all means say it was an accident; but we may as well hold no inquests at all – it is a perfect farce.

Hicks, working alongside the NSPCC, came to the conclusion that drink was partly to blame. Infants were most likely to die on a Sunday, he discovered, and he suggested 'overlying' by drunken parents falling on to their children in shared beds on Saturday nights. The death rate among children born to mothers in prisons was much higher, also, than for the children born to the non-alcoholic. But there is no doubt the deliberate smothering of babies was common at the time – especially so among one particularly vulnerable group: the illegitimate.

As a 'fallen woman', an unmarried mother in Victorian times had few choices. The chances were she would find little comfort or support at her family home, upon which she would be deemed to have brought shame. To make matters worse, under a 'Bastardy Clause' in the 1834 Poor Law Reform Act, illegitimate children were the sole responsibility of their mother – not their father – until they were sixteen. If a child's desperate mother could not support him, she had no alternative but to turn to the workhouse. Hardly surprising, then, that an enormous proportion of children born out of wedlock died young. One study – based on a sample of children born in Manchester between 1891 and 1894 – found that almost four out of ten died before their first birthday. That made the illegitimate child two and a half times more likely to die than the average child.[30]

Again, a read between the lines in any local paper would reveal a familiar but gruesome pattern: the *Bury and Norwich Post* reported, for instance, in June 1882, how a Mr J. Bloomfield, a farmer, noticed something in the village pond near Leavenheath in Suffolk. Having retrieved the object with a hoe, he found it was a girl child with her throat slashed. 'Elizabeth Murrels, a domestic servant in the employ of the headmaster of the Royal Grammar School in Colchester, was charged with the murder of an infant,' the article concluded.

This sort of thing had gone on since time immemorial. But in the 1890s a peculiarly Victorian scandal broke which ultimately would lead to reform. Searching for a solution to their problems, the mother of an unwanted child would often turn to a foster-mother – or, as she was more commonly known at the bottom end of the market, a baby-farmer. The notion of the 'farming' or 'sweating' of babies dug deep into the nation's fears about children's vulnerability – not to mention the concern, at a time when the education of girls was growing along with the clamour for the vote – that women of independent means could prove dangerous. And, of course, most of the children taken in by this particular class of professional woman were born outside wedlock.

There was nothing new or even necessarily disreputable about the practice of baby-farming in itself – Jane Austen and her siblings were all 'farmed out' until they were toddlers, for example, and came to no harm from it.[31] But the Victorians' draconian poor laws, along with their equally draconian moral sensibilities, had driven many a desperate unmarried mother to 'farm out' her baby with a woman of unknown provenance. One option was to pay a one-off fee and to turn a blind eye to the inevitability that the child would sooner or later die of neglect or starvation, its appetite ruined by opium. It seems that a handful of these 'farmers' went so far as actually to expedite the process. A particularly notorious case cropped up on 30 March 1896 when a bargeman pulled a parcel from the Thames at Reading. It contained the body of a baby girl, who was later identified as Helena Fry. An examination of the wrapping revealed a label from Bristol Temple Meads Station as well as a name, Mrs Thomas, and an address. That led the police to a woman called Amelia Dyer, who had already done hard labour for the neglect of children left in her care. It emerged that, having collected the baby from Bristol, she had arrived home to Reading with a lifeless package. Subsequently, six other infants' bodies were found, all similarly weighted and thrown into the Thames. It was reported that over the years Mrs Dyer might have killed as many as 400 babies. She pleaded insanity but was found guilty and hanged in June that year. The case caught the public imagination the way the witch trials of old must have done, and even sparked a popular ballad:

> The old baby farmer, the wretched Mrs Dyer
> At the Old Bailey her wages is paid
> In times long ago we'd a made a big fire
> And roasted so nicely the wicked old Jade.

The case led to a clamour for a change in the law, and the following year an Infant Life Protection Act was introduced, extending the registration of baby-minders to those looking after more than one child under five. Interestingly, adoptions were only to be reported to the authorities if the fee were less than £20, on the grounds that low-rent children were the most at risk. Conveniently, this protected the identities, and hence the reputations, of middle-class women who had illegitimate children.

As the Infant Life Protection Bill was debated in the House of Lords, the Bishop of Winchester rose to point out that the real issue, in his view, was not baby-farming, nor even the unmarried mothers who were forced to put their babies into the hands of such people, but the fathers who were allowed to walk away from their children without a backward glance: 'Blame could not always be attached to the unfortunate mother, some unhappy girl who had no thought of harming her baby, but who, earning a miserable pittance, was obliged to board out the child at the least possible expense. It seemed rather that the blame went further back to the father of the infant, who so often in callous selfishness shirked all responsibility.'[32]

The phenomenon goes to the root of a conundrum which has shaped our thinking about children and about childhood over the past 100 years and more. To put it crudely, though the death rate was high in the late nineteenth century, so was the birth rate. Therefore, the supply of babies tended to outstrip demand. The equation was far from simple, even then – the feelings of those desperately impoverished single mothers could never have been simple. Yet parents were often forced to harden their hearts in the face of tragedy – so much so that the extinguishing of a small, unwanted life must have seemed the best option to more than a few. The bigger issue, though – and it is one to which we will return – is the question of what a child is, or was, really for. To most Victorian parents, a child was not simply – or even mainly – an emotional asset. In the

poorer family children had to pull their weight, to make a contri-
bution to the household budget, if they were to be welcomed into
the family circle.

When Forster introduced his education bill in 1870, he could not
have foreseen this unintended consequence: by taking children out
of the workplace and turning them into scholars, the state was dimin-
ishing their economic value to their parents. The role of the child
in Western society was beginning to change, profoundly and irre-
trievably.

2   Cosseted Edwardians

'Mama used to tell me that she celebrated the Relief of Mafeking sitting astride a lion in Trafalgar Square. And that I was born a fort-night later,'[1] Sonia Keppel wrote of her birth. With the Victorian age all but over, Britain was preparing for a new, more frivolous era: 'The sky was clearing fast. From decorous grey it was becoming rather a blatant blue.'

The reign of Edward VII would be shoehorned into the years between two wars – the Boer War, which ended as Edward was crowned in 1902, and World War One, which loomed large on the horizon in the years following his death in 1910. And it would be, in Sonia's recollection at least, a brief interlude during which England would throw off the heavy garb of the previous century. Edwardian England wore its parental responsibilities with a lightness, a sense of fun, which had rarely been present before. And, for the first time, those who had the luxury of spare time began to use it – and to talk about using it – to nurture and enjoy their children.

Sonia's childhood was far from typical – she was born into a society family; I was her mother, the King's lover and her sister, Violet, the future lover of Vita Sackville-West. Yet her account of it contained much that typified this new era – its joyfulness, its femininity, and, most of all, the growing belief that childhood was an especially sacred time. Where the Victorians, with their adherence to the biblical notion of sparing the rod and spoiling the child, swung towards the 'original sin' narrative on childhood, the Edwardians began to take Rousseau to their breast. Indeed, they went further. Not only did they embrace the notion that childhood was a kind of idealized state from which adults should learn, but they also conflated this notion of infant purity with the increasingly popular view that innocence and simplicity were mainly to be found in the rural way of life. After the all-enveloping urbanization which had taken place during the Victorian age, there was a sense that something vital had been lost and needed to be recovered. Life seemed too mechanized, too pressured, too unreal, and it seemed that maybe the child, somehow purer and closer to nature, could be the route to salvation. The bedrock of the Arts and Crafts movement – the belief that time-honoured rural skills and simplicity were inherently superior to the frenzy and shoddy workmanship typified by the new urban environment – soon came to be incorporated into this new philosophy of childhood. In the popular imagination of the period, the happy child was the child who was free to roam the countryside, enjoying the flowers and the fruits of the hedgerows. This child feasted on good, clean, wholesome country food, of the type which had been fed to the young – according to the myth – before the urban parents of the industrial age spoiled them with a diet consisting of little more than tea and bread.

If the ideal child of the Victorian era was pale, delicate and rarely heard to speak, then the ideal Edwardian child took on a distinctly more rosy-cheeked hue. While the child of the Victorians grew up in a world which fretted about whether he was innately sinful or whether he was pure but vulnerable, the child of the Edwardians had a far more robust outlook on the world. A great national concern began to take hold about the importance of childishness and of play – not just as a key developmental stage, but also as a vital part of the fabric of society. *The Times*, in a leader in February 1909, worried that children no longer knew how to play independently, and praised the efforts of a famous novelist, Mrs Humphrey Ward, to reintroduce them to old-fashioned games through a network of play centres in London: 'We have discovered that our industrial civilization has been producing a new kind of Barbarian who does not know how to play. Nothing could be more beautiful and pathetic than to see the children of London slums dancing old country dances ... it is as if a native flower, long extinct, suddenly blossomed again in our meadows.' The innocence of childhood was similar to man's innocence in historical times, the paper added in a further leading article a year later. 'If the people of the Middle Ages were ready to believe that anything wonderful might happen, we are too apt to believe that nothing wonderful can happen. If they saw the future and the past in the light of their own childishness, we are inclined to see it in the dullness of our own darkness.'[2] The paper went on to warn that if England did not find a way soon to rediscover its inner child, then it would be subdued by 'some more childish race' that had not yet lost its joie de vivre.

So strong was this belief in the superiority of the rural lifestyle – and not without good reason, for the cities were often filthy places – that by 1909 the London charities were sending no fewer than 43,000 children to the country for holidays each year.

'We are making a blind and hazardous experiment when we allow so many thousands of children ... to grow up in places where they can experience so few of the natural joys of life,' *The Times* opined in a leader on the value of these holiday schemes in 1909. 'The enormous London of the present is a new thing, and we have not yet bred a race inured to it for several generations. The adaptability of all living things is such that very likely it will be possible to breed such a race with a low but enduring vitality and with an unnatural relish for the trivial excitements of town life.'[3]

For the first time, children became central to England's sense of self. They represented, in the public eye, all that was good, and pure, and timeless. They represented an escape from the mechanized world; an antidote to the niggling sense that while the economy had flourished under heavy industry, civilization had somehow begun to decline. One result was a flowering of children's literature which has endured to this day, bringing with it down the years its notions of how childhood should be. According to some accounts,[4] the literary children of the era were no longer mere 'incipient adults' but were beings in their own right. They had freedom to explore their own imaginations away from the adult world.

So while the fictional children of the Victorian era had been cloyingly moral, portrayed so often either as sinners or – more often – innocent victims, the Edwardian fictional child was a less biblical creation. J. M. Barrie's Peter Pan, for instance – who first appeared in 1902 as a character in a book called *The Little White Bird* – would epitomize this notion of the child. A boy who could fly into and out of the lives of his friends at will, he was a child with a magical power – he would never grow up. Peter was also a throwback to the age-old preoccupation with the lost child, of course, but Barrie placed the deep-seated fear of loss in a new and more positive context. Other authors of the day would take this notion further, turning childhood into an ever more idealized state. The children created by E. Nesbit, like Peter, were often able to have magical adventures – their own flying carpet, a rather grumpy sand fairy who could grant them a daily wish. In *The Railway Children* – notable too for having as a character a girl called 'Bobbie' with an exploring mind and a desire to be brave – the Waterbury children were able to right a wrong when their actions helped to bring home their father, who had been wrongly imprisoned. 'Oh Mother,' Bobbie whispered to herself as she got into bed one night. 'How brave you are! How I love you! Fancy being brave enough to laugh when you're feeling like that!'

Other authors, notably Beatrix Potter, whose tales began appearing in 1902, and Kenneth Grahame, whose *Wind in the Willows* was published in 1908, took up the idea of a connection between the child and nature in a more literal manner. The sensible Ratty chose, when possible, to stay on the riverbank and only to visit the Wide World when absolutely necessary. But while the tales harked back to a more innocent, even a medieval – Toad was incarcerated in 'the stoutest castle in all the length and breadth of Merry England' – age, they also took on a distinctly suburban, middle-class hue.[5] Grahame's characters enjoyed many of the same pursuits he himself would have experienced with his family, messing about in boats and picnicking by the river. When the modern world appeared it was as an intrusion, as it did when Toad's caravan was upset by a speeding motor car. The idealized child of the Edwardian age was uneasily suspended, then, between a world of rural simplicity and one of well-padded, semi-detached Home Counties comfort. When Grahame's readers first met Mole, he was busy spring-cleaning his spick little home: 'First with brooms, then with dusters; then on ladders and steps and chairs, with a brush and a pail of whitewash; till he had dust in his throat and eyes, and splashes of whitewash all over his black fur.'

When children in Edwardian fiction became savages, they were by necessity noble ones. The literature tended to idealize the primitive, and to hand to its child characters a freedom from the stress of modern life. In *The Blue Lagoon*, by Henry de Vere Stacpoole – a novel published in 1908 not for children but about them – two cousins marooned on a Pacific island survived on their own wits, diving for pearls, foraging for fruit. Eventually, the pair, full-grown into healthful beauty away from the impure air of the industrialized world – fell in love and had a son, their lovemaking 'conducted just as the birds conduct their love affairs. An affair absolutely natural, absolutely blameless, and without sin.'

The old Victorian preoccupation with loss and sickness had not completely gone, but the Edwardians wore it more lightly – appropriately, as the infant mortality rate was now dropping fast – and on occasion they allowed the child to take possession of it. Mary Whiteing, for instance, a plucky child born in Beverley, North Yorkshire, suffered frequent illnesses yet seemed always to be busy.[6] Mary was a keen supporter of Dr Barnardo's homes, as well as being an avid writer. After her death at the age of fourteen, her mother published a little book of her works in aid of the charity. The newspapers took up the story with an enthusiasm which perhaps would seem odd today for a small private publication with a short print run.

'In reading these verses we are sometimes reminded of Blake, who has captured the spirit of childhood as no other poet could,' reported the *Manchester Guardian*. 'The verses on "Night" seem to us remarkable work for so young a child, and other pieces, as well as the illustrations, show remarkable precocity.' The *Girls' Realm* added another paean of praise: 'Its note is the aspiration towards ideals of love, beauty and tenderness towards all created things which must ever set the pace for the march of humanity towards the light.'

'Occasionally there is something uncanny about the precocity of the child,' Barnardo's own publicity said, quoting a poem entitled 'To the One I Love':

> My love is like the red, red rose
> And I a bee who with caress
> Doth find the heart and nestle there
> To taste the joy of happiness.

The charity's blurb on the publication went on into a description containing much that epitomized the ideal child of the day: 'Our little authoress is not always dwelling on sad things. She can be gay and humorous; she can talk prettily of fairies, and plead the cause of dumb animals, of which she was exceedingly fond.'

The short life of Mary Whiteing, along with her poems and stories, briefly caught the imagination of a society that was turning increasingly to the feminine – not to the languishing femininity of the years just past, but to a healthier, warmer and more autonomous variety. At the Keppels' Grosvenor Street home, Sonia's mother, Alice, had her own drawing room decked out with chaises longue, lace cushions and screens: 'Whereas in Queen Victoria's reign 'paterfamilias' predominated and male taste prevailed, now, in King Edward VII's reign, the deification of the feminine was re-established.' Into this boudoir little Sonia would be admitted for daily visits to her mother, during which her adored 'Kingy' would often also be present: 'On such occasions he and I devised a fascinating game. With a fine disregard for the good condition of his trouser, he would lend me his leg, on which I used to start two bits of bread and butter (butter side down) side by side. Then bets of a penny each were made (my bet provided by Mamma) and the winning piece of bread and butter depended, of course, on which was the more buttery ... Sometimes he won, sometimes I did. Although the owner of a Derby winner, Kingy's enthusiasm seemed delightfully unaffected by the quality of his bets.'[7]

Despite the easing of the formalities of family life, little Sonia Keppel was still largely excluded from the world of adults. While they ate rich fare in a dining room that could seat seventy, Sonia sat with her French governess eating bland but wholesome food. Clothing, similarly, was wholesome but dull: 'In our youth, Violet and I were dressed by Mr Nichols in Glasgow, and Woollands in Knightsbridge. Usually our Easter toilettes consisted of new coats, straw hats and light dresses. Violet's hat was secured under her chin by an elastic band; mine was tied on by a large bow of white moiré ribbon. Both of us were equipped with black, buttoned boots. Violet wore black cotton stockings with hers; I wore white cotton socks. Mamma turned a deaf ear to Nannie's hopeful comment that Mrs Wilfrid Ashley's children had real lace on their knickers.'

The changing attitudes of the age were partly inspired by this sense that mechanization and development had swept away part of the nation's humanity, but they also sprang from an early flowering of ideas that would come to dominate thinking about childhood in the twentieth century – the growth of child psychology, and the deepening influence of Sigmund Freud. Freud's works, although published in this period, did not really reach the public consciousness until later. There were hints at what was to come, though, in the child-rearing manuals which began to appear during this time.

'Psychologists have of late insisted much upon the importance of the first few years of life from an educational point of view. The younger the child, the more plastic its mind and the deeper are the impressions made upon it,' explained Edward Vipont Brown in a leaflet on infant care published in 1905.[8] The pamphlet advocated strict routine and plenty of parental attention: 'I fear parents do not realise sufficiently the importance of their post, that they have not understood that "the child has to begin as a God in the faint hope he may end as a man . . ." Many of those who can afford the time to bring up their own children look upon it so spent as wasted.' In the spirit of the times, the booklet's theme was one of a return to a more natural approach: 'God made the fresh air, man made the close room, and God was incomparably the better workman . . . We have everything to learn by studying nature and her laws, and we can in no wise improve upon her handiwork.' Scientific advice, too, pointed in the same direction, for doctors had begun to note that the death rate was much lower among breast-fed babies.

Writers on childhood at the time – and they were beginning to proliferate – advised strongly that the upper-class children who spent most of their lives with nannies and governesses should be enabled to meet their parents at least once a day. Along with this new cult of childhood came, almost inevitably, a cult of motherhood. To be a mother was suddenly no longer just a grim fact of life – though it still was, for many – but something to be aspired to. 'The wise educator is ... one who, unconsciously to the children, brings to them the chief sustenance and creates the supreme conditions for their growth. Primarily she is the one who, through the serenity and wisdom of her own nature, is dew and sunshine to growing souls,' wrote Ellen Key in an influential tract on motherhood in 1914.[9]

Children, in this new age, were becoming individuals, with individual needs. And the greatest of those needs was the need to have the undivided attention of their mothers. 'Were it possible to banish all friends and most relations for the first three years of a new life, that life would be stronger and better,' explained a handbook published by the London County Council during this era.[10] 'Because the child is tiny it is petted and honoured, aunts claim a special licence to allow the infant everything it wants ... this matters vastly, parental love and authority are weakened.'

'Babyhood does not last for ever ... it will be worth going without a nurse's help,' added another childcare expert, Hilary Pepler.[11] To Pepler, this was not just about the child's immediate needs, but about its need to grow up with the proper middle-class manners: 'A lady-nurse, with evident love for children, might be allowed more liberties but until we have "levelled up" and all have enjoyed the same humanizing education, and until there are many more refined homes in the land, it is best to confine your Cockney to the kitchen, your would-be nursemaid to the laundry.' Echoing the views of Sonia Keppel's mother, Pepler advised that clothing should be warm, functional, neat and devoid of such fripperies as lace: 'Avoid vanity in dress and dispense with superfluous garments is the motto.'

This new blossoming of the feminine and the maternal did not mean, however, that parents were exhorted to listen to their children and follow their desires. Far from it – in general, the advice of the day was that a child would be spoilt for life if proper boundaries were not set. 'Some mothers, if the baby cries, will stop in the midst of the washing operations to feed it; this is a bad habit which should never be commenced. The baby will very soon become a tyrant if the mother gives in to it, and it is never too early to begin to discipline the small body,' wrote another contemporary childcare expert, Mrs Frank Stephens.[12]

Olive Everson, growing up in the shadow of a 'Big House' in Suffolk in the early years of the twentieth century, described her relationship with her parents as loving, if a little joyless. She was led to believe her family were 'a cut above', she wrote later.[13] Her grandmother had been a teacher in a village school, and there was a family rumour that there was blue blood in their veins because Olive's great-grandmother had been 'done wrong' to while working as a servant. Olive's parents were 'people who took their responsibilities seriously, and were conscientious parents', she wrote. 'When punishing was necessary it was mother who generally smacked us. This happened quite often, but our father seldom raised his hand to us. The fact that he knew about something bad that we had done was sufficient for it not to happen again. Mother … did wonderful things in the way of adapting discarded adult garments to make attractive clothes for us to wear. She was constantly making and mending.'

Sonia Keppel's mother had none of this drudgery to face, and consequently her daughter recalled their relationship as having a great deal more fun in it. During a bout of rheumatic fever, she was confined to her bed: 'Of course mamma had her own way of accelerating my recovery. Ignoring the pain of bruised knees and torn stockings, she invented a race. When my throat was at its sorest and my medicine very difficult to swallow, at a signal from Nannie while I started to drink it Mamma started round my room on her knees. With the odds heavily in my favour, inevitably I won but I so enjoyed the contest that sometimes I let her get slightly ahead.' When Sonia was bullied by a brute of a girl called Lois, her mother took the offender on one side and threatened to stamp on her toe if she did it again: 'Unbelievingly, Lois did it again. Mamma stamped, accurately and hard, and Lois was carried screaming from the room.'[14]

In addition to the yearning for a simpler age, scientific advance was also leading to a closer focus on the child. In *Practical Motherhood*,[15] Helen Campbell tackled the effect of Darwinism and evolution on child-rearing. In this practical guide, she said it was essential that evolution should be properly understood if mothers were to grasp the way their children's minds worked. 'Human nature is ever climbing up the world's great altar stairs that slope through the darkness to God,' she explained. Parents must use routine to establish patterns of behaviour in their children: 'The clay is soft and moist, now make haste and form the pitcher, for the wheels turn fast.'

The notion that childhood was a vital time, when early mistakes could lead to later disaster, was taking hold of the public imagination. In America, universities were already setting up child study departments, and the keeping of notes by Charles Darwin on his own children had led to a vogue for similar observations by other parents. Louise Hogan's *Study of a Child*, in which she described every development, planned her son's surroundings to suit his needs, made nightly plans to ensure that he had sufficient spontaneous play each day and refused to engage servants if her son did not like the look of them, would certainly challenge the notion that over-anxious parenting was the exclusive preserve of the twenty-first-century middle classes. Using this type of observation, childcare manuals began to include important 'milestones': 'At six months your baby should be crawling, at ten months standing, at a year he should have two or three words.'[16]

A major implication of all this was that mothers needed to devote themselves to their children rather than to work, education or – of course – political activity, the latter particularly relevant as the suffrage movement reached its height in the years before World War One, with middle-class mothers prominent among its leadership. This was a central theme in Ellen Key's book *The Renaissance of Motherhood*: 'Has our race ever been afflicted by a more dangerous disease than the one which at present rages among women: the sick yearning to be "freed" from the most essential attribute of their sex?' she asked. 'Many women now advance as the ideal of the future, the self-supporting wife working out of the home and leaving the care and education of the children to "born" educators. This ideal is the death of home-life and family life.'

The backlash against all this intense focus on the child soon began. 'The general tendency is in the direction of bringing children into too great prominence in making them the most important and first-to-be-considered members of the family,' noted the *Archives of Paediatrics* for 1898. The worst mistake parents could make, it said, was 'the habit of too great camaraderie with their children, and the growing tendency to remove the barriers between childhood and age ... this cannot fail to cause harmful effects during childhood, and frequently produces a neurasthenic and nervous temperament in later life'.[17]

The child development movement took the brunt of the blame: 'Nowadays there are unhappy children who are studied all day long,' wrote Lizzie Allen Harker in a fictional account of the movement in 1903,[18] 'who may not even make mud pies in seclusion but must perforce and in gangs shape something out of grey India-rubber, and sit at a table to do it. What can they know, poor things, of the joys and terrors to be found in a dwarf-infested shrubbery, just at sunset, on a chill October day?'

And while some, like Harker, objected to the intensity of this focus on motherhood, others – including the poet John Masefield – simply disliked the feminizing of childhood. 'I would make it a criminal offence for mothers to attempt to impose their personality on their children,' he wrote in 1911.[19] 'Certain things have been proved to be of use in this world. Hardness. Truth. Keenness and quickness of mind. Indifference to pleasure. Honesty and energy in work. Hatred of dirt in all its forms. I believe they can best be taught by men. You can't get them from the average mother. They aren't in her. The world has gone steadily downhill in all manly qualities since the "mother's personality" became what is called a "factor in education".'

The best kind of childhood, then, was spent outdoors in the countryside, largely free from the ministrations of the adult world but always under its watchful gaze, and with regular parental interventions. This growing obsession with the virtues of the countryside and fresh air had its roots in mythology, then, in a desire to return to something that resembled the core of what the nation thought of as 'Englishness'. 'The English are by nature a country people. The very manner in which they neglect their towns proves that,' *The Times*[20] explained. Yet there was an even more pressing, more pragmatic urge to find a healthier way of life for the next generation: the very future of the Empire was at stake.

3   Scout's Honour

As Sonia Keppel's mother had celebrated the Relief of Mafeking astride a Trafalgar Square lion in May 1900, Robert Baden-Powell – commander of the British troops – had been reflecting on a job well done. The siege had lasted 217 days and its victorious end turned him into a national hero. Yet a few years on Baden-Powell had concerns on his mind, too – about the future of Britain's young. His intervention would have a profound effect on attitudes to, and the lives of, millions of children and young people – an effect whose ripples still spread today.

The youth of Mafeking had done sterling work during the siege. Organized into a well-run cadet force in khaki uniforms and wide-brimmed hats and with a thirteen-year-old named Warner Goodyear as Sergeant Major, they had acted as lookouts and had carried messages, often as far as a mile over open ground. Back in Britain, and with time to reflect, Baden-Powell now wondered whether the children of the English slums would have been up to the job.

Even before the Boer War, the future founder of the Scout movement had been worrying about this issue. He had been very struck by a book called *Degeneration*, which had made quite a stir in the early 1890s. Its author, Max Nordau, had claimed that a wave of degenerate writers and artists – Oscar Wilde and Henrik Ibsen, to name but two – was symptomatic of a deeper malaise. Socialism, anarchism and the demand for women's rights were corroding the values of European societies, Nordau said. As a result they were 'marching to certain ruin because it is too worn out and flaccid to perform great tasks'.[1]

In fact, Britain's eventual victory in the Boer War masked the fact that throughout the conflict there had been concern about the physical fitness of many of the British troops. In 1900, the army had been forced to cut the minimum height requirement for infantry soldiers from five foot three and a half inches to five foot three, yet even so almost three out of ten prospective recruits were rejected.

Now, Baden-Powell became a leading voice in the national debate about where the youth of Britain's industrial cities was headed. In February 1904, in an address to the Liverpool Patriotic Society, he described working-class teenage boys as 'loafers' and 'wasters'. They drank, smoked and watched – rather than played – sports. They gambled and spent hours on street corners. Even the public schoolboy was not immune to slouching around with a cigarette in his mouth and his hands in his pockets. The message hit home, not least because it chimed with an already rising note of alarm in the public discourse on the issue. An official committee had been set up to investigate whether – despite advances in public health – Britain's physique was deteriorating. If it was, Baden-Powell and others pointed out, it would endanger not just the economic wellbeing of the nation but also its defence, and the future of its Empire.

A walk around any inner-city area would have confirmed the impression – life had not been easy for working-class families in the last years of Victoria's reign. The disruption to colonial trade during the Boer War had led to unemployment and a drop in wages, and the quality of the food eaten by the poor had also deteriorated. White bread had largely replaced wholemeal, and this alone was a major factor in determining children's condition, for bread – along with unfortified margarine and cheap jam, which sometimes contained so little fruit that it contained wood chips to mimic pips – formed the basis of most children's diets. In Dundee, one observer reported that 'a combination of hot strong tea and soft bread is fatal to the teeth as well as bad for the digestion. Yet this is the most frequent diet taken by the working classes.'[2]

Edith Sowerbutts, who was born in Suffolk in 1896 but grew up in London, recalled later her shock at seeing children her own age in Camden Town and Bloomsbury, dressed in rags:[3] 'I became sharply aware of poverty,' she wrote. 'Around the streets were pasty-faced, ragged, barefoot children, verminous and smelly. They stank not only of body dirt, but also had that unmistakeable odour of the badly under-nourished and unhealthy. Little urchins who played in the streets when I was a child were puny and pallid, often had rotting grey teeth and always hair full of nits.'

By contrast, the diet in the Suffolk countryside, where Olive Everson was growing up in the environs of a 'Big House', was stodgy but plentiful: 'On our breakfast toast we usually had dripping from the Hall kitchen. We children liked cocoa to drink at breakfast. The meat joint was for weekends of course, but there was some kind of hot meal each day. We had bread and butter pudding, currant duff, treacle pudding. A general favourite was suet pudding, half of which we usually reserved for the second course, to be eaten with golden syrup. Once a week we had pea soup, very thick . . . on Friday when the Dutch oven was in use there was lovely, tasty potato pie.'

Seebohm Rowntree, who had previously noted stark differences in height and weight between the children of the rich and of the poor, pointed out that country children fattened on a diet such as Olive enjoyed had, up until recently, been replenishing the puny population stocks of the towns. But now the stock of strong country-folk was dwindling.

'Already the country dwellers have given up their best, and the prospect, from the point of view of the maintenance of the national physique, is not bright,' he wrote.[4] 'It is doubtful whether the health conditions in the cities are being improved as rapidly as the vitality of the country districts is being exhausted.' Rowntree was concerned, too, about a moral decline in the population: 'Work on the land, in constant contact with natural objects and often in comparative isolation, produces a solid strength of character which our English nation can ill afford to lose ... The town dweller suffers from living too quickly and living in a crowd. His opinions are the opinions of the crowd – and a crowd is easily swayed, for evil as well as for good.'

The idea of the countryside, and of a sort of natural connection between the innocence of children and a perceived purity in the rural environment, had long held a powerful place in European culture. And, gradually, as urbanization proceeded apace, it had gained almost the status of a lost land – a repository, in the popular imagination, of all that had previously been good and desirable about Englishness. But while the devotees of the Arts and Crafts movement filled the rural idyll of *their* minds with free-spirited elves and sprites, left to run free among softly wooded glades, the followers of Baden-Powell had quite another idea. Their England was a far more militaristic, colonialist land. And just as the German *völkisch* movement moved on from an early Romantic nationalism, its interest in self-sufficiency and anti-urbanism to a much harder-edged form of patriotism, so the English notion of the rural ideal began to move in the same direction. Europe was gearing up for war.

The state of Britain's children became a central theme in an increasingly fraught debate about the future of the nation – and to some extent, the facts seemed to support the doomsayers. For generations, there had been around thirty-four births each year for every 1,000 people, and in the mid-Victorian period this had risen slightly. But families were now getting smaller, and by 1914 the birth rate had dropped to twenty-four per 1,000 – a decline of 33 per cent in forty years. This would not have mattered much – after all, the death rate was falling too – except for one factor. The poor, unable to take advantage of contraception, were continuing to procreate at a much faster rate than the rich. It was middle-class families that were getting smaller. Sidney Webb, joint founder of the Fabian Society, published a tract claiming that the number of babies born in England and Wales had fallen by 200,000 in two decades: 'It is the differential character of the decline in birth rate, rather than the actual extent of the decline, which is of the gravest import. Volitional regulation of the marriage state is demonstrably at work in many different parts of Great Britain, among all social grades except probably the very poorest.' Both the *Daily Mail* and the *Lancet* weighed in to sound the alarm, describing the falling birth rate as 'an ominous threat', a 'menace' and 'a national calamity'.[5] Yet these eugenic fears would prove unfounded, for none of those who chose to comment on the problem had considered the differential death rate. In the event, the balance would be maintained – the children of the poorest remained almost three times as likely to die in their first year as the children of the wealthiest.

Even so, the government's Interdepartmental Committee on Physical Deterioration, which reported in 1904, prescribed radical action to boost the health of the working class. A slum clearance programme was needed, it said, and the state might have to intervene in the lives of those who were incapable of an acceptable 'standard of decency': 'In the last resort this might take the form of labour colonies with powers of compulsory detention. The children of persons so treated might be lodged temporarily in public nurseries or boarded out,' it suggested. Feckless parents might be held liable for the costs of this, and subjected to forced labour until they had paid off the debt.[6]

Others had radical solutions in mind, too. S. C. Johnson, a contemporary historian, suggested mass emigration:[7] 'Population, we know, increases more freely in the colonies than at home; therefore, if a number of the inhabitants of the United Kingdom are permitted to emigrate, it is logical to argue that the empire will benefit numerically and, consequently, in military and commercial strength.' Naturally, the colonies would be expected to come to Britain's aid in any future military conflict, he said.

Britain was already, and would remain, a major exporter of its population, but in the event no such radical measures were taken, and indeed there were already some signs that the health of the urban population was improving. Child mortality was dropping, even in the poorest areas, and the average life expectancy was rising, thanks to improvements in public health and medicine.

As before, charities continued to plug many of the cracks in the fabric of inner-city life. In Dundee, the school board authorized head teachers to offer 'penny dinners' of soup and bread to the neediest children. For the first time, childcare manuals began to be distributed among poorer families,[8] many of them by organizations such as the Ladies Sanitary Association and the Infant Health Societies of Marylebone and St Pancras. Some of the advice was brutal. In *Mrs Blossom on Babies*[9], Helen Hodgson, a Durham health worker, advised that dummies were 'an invention of the devil to tempt mothers to harm their children. If the Lord had intended little babies to be always sucking something, he'd have sent them with dummies round their necks already.' More liberal was the St Pancras School for Mothers, set up in 1907, which offered a 'Babies' Welcome' where infants could be weighed and examined free of charge by a doctor. Breastfeeding was recommended, and breastfeeding mothers were offered free dinners.

At around this time, pasteurized milk began to be more widely available, as dairies were set up under the leadership of an American paediatrician called Luther Emmett Holt. Holt was the Gina Ford of his day, and his *Care and Feeding of Children*,[10] originally written as a training manual for nurses in the New York Babies' Hospital, was revised twelve times during his lifetime. Recognizing that contaminated milk was a major cause of ill-health among children, he established a chain of laboratories to deliver pasteurized milk in sealed bottles to doorsteps in the United States. In 1914, he began doing the same in England, from a dairy at Wembley.

But measures designed to improve the nation's health, and in particular that of its children, were not universally welcomed. As doctors pressed for more vaccination – smallpox jabs had just become compulsory and had massively reduced the incidence of the disease – parents pressed for a right to choose. There was concern that the use of infected calves' lymph in the vaccinations would transmit tetanus, syphilis, tuberculosis and other diseases. Anti-vaccination societies began sending postcards to new parents, urging them to withdraw their babies from the schemes.

Such was the ferocity of the protests that the government was urged to withdraw the penalties it had previously imposed on recalcitrant parents. Sonia Jex-Blake, one of the pioneers of women's medical education, was horrified. 'In civilised communities the well-being of the many must override the suicidal hobbies of the few,' she wrote.[11] 'Just as people should be stopped from setting their own houses on fire because of the danger to other people in the street, so parents should be forced to vaccinate their children for the general good.' Gradually, the fuss would die down, and children's health would continue to improve – until the vicissitudes of the next war came along to cause another setback.

And here, Baden-Powell came into his own. Already, a group of Cheshire choirboys, who had been corresponding with him about non-smoking pledges, had set up a Baden-Powell League of Health and Manliness. Now the former commander became Vice President of the Boys' Brigade, which had recruited several thousand members since its inception in Glasgow in the 1880s. Baden-Powell saw a way forward – the Mafeking cadet model could help save the Empire, he thought.

The first Scout camp was held on Brownsea Island, Dorset, in the summer of 1907 and featured nature-study, hunting, the art of camping and yarns told around the campfire by Baden-Powell himself. The following year, *Scouting for Boys* was published, and included the first of many 'Camp Fire Yarns' written by Baden-Powell: 'I suppose every British boy wants to help his country in some way or other,' he wrote: 'Perhaps you don't see how a mere small boy can be of use to the great British Empire, but by becoming a Scout and carrying out the Scout Laws every boy can be of use. "Country first, self second" should be your motto.'

Fun, ancient and modern

'My brother Leslie was continually falling into ponds,' Olive Everson recalled. 'In winter he would slide on too-thin ice, and in Summer, wading in streams in order to catch "tiddlers", he would suddenly find himself in deep water and arrive home soaked and miserable. My mother never knew what to expect at the end of the day, when he was due to arrive home ... he loved to go off on his own for a day's fishing, with a bent pin, a worm and some string.'[12]

Baden-Powell tapped into some powerful forces when he founded the Scout movement. There was the age-old tendency for boys – who always had more freedom – to go off exploring their environment, and also this renewed sense that there was something fundamentally character-building and life-affirming about allowing children to roam the countryside, to breathe its healthy air and even occasionally to come into contact with cold water or mud.

The first weekly comic strip, which had appeared in 1884, had featured a raffish character called Ally Slope, who was always getting into scrapes. But it was during the Edwardian period that children's comics began to come into their own, with Alfred Harmsworth's Amalgamated Press launching the *Daily Mail* on the profits from its *Comic Cuts* and *Illustrated Chips*.[13] But the big excitement of the age, for the working-class child at least, was the cinema. The first films were shown in the late nineteenth century at travelling fairground shows, and graduated to small shops known as 'Penny Gaffs'. By 1909, larger cinemas were being built, licensed by local authorities.[14] Yet these picture-houses were a working-class domain, not considered entirely safe or respectable for the more affluent child. Elsie Oman, born around 1904 into a very poor family in Salford, remembered her local picture-house as a chaotic place:[15] 'Sometimes Auntie would give my cousin and I a penny each to go to the pictures matinée – "the bug house", we called it. Sometimes we got a free orange or a comic as we entered. It was like a madhouse inside. Some children got their entrance fee by taking empty jam jars or bottles back to the shops – they got a penny for three. The place reeked of oranges and every now and then lumps of peel would come whizzing round our earholes … it was a good job they were silent pictures, as with the noise of the children it would have been difficult to hear.'

The premises in which films were shown to children were often unsanitary and even unsafe. But it was the content of the films, and their possible effect on the morals of the children of the urban poor, which now began to cause serious concern. The first known case of a film being blamed for encouraging juvenile delinquency occurred in 1913:[16] a magistrate named Mr Wallace, dealing at the London Sessions with a boy who pleaded guilty to burglary, blamed the pictures for the offence, according to the following day's newspaper: 'Many of the lads who came before him owed their position to having been influenced by pictures of burglaries and thefts at such shows … these shows, as far as young boys were concerned, were a grave danger to the community.'

Similarly, the following year a group of boys who came before the Sutton Coldfield magistrates accused of theft were bound over not to enter a picture-house for twelve months: 'The chairman said the town had been made notorious as a den of young thieves, and shopkeepers had been terrorised. A petition, signed by clergy and ministers of religion and by the local branch of the Women's Temperance Association, was presented, suggesting the closer supervision of picture theatres. They urged that no picture should be allowed to be shown which represented violence and wrongdoing, and objected to certain posters.'

Yet the cinema was here to stay. In 1914, research by Manchester's Director of Education, Spurley Hey, revealed that half the city's pupils were attending at least once a week. Indeed, Mr Hey told a commission of inquiry, many of them were prepared to beg or steal to do so. One enterprising group had formed a begging circle for the purpose, which had met its demise when one member had stolen the group's hidden boots and stockings – removed to increase the impression of poverty – and had pawned them for cinema tickets. But *The Times* weighed in on the child's part. Criticism of the cinema as immoral was 'an expression of the type of mind which regards all pleasure as evil', the paper said in a leader column in January 1914. But the biggest question was: What would children do instead if the picture-houses were closed to them? 'Are their homes better ventilated than the palaces, or the street corners less draughty? Will they go to bed any earlier, or sleep any sounder for being left at home?'

Sonia Keppel, growing up in a wealthy household in London, would have had no such japes. However, her mother would occasionally take her to a matinée at the theatre, which in itself was a far from sedate experience.[17] 'Clearly I remember that it was a matinée about Nero, fiddling madly before the burning of Rome. A deafening thunderstorm went on in the background, through which Agrippina shrieked valedictions to her insensitive son. Alternately, the stage glowed red from the flames consuming Rome, or was blacked out altogether while the thunder lasted, or flared white with the lightning. Through all these extremes of heat and shade and light I clung to Mamma, protesting loudly that I was not frightened.'

Nor was the experience entirely free from violence: the Keppels had taken along a friend, Sir Hedworth Williamson, 'who appeared to treat the appalling scene in front of him with comforting levity'. Halfway through the performance, a lady arrived late and groped her way to a seat in the row behind. 'Then she took the long pins out of her hat and pinned it to the back of the seat in front of her. On the stage the lightning flared, and by its light I beheld the terrifying spectacle of Sir Hedworth Williamson impaled, like a gigantic butterfly, on the back of his seat. And a doctor had to be sent for to dress the wound and to treat him for shock.'

The Keppels evidently gained endless amusement from retelling the story later. Yet these excursions with her mother were rare, Sonia said, and mostly she 'accepted the current theory that a child must not be too much with its parents'. Yet, despite her admission that she longed to spend more time with her parents, she described the times she did spend with them – shopping trips, even a holiday in St Moritz – as times filled with fun and affection. The Edwardian age, Sonia said, was a time when the heavy mantle of Victoria's solemnity was lifted, and when both children and adults indulged – at least sometimes – in childish behaviour.

The world intrudes

Yet this was a turbulent age, with Britain preparing for war and with tension mounting over women's suffrage, Irish home rule and the reform of the House of Lords. And children were not immune to their odd outbreak of social unrest. In 1911, a wave of school strikes swept the country, during which pupils refused to work in protest at perceived injustices in their schools. It all began in Llanelli, in south Wales, when pupils had marched out of their classrooms in protest at the hitting of a child by an assistant teacher.[18] Similar strikes followed across the country, highlighting grievances over hours, leaving ages, holidays and discipline. By the end of a week, pupils had walked out of lessons in Liverpool, Sheffield, Birmingham, London and Glasgow, as well as in other cities. In the East End, school strikers armed themselves with iron bars, sticks and belts, though eventually their protest ended peacefully. *The Times*, while condemning the action, took a notably relaxed stance. Describing the outbreaks of unrest as 'a popular method of escape from the dullness of discipline and scholastic routine', the paper's leader-writer pointed out that none of this was new: 'The incident may serve to remind us, and especially those who are disposed to regard ill-disciplined boyhood as the peculiar product of twentieth-century legislation, that schoolboy strikes are probably as old as organized education itself,' the paper said. A school striker had lost his life at the Edinburgh High School in 1595, and those of a classical bent would recall that a similar incident had taken place in one of the Mimes of Herondas.

Parents could occasionally be part of the problem when school-children failed to behave, the paper added – 'Difficulties have arisen from time to time from the fact that parents of elementary school children, while anxious for good discipline, object to the use of ordinary instruments for maintaining it' – and maybe the strikes would lead them to discipline their own children better in future: 'These school strikes may serve a useful purpose if they induce parents to realize the limits of peaceful persuasion as an educative force.'

The class divide, which remained stark, loomed large in the lives of many children. Olive Everson, in Suffolk, was very aware of her social position.[19] 'Grannie was a person of refinement,' she explained, because she had taught in a small village school, while Olive's father was a worker on a country estate. Yet the Eversons were very aware of the social gulf that divided them not just from the family in the 'Big House' but also from those who owned their own land: 'I had a school friend whose parents lived at a farm. I often went there for tea, and on one occasion to their Christmas party,' Olive wrote. 'Relatives of the family were there in full force, and one elderly friend of the family was a lady who lived at the Manor Farm. Sitting at the far end of the table she directed her glance at me, the little girl whose father was merely a farm worker, and in a loud tone heard by everyone she remarked: "You don't get anything like this at home, do you dear?" I could only have been nine or ten years old, but I felt most embarrassed and resentful.'

Twice a year, 'her ladyship' would visit the village and leave parcels of her children's outgrown clothes. And at Christmas the wives would be sure to show their gratitude as they queued in the courtyard of the House to receive their annual joint of beef. Due respect was shown – on Sundays, when Olive sang in the church choir, she was exhorted by her parents not to try to crane her head to see 'the family' in their special box pew.

Sonia Keppel, meanwhile, remembered being regularly incarcerated inside just such a box pew during her family's regular visits to aristocratic friends in the country, and being completely unable to see out. Her mother, Alice Keppel, had a social conscience, though, and rather enjoyed embarrassing her wealthy friends by showing it. Often, Lord Alington, who owned large amounts of property in the East End, would call to invite Alice out for a drive: 'One rather dull day, he called for her and as usual asked her where he should drive her. "Hoxton, please," she said.' It transpired that Lord Alington had never actually been to Hoxton, despite owning large parts of it, and had no desire to go. But to Hoxton he now went, unable to refuse a lady's request: 'From her subsequent description the drive was funereal. Along dreary streets the horses clopped slowly, the smart equipage jeered at or sullenly watched by dull-eyed men and women and miserably-clad children. Through an occasionally open doorway the inmates of the carriage got a glimpse of disheartening squalor. Many of the window-frames had lost their glass, and the holes had been stuffed up with old rags or newspaper, or just left empty. At the end of it Lord Alington was speechless and miserable. As he dropped her at home, Mamma thanked him enthusiastically. "I do think it was charming of you to let me see Hoxton as it is now," she said. "Next time I go there, I shan't recognise it."'

On another occasion, during a Christmas shopping trip to Oxford Street, Sonia was entranced by a baby doll in a toyshop window. But so, too, was a ragged and dirty little girl of about her own age who was also staring at the doll from the pavement: 'Leaving me on the pavement and with bewildering speed, Mamma went into the shop, bought the doll and came out with it, still as it was, without its wrappings. Instinctively the child lifted up her thin little arms for it and Mamma laid the doll in them ... Mischievously, Mamma looked down at me, purple and furious. "I thought she needed it more than you did."'[20]

Sonia Keppel was ten when King Edward VII died of bronchitis and a series of heart attacks. The little girl had not been told the truth about her mother's relationship with the monarch: 'I was aware of some secret which even Violet shared, but which I was considered too young to understand.'[21] The King's death precipitated a family crisis for the Keppels. Alice and her husband George fled their home in the night; Sonia was taken the next day to join them at the house of some friends. Shortly afterwards, Alice set off on a tour of the Far East, and continued travelling for some time. Sonia would spend months in Germany with her nanny and governess, and would not see her parents for the best part of a year.

Despite the fact that the open secret of her mother's affair was spoken of only in whispered asides in her presence, Sonia's descriptions of daily life gave a sense that she was aware of much more than she could say. Her description of her nanny's daily ablutions make eye-opening reading: 'Surprisingly, under her martial exterior, Nannie had a snail's soft body. In the early morning light, under her voluminous nightgown, I could descry the pink folds of it. At one moment I could see the outline of a huge shoulder above the bath, then its eclipse behind a bath towel, then its emergence again for a tantalising minute, as she put on her bodice and stertorously pulled up her stays. There followed the camouflage of her petticoat, concealing the pulling on of knickers, more whalebone, more starch, clamping down a vast bosom, the fastening of sharp buckles and a brooch, like the riveting of armour.'

To a growing child, these glimpses of an unseen world seemed entirely natural. Olive Everson, growing up in Suffolk, recalled hearing a story about an elderly couple living in a nearby cottage: 'How we knew that the wife was one of those who accepted money for services rendered, I have no idea, but I expect brother Leslie had heard it from his mates at school. Her fee was said to be 1/-.' The children of the village gossiped in this way about several local women, the price of each being general knowledge – two shillings and sixpence for the youngest and most attractive: 'On Saturday and bank holiday evenings, when often local fishermen were home from a trip at sea, with pockets full of cash, these ladies would make for the Huntingfield Arms. At closing time they would take their clients for a walk up a secluded lane nearby,' Olive recalled.

If the cult of childhood in the Edwardian era was partly precipitated by a reaction to the stresses of urbanization, it was equally a reaction to a sense of a civilization in a different kind of decline: that of sexual degeneracy. There was a peculiar kind of double-think attached to sex during the period – everyone knew it went on, and yet a kind of collective innocence was feigned – sometimes to a start-ling degree. When J. M. Barrie published *The Little White Bird* – precursor to *Peter Pan* – in 1902, *The Times Literary Supplement* gave it a glowing review.[22] It was 'an exquisite piece of work', the paper said, and 'one of the most charming books ever written': 'If a book exists which contains more knowledge and more love of children, we do not know it.'

Yet the book contained passages which would never be published in today's more knowing world. At one point the author describes spending a night alone with a child: 'David and I had a tremendous adventure. It was this – he passed the night with me ... I took [his boots] off with all the coolness of an old hand, and then I placed him on my knee and removed his blouse. This was a delightful expe-rience, but I think I remained wonderfully calm until I came some-what too suddenly to his little braces, which agitated me profoundly ... I cannot proceed in public with the disrobing of David.'

Sonia's experiences in the years before the outbreak of war provided a striking counterpoint to this apparent state of denial. Entering her teens, she became increasingly aware of an exotic tinge to the artistic life of the capital, and to the performers who could now be seen there: 'In London, nothing like Nijinsky's lithe and sensuous dancing had been seen before, and Karsavina's interpre-tation of "Scheherazade" was voted to be equally seductive and disturbing. Many of those who saw their performance were power-fully affected by it, and some of the most unlikely people suddenly saw themselves as pagan gods and enchantresses,' she wrote. These influences were even percolating through the ceilings of the Keppels' home, through the activities of Sonia's older sister, Violet. By 1913, Violet had 'come out', into society, had put up heavy gold lamé curtains in her bedroom and was mixing with a racy crowd: 'She had Persian jackets for her friends to put on when they entered, and a huge feathered turban, along with incense.' It was this kind of avant-garde artiness to which Max Nordau had taken grave exception a couple of decades earlier in his influential book, *Degeneration*[23]. But now, as the young contemplated the prospect of war, it seemed to take on a new kind of intensity. At the home of a family with whom the Keppels spent Christmas, the teenage son had taken over a housemaid's cupboard as a 'studio', within which strange events were staged: 'Over the fireplace, Pan supplanted the sphinx,' Sonia remembered. 'And panthers and Nubian slaves seemed to be inextricably mixed up on the walls. Through the doorway, alluring strains of Rimsky-Korsakov's ballet music used to filter, toned down on the gramophone. Then more prosaically a strong smell of oranges. And then incense. Then someone would begin to read, slowly and sonorously. It did not sound much fun.' Years later she asked a shy boy who had been admitted to the broom cupboard to tell her what had occurred within. 'He had a slight stammer, and indignantly he spluttered out: "It was damned dull! They t-took off m-most of my clothes. And made me eat fruit!"'[24]

Yet when the long-anticipated war finally came, sweeping rich and poor together into the trenches, both were equally ill-prepared. Sonia and her family were on holiday in Holland when war was declared, and were forced to pack and leave in a hurry as the Germans invaded Belgium: 'The usual routine had been upset. Ordinarily, our packing was conducted almost invisibly . . . but . . . it had spilt everywhere and Papa and Mamma had packed as urgently as anyone . . . the meals had been equally disjointed, served by Mr Hillsden and one footman in incomplete livery, looking rather harassed and without their gloves.' The family found itself on the last boat back to England, which was besieged by crowds of people trying to board. Fortunately, the purser recognized them, and allocated them two cabins. 'Through the porthole of Mamma's and my cabin, I looked down on to less fortunate passengers jostling each other on the deck. One harassed mother was trying to cope with two crying children.

Inanely, I asked Mamma: "Where will those children sleep?" And inevitably, purposefully, Mamma replied: "There's plenty of room for them to lie down on the lower bunk in here."' Back in London, they found the house shuttered and cold, and repaired to the Ritz for breakfast.[25]

Meanwhile, in Salford, Elsie Oman's father had arrived home on leave from the merchant navy, full of excited anticipation: 'He had brought plenty of money home . . . he spoke about Germany, France and Belgium. The men seemed to be enjoying the thought of war . . . they thought it would be a picnic away from this dull life. They would be sure of good food and a uniform and sixpence a day and their wives and children would get an allowance, so everything in the garden would be lovely. So the men were all clamouring to join up, and it was said that as long as you were "warm" you were passed A1. They even took little men in and called them "bantams". The men soon found their mistake. We were no more prepared for war than Soft Nick.'[26]

The fathers go to war

'One wonderful evening we brought home a Shetland pony in the back of the car; it was four months older than me. The next morning we were brought down early from the nursery: Our Father was standing in the hall dressed in a tunic with gold buttons, riding breeches and tall, shiny brown boots. He hugged and kissed us, and our mother – and then he drove away. It was August, 1914.'[27]

For Hermione Llewellyn, born into a wealthy mine-owning and brewing family and watched over by nannies, this absence might have made little difference in practical, everyday terms. Yet all over the country, in all kinds of homes, similar scenes were being played out. Fathers were departing to join up, dashing in their new uniforms and apparently destined for great adventures. The departure of so many men from so many homes left a deep impression, and letters home were anxiously awaited.

Hermione's father was stationed in Norfolk with the South Wales Mounted Brigade, and the family was even able to rent a house nearby for a time. Yet the mood darkened when the men sailed for Egypt in the autumn of 1915: 'It was dreadful – we'd never before seen our mother cry.'[28]

In the early days of the war, most children were sheltered from the dread their parents must have been feeling, and letters home were usually upbeat. The letters of Private A. F. Uncle, written from Morn Hill Camp in Winchester to his daughters, Daisy, Ivy and Rosie, in London were typically cheerful: 'Don't worry about me, I am with a lot of jolly fellows and get plenty to eat. You would like to be a soldier – they give you DRIPPING on your bread for breakfast and tea nearly every day.'[29] And then, slightly more pensively as he departed to take part in the action: 'You will no doubt have received the parcel of togs and so know that I am now well away. I know you will be wondering what has become of me. Whatever happens its no use grumbling – here I am and here I must stay, so I shall endeavour to make myself as comfortable as possible.'

Elsie Oman in Salford, now a parentless teenager, for her mother was dead and her father away in the navy, followed developments along with her best friend, Vera, avidly but without any deep sense of fear: 'It made life much better for me. Vera and I had a good natter in the playground. Her mother used to buy papers and let Vera read them and her Mam and Dad would let her join in the conversation, so she had lots to tell me about the situation and it was becoming a new interest in life.'[30] And with the men gone, the world began to become a more feminine place: 'People seemed to come alive and as the men disappeared the women took over. They became tram drivers, conductors, postwomen, land army women on the farms, helped in the army, air force and navy – wherever there was a man shortage, the women were there, even on munitions,' Elsie recalled. Aged thirteen, she was now able to leave school and get a job in a sugar mill earning twelve shillings and sixpence a week. The now largely female workforce took her to its heart: 'It was wonderful to mix with young people who were laughing, singing and cracking jokes with one another. Despite being worried to death about their fathers, husbands, sons or brothers in the war, they tried to look on the bright side.'

Olive Everson, growing up in Suffolk, noticed only minor differences to her daily routine: 'It didn't affect our small village to any great extent – at least not the children. We noticed that some of the young men went away, and that our parents were careful to black out the windows at night because nasty things called Zeppelins dropped bombs from the sky. Ration books were necessary to take with us when we went to a shop. Flour, to make it go further, was adulterated with other substances and our mother's home-made bread no longer tasted as before and was a light brownish colour and sticky in the centre. My father was just too old to be conscripted and in any case he was engaged in work of national importance. He joined the volunteers and wore his uniform at weekends.'[31]

Yet for many families, especially in the poorer parts of the big cities, the early months of the war were a time of desperation. Many lost their main breadwinners quite suddenly, and the economy took months to settle into its wartime routine. Sylvia Pankhurst, who had been running a women's suffrage campaign in the East End of London, was shocked by the state in which she now found some of the children she knew in Stepney and Bow: 'I met little Rose Pengelly, one of our junior Suffragettes. "What are you doing in Ranwell Street?" I asked her, knowing the chronic poverty of that little alley. "All out of work, all helping each other," she chirruped gaily, flashing a merry smile to me, from her clear green eyes, her red plaits tossing. Yet I saw she was pale, and her gait not as buoyant as usual.'[32]

The wife of a ship's 'greaser' told Sylvia the government had commandeered her husband's ship, and since then she had had no money nor any word as to his whereabouts. She had six children, and the family had gone four days without food. Sylvia said she saw 'a wilted look' growing upon the children: 'They seemed like fading flowers.' A photograph taken at the time by Sylvia's friend Norah Smyth spells out the appalling hardships faced by some East End families in the early months of the war. In it is a child of maybe eighteen months, clearly close to starvation, legs stick-thin and hands clutching one another, almost claw-like in their frailty. The child – impossible to tell whether a boy or a girl – has only tufts of matted hair and its expression is a haunting mixture of curiosity and terror.[33]

Soon, the former Suffragette headquarters in the Old Ford Road had become a feeding centre for babies: 'Here, and in the passage through the house, the queue of distressed mothers extended: Already the babies were ill from starving; they could not digest the milk now we had got it for them.' Later, Sylvia would open a nursery in an old pub, renamed the Mother's Arms, along with cost-price restaurants and a toy factory. Yet many of the children were already in too poor a state to be helped: 'Several times it happened that after a baby had been nursed patiently to apparent health, and had been sent away to the country to assure its stability, it would return home, catch a chill or some childish ailment, collapse and die, quite suddenly, as though the physical well-being we had built for the little body had been merely a house of cards.'[34]

Sidney Day, born not far away in north London, was six when war broke out. His father spent almost the whole time in France, driving the horses that pulled the infantry guns. Sidney remembered regularly going without. 'While me Dad was away, me Mum had to keep the seven of us on rations. I would go round and get food from Buckingham's shop. Mum would say, "Take the cup with you and get an haporth of jam, a pennorth of sugar, a bit of tea, a tin of evaporated milk and a lump of margarine." We hardly ever seen any meat.' If Sidney thrived, it was largely through his own ingenuity: 'Every day I nicked something from the shops and stalls around Archway, specially the greengrocer's. If you are hungry you got to live.'[35]

Another major issue, Sylvia reported, was the growing number of illegitimate babies for whom there was little or no support. The army's separation allowances did not extend fully to unmarried partners and their children. The navy deducted sixpence from the daily pay of each sailor to send to his wife and children, but 'in respect of a bastard child, fourpence'. In many cases, even this paltry sum did not come through. Many of these now-absent young men would have married their sweethearts if they had known they were pregnant or had had the time to do so, Sylvia said – though there were also reports that men ordered by the courts to support their children were escaping their responsibilities by joining up.

Soon, though, even the most affluent homes were coming to terms with the horrors of war. Hermione Llewellyn, her mother and her brother Owen returned to her grandmother's large house after her father's departure for Egypt, only to find it had been turned into a hospital. Each week ambulances would arrive bringing bandaged soldiers: 'Owen kept asking who had hurt them and they always said, "The bloody Boche."'[36]

'Sometimes in our house grown-ups talked French, or stopped talking at all, when Owen and I were around. One day when Cook was having her afternoon rest Owen and I looked at her newspaper on the kitchen table: we saw dreadful pictures of men without arms or legs, and there were pictures of men all huddled together sleeping. Owen was five and owned a tricycle and explained it all to me: "There's been a quarrel between the Kings and Emperors," he said. "And now all the good men are fighting all the bad men." He told me the sleeping men in Cook's newspaper were dead but they were heroes and would go to heaven.'[37]

War work

Harry Watkin was six when the war started, the second of ten children born into a poor family in the slum district of Hulme in Manchester. Even at this tender age, and in the absence of a father who had joined up, it was his job to run most of his mother's errands. Later, he would remember thick fogs, broken only by candles carried in jam jars, and queues for everything.[38] 'The longest and slowest-moving queues in which I waited were those at the Medlock Street gasworks to buy coke. It was overall a wearisome task. First a wagon had to be borrowed from Jack Booth's coalyard in Duke Street. I had to beg, looking as humble and as grateful as I could, for the loan of one. They were very strong and heavy with iron handles and wheels and made a noisy clatter as they bumped along over the flags and setts. These coke errands meant half a day off school and I would take one of the children with me, riding in the wagon.'

Many children had work to do in wartime. In addition to his regular domestic duties, Harry took part in a national scheme to raise funds for refugees, which involved selling scent cards: 'They were coloured and strongly perfumed and every boy at school was given about a dozen to take home and sell. Well, I didn't even consider asking mother to buy one and I wouldn't have dreamt of trying to sell any to our neighbours – one never bothered with or spoke to women unless specifically sent by mother. So I just kept the cards until we were told to return all money and unsold ones. Obviously mine were soiled and creased, for there was no place in our house where they could have lain untouched. In spite of that I was given another batch. The procedure and result were as before.'[39]

Elsewhere, too, children were being pressed into the service of the war effort in all kinds of roles. If the Scout movement was ever to come into its own, now was the time. It was set up to build the physiques and the characters of the nation's youth – particularly the poor – for just such an eventuality as this. By 1918, it would boast 300,000 members, and a quarter of a million current or former Scouts would have served in the forces. Girls, too – in 1909 Baden-Powell had conceived a theory that middle-class girls needed to be less mollycoddled and more able to manage, if necessary, without the help of servants. 'You do not want to make tomboys of refined girls, yet you want to attract and thus to raise the slum girl from the gutter,' he had written in his *Headquarters Gazette*, adding: 'Girls must be partners and comrades rather than dolls.' And so the Girl Guides had come into being.[40]

If World War One has a major significance in the history of the English child, it is perhaps connected with this: the very notion of childhood now began, through children's war roles and through the growing influence of the Scout and Guide movements, to change. Even as the 'ideal' child's physical presence had begun to grow stronger in the years before the war, ultimately he had remained a somewhat wraithlike figure. Now a far more robust child began to solidify in the public imagination: a stout, capable child who had been trained in practical skills and who was willing to step up to the mark in a time of national emergency.

Baden-Powell's role in this transformation would be hard to over-estimate. Even before war broke out, he had offered the services of the Scouts as lookouts who could watch trunk lines and telegraphs between London and the coast to prevent sabotage by German infiltrators. Soon, Scout troops were also watching reservoirs, acting as messengers in public offices, hospitals and Red Cross centres, and helping the coastguards. By 1915, the Scouts were also serving refreshments to the troops in France from specially constructed 'huts'. Within months of the outbreak of war, thousands of Scouts were away from home on extended tours of coast-watching duty which lasted for many weeks at a time.

'We had the order to mobilise from the superintendent of police on August 6th at 11 a.m. and at 2 p.m. we started,' reported J. Barcham Green, Scoutmaster of the 11th CK Troop from Kent in November 1914, after a three-week tour watching the Deal to Dover road:[41] 'We went on duty at 6 a.m., watching the telegraph line and following suspected persons, of which there were a host. Our duty ended at 8 p.m. when the police took it over till 6 a.m. During our stay of three weeks we handed many suspected persons over to the police and military, had two aliens registered, tracked and shadowed many innocent persons whose movements were suspicious, mended various punctures and broken down bicycles and made many good friends. The Scoutmaster was arrested one fine afternoon while watching for a spy who was said to be disguised as a Scoutmaster, and he (our Scoutmaster) had a busy time explaining his identity.'

By December 1914, it was estimated that 100,000 Scouts had been employed in war work. And in that month, too, the first deaths of Scouts were recorded. The lists, which were printed each month in the *Headquarters Gazette*, would total 10,000 by the end of the war, some in air raids at home and some in action with the forces abroad. Baden-Powell has since been accused of helping to brainwash a generation of young men to go willingly to their own slaughter.[42] It is an accusation which is easy to make, for the Scout movement's founder certainly threw himself with gusto into the preparation of his charges for war.

'At present, only men of 19 and over, and of rather big size, are being enlisted for the service,' he wrote in the *Headquarters Gazette* in November 1914. 'The time may shortly come when the standard may be lowered, and younger men of smaller size admitted. I want all Scouts to Be Prepared for this and to have our Scouts Defence Corps ready, so that the moment the door is opened we can step in, trained and ready for service. The candidates should perfect themselves in the following duties: Rifle shooting, judging distance, signalling, pioneering, entrenching, drilling in accordance with the Army "infantry training", Scouting, first-aid, camp cooking.'

The Girl Guides were doing their bit, too, with Baden-Powell's sister Agnes at their head. But there were strict limits. Too much physical activity could fatally damage a girl's 'interior economy', Agnes explained.[43] 'Do you know that there are more girls nowadays with hairy lips than formerly, and I believe it is due to the violent exercise they take?' Guides were urged not to use vulgar slang such as 'topping' or 'ripping' or 'what ho!' and were put to work during the war training as volunteer nurses. The *Handbook for Girl Guides* suggested that 'really well-educated women' could also take up translating, dispensing to a doctor, stockbroking, house decorating, accountancy or even architecture as careers.[44]

The Girl Guides did have one notable victory over the Boy Scouts – early in the war, the nascent intelligence service had recruited a few of the boys as messengers, but had found them prone to getting into mischief during the long hours of forced inactivity. They turned instead to the Guides, who continued to supply them with girls aged between fourteen and sixteen throughout the war.[45]

On the land, too, children were everywhere pressed into service. This had been common practice before the war, with some areas fitting school holidays around harvest times, and children in many rural areas simply missing school when they were needed to pick fruit or work on the family farm. Now, a huge effort was made, in particular through the Scout movement, to recruit boys to work on the land. By June 1918, forty-six Scout troops from the East End were supplying about 300 boys to help farmers in Peterborough with their crops, for instance. But this was not universally regarded as a good thing, for many commentators tended to feel children were too easily exploited as cheap labour.

In one of his last parliamentary speeches before his death in September 1915, the Labour Party founder Keir Hardie – a vehement opponent of the war – spoke out against the practice. Education authorities all over the country were quietly allowing boys of eleven or twelve to leave school early so they could do agricultural and even manufacturing work, he said. He feared that if this were allowed, it might continue after the war and erode a century of progress in protecting children's rights: 'Once the principle is laid down it may become permanent,' he said, accusing the education authorities of 'robbing the child of the education which the law has provided for it'.

Yet with an estimated 60,000 agricultural workers now away at the war, and hundreds of thousands of jobs in other trades now vacant, Hardie and his supporters were left shouting into the wind. Children were legally allowed to leave school at thirteen with permission, and many did so much sooner, especially during the war. The President of the Board of Education, Joseph Pease, declared himself unable to do much about it. After all, he pointed out, many thousands of children were out of lessons because their schools had been comandeered by the forces.

Dora Dewar, a young teacher who worked near London's docks at Custom House during the war, recalled later that her pupils began to disappear as soon as spring was in the air: 'After Whitsun the great exodus began across the Woolwich ferry into Kent, first for pea-picking, then for the cherry picking and other soft fruit, then for the apples and pears and last of all the hops. They camped in tents and huts and had a glorious holiday and came back in early October like a horde of brown, shiny, smelly gipsies.'[46]

For other teenagers, there was no such happy ending to a spell of war work. Sylvia Pankhurst's young friend Rose Pengelly, by now aged sixteen, found a job in one of the factories which were crying out for women and girls to fill the places of the absent men. One Thursday just before Christmas 1915, she came to Sylvia's welfare centre to dance for the younger children. 'On Saturday she should have danced again – but the knife of the machine she was working descended on her pretty right hand, rending and mangling the thumb and a couple of fingers. Her new employer making no offer to pay a cab fare, she walked to the station, took the train to the London Hospital and there sat in the out-patients department till late in the evening, when her crushed thumb and two fingers were amputated.'[47]

Boy combatants and civilian casualties

Legally, the minimum age for enlistment in the army was eighteen, and soldiers were meant to be nineteen before they could serve overseas. Naval cadets could join at fifteen, but most did not see active service until they were older. But in truth many teenage boys were swept up in the jingoistic atmosphere of the time and managed to persuade the recruitment officers to turn a blind eye to their real age. The youngest fatality is reputed to have been John Condon, who was killed in May 1915 and who was said to be just fourteen years old – though there has been some dispute about this.[48]

Most boys joined for the glory and the excitement, yet the food was also an incentive. When Albert Farley, aged fifteen, sent his first letter to his family in London from a shore base near Chatham in Kent, much of his letter was taken up by a full description of the clothing and the meals he had been given: 'I am getting on all right with the bananas, salmon, sardines, bully beef, peas, pickle onions, shrimps for tea, cocoa for supper,' he wrote. 'Perhaps fried fish and salmon 2nd course dinner, bananas, apple, custard and plums on Sunday.' Albert reported, with all the wide-eyed enthusiasm of a pupil writing home from boarding school, that he also had four new 'duck suits', three hats, a toothbrush and two sets of singlets and drawers: 'Everything A1.' Albert died four months later along with about 400 other sailors when HMS *Natal*, the ship on which he had become a stoker, caught fire while at anchor in the Cromarty Firth and was ripped apart by a series of explosions.[49]

But the most celebrated of these boy combatants was Jack Cornwell, who, like Albert Farley, was fifteen when he joined up and sixteen when he died. Unlike Albert, Jack became a national hero and was posthumously awarded the Victoria Cross. He died standing alone at his exposed post on the deck of HMS *Chester*, awaiting orders while under fire during the Battle of Jutland in May 1916. In different times the reaction might well have been that Jack Cornwell was too young to fight and that he should never even have been there. Yet the navy did not even attempt to play down the significance of Jack's extreme youth. Far from it: the boy's tender age was used to highlight his act of heroism. The *Daily Sketch* splashed his photograph across its front page. The *London Gazette*, recording the awarding of the Victoria Cross in September 1916, reported: 'Mortally wounded early in the action, Boy, First Class, John Travers Cornwell, remained standing alone at a most exposed post, quietly awaiting orders, until the end of the action, with the gun's crew dead and wounded around him. His age was under sixteen and a half years.'

Jack Cornwell had been a Boy Scout, and the movement, too, was eager to honour his life and death. The *Headquarters Gazette* reproduced a letter written to the boy's mother by the captain of his ship: 'I cannot express to you my admiration of the son you have lost from this world. No other comfort would I attempt to give to the mother of so brave a lad, but to assure her of what he was, and what he did, and what an example he gave. I hope to place in the boys' mess a plate with his name on and the date and the words, "Faithful unto Death".' Money was raised for an impressive memorial in Manor Park Cemetery in east London. A few months later Jack's father, Eli, who had joined the army, was buried in the same grave. Jack Cornwell is also remembered in a memorial in Chester Cathedral.

None of those young recruits could have known what they were going into. C. J. Arthur, who was fifteen when the war broke out, had joined his school's cadet battalion in 1914. A few months on, he recorded later, he told his commanding officer he was going to join up: 'Good,' he said. 'What age do you want to be?' Armed with a letter, he presented himself to the colonel of an infantry battalion, who told him to get his hair cut and made him a lancecorporal. Ten weeks later, he was promoted to sergeant, and in 1916, still aged just seventeen, was sent to the trenches in France. When volunteers were sought for a raid, he pushed himself forward: 'The major had seen service in Gallipoli, and was not nearly so bloodthirsty as we new soldiers, and he promptly asked me if I wanted to end my young life. Being facetious, I answered that I thought there was a war on. I had my wish ... one of the casualties was the company sergeant-major, whose place I had to take before I was eighteen.'[50] Arthur recorded that he had 'lost at least half my bravado' by the time he had survived the Somme, but unlike so many others he did outlive the war.

At home, too, the casualties were mounting. Although the death toll from bombings was not so high as it would be in World War Two, it was still significant. An official report published after the war recorded the total numbers of children killed at home, in aeroplane and Zeppelin raids, and in bombardments of the east coast from the sea, to have been almost 300. A total of 770 children were known to have been injured.[51]

The worst atrocity occurred on 13 June 1917, a hot, hazy day. Residents of London's East End reported looking up to see a couple of dozen silver planes 'like big dragonflies' in the sky. The shrapnel bombs they were carrying would kill a total of 104 people that day. Among them would be a class of five- and six-year-old pupils who were in lessons at Upper North Street School, Poplar, when one of the bombs hit and devastated their classroom. Sixteen of them would die. Rose Moorhouse was among the survivors: 'We didn't hear anything, no noise, no bomb falling,' she recalled later. 'Next thing I remember was that I felt heavy, I could scarcely breathe. I kept falling into unconsciousness, then waking up, to hear the sound of myself moaning.'[52] Rose was buried for three days while her older brother Jimmy kept returning to the site to dig for her, convinced she was buried alive there. On the third night, he heard her moaning and, along with a policeman, managed to dig her out.

The event caused widespread horror and dismay, and a fund was set up to erect a memorial – still standing today – and to send the victims' surviving siblings out of London for a holiday. Yet some fatal raids were met with a much more prosaic response. C. Ward, a Scoutmaster from Hartlepool, reported in 1915, for instance, on the German bombardment of the town in February that year. As firing began from the sea, the town's scouts were dispatched on bicycles to call up 'special constables' from outlying areas. 'I felt quite proud of the scouts, they seemed to think only of duty, heedless of the bursting shells all around them they really behaved like seasoned veterans under fire – quite cool, calm, and collected,' Mr Ward reported in the *Headquarters Gazette*. A scoutmaster and three scouts were killed while doing 'good turns' running messages, he said. Yet there was a silver lining – recruitment had received a boost as a result: 'The visit of the Germans has certainly given a fillip to the scout movement locally.'

Not everyone was so brave under fire. *The Times* reported in December 1915 that London's Chief Inspector of Schools had read out a series of children's essays about their experiences of Zeppelin raids: 'My father was frightened during the raid and he ran into a beer shop and got under the counter and stayed there until it was all over,' one such essay reported. Another added: 'A man came into the public house and said: "Give me half a pint. If I am going to die, I will die drunk."' Most of the children recorded how exciting they had found the raids, though, and many of the boys spent time afterwards hunting for souvenirs.

As the war went on, even those not directly affected could no longer ignore the horror of what was happening overseas. Elsie Oman, now working in a sugar factory in Salford, remembered seeing wounded soldiers who were being billeted in a local school because the hospital was full: 'There were quite a lot of wounded young soldiers on crutches with legs missing, some with arms off and some blind. In fact some of them looked too young to be in the army. It made a shiver go down your spine to watch the poor things hobbling about in their hospital blue.'[53] And the arrival of a Post Office messenger was greeted with dread: 'Sometimes when we were going to school or on an errand we would see the messenger boy from the GPO and that meant a telegram for somebody. We would stand and wait to see which house he would go to. They were coming very frequently and nine times out of ten they would bear the familiar words: "Deepest Sympathy".'

In north London, Sidney Day's father would come home on leave with the smell of the front hanging around him. 'When he had leave from the army he would come home, straight out of the trenches, mud everywhere, filthy. The poor old bugger had puttees wrapped round his legs up to his knees and the mud was all caked in where they hadn't been taken off for weeks and weeks. His legs looked like ladders from the marks round them made by the ties.'[54] Sidney's father survived the war and came home, his lungs permanently scarred by gas but, as Sidney noted, better off than an uncle across the street, who had lost most of his jaw.

Sonia Keppel's wealthy and well-connected father was in France, too. His early letters, she said, were 'full of almost boyish adventures which I, at least, could share. Unlike me, Mamma and Violet were not taken in.' Now these letters began to change and 'although they nearly always contained something to laugh at, through them now seemed to ooze a trickle of mud from France'. On his fiftieth birthday, the family sent a hamper from Fortnum's, and he reported that he and his men had enjoyed it but so, too, had the rats. When he came home on leave Sonia was shocked to see his changed appearance. 'I grew up a lot ... suddenly the positions were reversed. Now here was Papa, dependent on me. "Is it awful at the front, Papa?" once I asked him. And he nodded back at me, gravely smiling. "Not too good, Doey," he admitted, pressing my hand. "Not too good."' Fortunately for Sonia, her father was transferred to Ireland just before most of his battalion was wiped out at the Somme. Sonia's sister, Violet, was not so lucky. Three of the friends with whom she had enjoyed high jinks before the war – including a particularly close friend called Billy – were killed in the space of three months. 'Much has been written of the lost generation and of the irreparable gap it left,' Sonia wrote. 'And almost the most tragic part of it was that it was lost so quickly, largely within three years ... I can remember Billy, on a day of spring sunshine, playing beautiful tennis and then, flinging down his racquet, making quick, skilful sketches.'

The armistice was greeted with relief and an official stiff upper lip. In Hulme, Harry Watkin's headmaster brought the news to his pupils: 'Mr Holmes came into our classroom and told us that the war was over, but if we wished to applaud it must be done quietly. Then came his instructions. The few boys who were wearing stiff Eton collars should tap on them with their finger tips [instead of clapping]. He then solemnly made his announcement and we responded. We had the afternoon off.'

And Hermione Llewellyn's dashing father, who had gone off with his horse to Egypt at the start of the war, was coming home too: 'When the telegram arrived we were with our mother picking lavender in the garden. Nannie brought it out from the house: she held the envelope out by one corner as if it was a firework which might explode. Our mother opened it carefully and slowly: we all watched and saw that her hands were shaking. She seemed to take ages to read such a little bit of paper. And then she stooped down and scooped all three of us into a bundle and cried: "Your father is coming back. He's coming home soon. He'll be here soon, soon, soon . . ." We ran all the way to the Hall to tell Gran and she and our mother hugged each other and cried.'

4   Between the Wars

'The war ended and me Dad come home,' Sidney Day would write later.[1] 'After he got gassed in France he never could breathe through his nose properly again. Sometimes he was in so much pain with his nose he would come home from work at dinner time and put his head over a bowl of hot salt water and sniff it up. That was the only way he could shift it. Me mum's brother, Rob, who lived right opposite us, was much worse off. He lived with his wife Ginny and their kids . . . he had half his jaw blown off in the war. For a pension he got the big amount of two and sixpence a week. The poor old bugger only had half a jaw and looked a sight, but he got used to it at the death. He still knew how to drink a pint of beer.'

For the Day family of Archway, north London, life would go on – indeed, the six-year-old Sidney seems to have taken it in his stride. 'Me dad was never sober when we was kids, but he was a proper father. He showed us where to go scrumping, where to go bird catching, where to go fishing. We collected walnuts in the season and pickled them. We made horseradish sauce by digging down deep for the root, grating it and mixing it with vinegar. We always had a pocket of beech nuts or cob nuts in the autumn. We made elderflower wine in spring,' he wrote.[2] Yet somehow the mud that squaddies like Sidney's father had brought home from the trenches had besmirched this idealized Edwardian notion of childhood, and nothing could ever really be the same again.

Among the adults of that generation – the parents of the children who would be born between the wars – there would always be an abiding sense of dread. This was the generation that had survived one war and lived with the fear that before long – perhaps just as its children grew old enough to be called up – there would be another.

Some, once the war was over, threw themselves into the frantic partying which would come, in the eyes of posterity, to characterize the world of privilege in the 1920s – the world of the flapper and the age of jazz. One history of the period is entitled *We Danced All Night*;[3] another, *The Morbid Age*.[4] The two titles, taken together, seem to sum up the spirit of the times.

Emma Smith, born in Newquay in 1923, would grow up in an atmosphere of troubled respectability:[5] 'My mother stretches her hand across the table towards my father. It's her way of saying she's sorry to him for something. I don't know what. I sit in my high chair and watch. Her hand lies on the tablecloth, palm upwards, open. She wants him to take it, but he lets it lie there … Then at last he does put out his and allows her to take it, but I see the look in his eyes and because it's a terrible look, I remember it. Later, much later, I learn the word that describes the look. It is hate.'

Emma Smith – born Elspeth Hallsmith – was the daughter of a bank clerk who dreamed of being a famous painter. Her parents had married – unhappily – in 1919, soon after her father had been released from a German prisoner-of-war camp. And although the war was ancient history to children such as herself and her sister Pam, it seemed to hang around: of the groundsman at the local tennis club, she wrote: 'Our father and Wilton are different in every particular except for being, both of them, very silent men. Wilton doesn't call all the members of the tennis club "Sir": he chooses whom he will respect. There are those who say that the groundsman is bolshie.

He looks at them with contempt, in the same way as our father regards his bank manager, Mr Oxley, with contempt. Our father and Wilton were both in the Great War. They have this in common. Is it the Great War that Wilton is thinking about as he silently, broodingly mows the grass of the tennis club courts? Is it because our father was awarded a medal, the DSO, that Pam and I are allowed the out-of-season privilege of playing on the creosote-smelling step of the tennis club pavilion?'[6]

The 1920s were a period in which, it seems now, shadows hung heavy over family life. For Hermione Llewellyn, born into a wealthy mining and brewing family, there would be a dizzying downward spiral into excess, followed by debt, followed by disaster. Hermione's dashing father, back from the war, was determined to live the life of the landed aristocracy. He had bought a country manor called Combend, several fast cars, plentiful quantities of livestock and numerous horses and dogs. No one had ever counted the cost, until one day it all came to a sudden, painful end. Hermione's mother was forced to break the news one teatime.

'We'd raced up the secret stairs to the story-time room and found her looking so pretty in a tea gown, with a leather-bound copy of *Huckleberry Finn* on her lap.[7] She began to read but suddenly tears streamed down her cheeks and then, with difficulty, she said: "Combend has been sold – our house and land ..." "Why, why, why?" we asked, but she wept so much she could not answer. Nor did she ever answer that question – to any of us.' There followed a painful process of negotiation, in which the children were forced to give away most of their toys and pets before moving to a much smaller house: 'On 17 March, when all was settled, we drove slowly, like a funeral cortege, along our drive; I felt sick and sad and also uncomfortable. I had hidden two of my mice and four Roman snails in small cardboard boxes in my knickers; for once it helped that I was rather plump.'

The 1920s were a time of collective denial, of a sort of national attempt to find meaning, or at the very least joy, in a world that was badly soiled. This was an age in which survivors' guilt touched every adult, particularly the men, and in which children experienced a dislocation – a feeling that they could never quite know, or understand, what ailed their parents. In many households, the psychological scars of war and its aftermath were unspoken but ever-present.

For the Llewellyn family, the tension that lay just under the surface of everyday life became increasingly hard to deny. Hermione, packed off to boarding school at the age of thirteen, was surviving quite well until her letters from home suddenly stopped: 'As the weeks passed, I grew frightened . . . huge carbuncles appeared on my thighs and before long I could not walk or run normally. When one burst, it was so enormous and frightful that it hit the ceiling. Bunny [the school matron] insisted I tell her what I was thinking about. She said one's mind can affect one's body.'[8]

The matron phoned Hermione's grandparents, and was informed that her parents had separated. No one knew where her father was, and her mother was seriously ill in an asylum in Bristol. She had descended into mental illness, from which she would never recover. The response – both from the matron at Hermione's school and subsequently from the family – was indicative of a fundamental change which would ultimately come to alter the mindset of all Western societies. Somehow, humanity had begun to creep in. The work of Freud and his contemporaries, which had made little impact on the wider public when it had first appeared in the early years of the twentieth century, was now beginning to be absorbed into the fabric of human interaction. What was happening – perhaps little recognized at the time – was a portent of a huge, almost geological, shift. Until this point, judgements about human beings and their inherent flaws had tended to be made through a prism with a distinctly religious tint. As the Enlightenment debates about whether children were ultimately born good, needing protection from the corruption of the world, or evil, needing stern instruction to enable them to operate by a moral code, demonstrated, the world's view of the child – indeed, of mankind itself – had up until now been largely biblical. Now, the notion of the child as an individual began to creep in. This philosophy was still nascent, of course, and the theories of human development which had begun to be accepted were largely driven by biological determinism – each child had to go through certain stages of development, and if those stages were not passed satisfactorily, then disaster could strike. If each hurdle were not, as it were, jumped, then the child's development could be arrested.

That Hermione's school matron had already absorbed the theory that physical ailments could have psychological causes is interesting. Perhaps the recognition of 'shell shock' after the war was helping the notion of the psychological to creep further into the public consciousness; perhaps she was a woman ahead of her time. But, certainly, there was a new awareness surrounding issues about mental health. Hermione's father reappeared, and did his best to help his ailing wife towards a cure. The standard procedure among the wealthy classes at the time – and the one the Llewellyn family adopted – was to take the afflicted one to Switzerland for a cure. Hermione, now aged twelve, was removed from her boarding school to spend her days – and nights – helping to care for her seriously disturbed mother. But to no avail: 'Our nights became terrible. When it grew dark she had hallucinations and thought dreadful creatures were crawling across the walls and ceiling of her bedroom. She dared not go to sleep lest they harm her . . . my father and I took turns to sit up all night in her bedroom to try and comfort and reassure her, but gradually we both grew exhausted from lack of sleep . . . eventually our kind and clever Swiss doctor persuaded our father that she should move to a nursing home at Nyon on Lake Geneva.'[9]

The importance of this growth in psychological understanding for the way humans saw – and still see – their children can hardly be overstated. It was the beginning of a profound change in attitudes to children and childhood which would gather pace throughout the rest of the twentieth century. And its profundity sprang from the new sense, ushered in by Freudian psychology, that a child was neither a blank slate upon which to be written nor a creature of biblical sin, but an individual. The notion that children had psychological needs, as well as physical needs, would bring deep and lasting change in the way they were reared. And indeed it was not long before these new ideas began, tentatively at first, to extend their roots into the world of parenting. In 1929, the *Guardian* reported that the Chelsea Babies' Club was hosting a series of lectures on child psychology for mothers. The aim, the paper said, was to give middle-class women access to the sort of advice which those from poorer backgrounds were already receiving in state-aided welfare centres: 'One of the chief duties of a mother is to teach her child to grow away from her and to become an individual,' the article explained. 'The child must learn to do without his mother as early as possible, though still regarding her as his best friend ... one of the most important conditions of successful child development is that of absolute harmony between the parents, which will not easily be achieved unless both parents have lives of their own.' Even more strikingly, the article also explained that a mother would not be a good mother – and indeed could suffer mental breakdown – if her own talents and desires were thwarted. A professional mother with a life outside the home was considered entirely a desirable thing.

Changing children

Why this new focus on children? Perhaps the shrinking of the family had led parents to begin to see their children's individuality, just as the growing influence of Freudian psychology had led to a new, more child-focused approach to parenthood. It would be wrong, of course, to suggest that the experience of the average child changed overnight. Yet it did change, incrementally, over the following decades. Children, increasingly, were permitted to hold opinions, and even to express those opinions in public. During this period, the *Guardian* ran two long pieces of advice to parents from a fourteen-year-old girl named Catharine Alexander: 'If your children are artists and you live in a large house, try to give them each a room to work in. If you live in a small house, don't all cram into one hot, stuffy little room . . . The children become pasty and white and spotty and have bad complexions. The parents become consumptive and die off in the end,' she advised.

If there were to be fewer children – and there were, thanks to the international birth control movement, pioneered by Marie Stopes – then they were going to be stout, uncomplicated children who breathed plenty of fresh air and developed healthy lungs and chunky calves: 'Send them to school as soon as possible, where they will be punched and cuffed into shape, and sent back to you a happy, strong, healthy, ordinary child . . . I should let your children have fairly large appetites, for it keeps them strong and healthy,' Catharine Alexander advised. And Sir Frederick Truby King, who was fast becoming the childcare guru of his day, had rather similar thoughts: 'Ask any capable farmer what steps he takes to ensure the health and safety of the mothers of his flocks and herds, and he will tell you free range in the open air and daily exercise are the first essentials, and without these both mother and offspring suffer . . . Pure air and sunshine have almost as much effect on the health and strength of both mother and child as good food . . . Regulated sunbathing is highly beneficial.'[10]

The children's literature of the period tended to reflect two ongoing trends: the continuing sense that the healthy, wholesome child was a country child; and the fear that the nation would soon be swamped again by war. So the Walker children of Arthur Ransome's *Swallows and Amazons* novels were allowed to rampage cheerfully across the Cumbrian countryside with little parental control; yet in the background lurked always a sense that this was an idyll that could be lost. Mr Walker was always away – or about to be called away – because he was a naval commander. In one notable episode, a telegram to his base in Malta about whether the children should be allowed to sail to an island on Coniston Water brings the response: 'BETTER DROWNED THAN DUFFERS IF NOT DUFFERS WON'T DROWN.' Richmal Crompton's William Brown, meanwhile, lived a rather more suburban life, his scrapes generally of a lesser order – the Walker children drift out into the North Sea in one memorable sailing episode in a later novel, and find themselves in Holland, while William's most violent episodes are mere scraps with the Outlaws' arch-enemies, the Hubert Lane-ites. But a key feature of both Ransome's and Crompton's works was the stable family life to which the children always returned. The Walker children always greeted the arrival of their father with unbridled joy, despite his long absences, while William's family – aunts, siblings, placid mother and forbidding father, are treated with a sort of humorous accept-ance. In an age of fear and uncertainty, the emphasis on the impor-tance of family, of hearth and home, tends to grow. And that was certainly a feature of this particular era.

While the urban poor – or at least some of them – now had access to clinics and while the mothers of Chelsea could attend lectures on childcare, the mother who was bringing up her family in the rapidly expanding suburbs had Truby King by her side. His book contained a picture of a boy, aged four, 'reared according to the principles advo-cated in this book'. He was blond, his hair combed to one side and shining, and he was wearing well-pressed shorts with a shirt and tie. Everything about him spelled healthfulness and wholesomeness.[11]

There were shades, in all this, of the political future of Europe in the coming decades. Marie Stopes and her birth control campaigners were not only about helping parents to bring wanted children into the world, but also about ensuring that the wrong kinds of children were eliminated. The birth control movement was connected to a growing interest in eugenics, and to the general fearfulness of the age.[12] Its proponents were fired up by the Malthusian belief that population growth would always outstrip the supply of food and other resources, and would be counteracted by war or by disease. Stopes had joined the Malthusian League, whose motto was: 'Non Quantitas sed Qualitas', or 'Not Quantity but Quality', in 1917. Later, she left to form the Society for Constructive Birth Control and Racial Progress. She opened the first birth control clinic in London in 1921 – in Holloway, not far from where Sidney Day and his rumbunctious, impoverished family were eking out a living. Indeed, Day acknowledged that numerous babies were a fact of life in this district: 'Me dad . . . loved his pint, they all did. That was all they had to do, let's face it – drink and make babies . . . Me poor mum, what with all the washing, ironing and cooking, she was worn out before she died, poor old sod.'[13]

In May 1921, at a meeting in the Queen's Hall, Stopes lectured her audience on the perils of allowing 'wastrels' to breed. Over the coming years, the pre-war fear that the quality of the population was inadequate to the task of maintaining an empire would again come to the fore. In 1931, a Sterilization Bill would be unsuccessfully introduced in the House of Commons, and during the 1930s a number of eminent people would promote the view that population must be regulated in order to ensure good stock. In 1934, an official committee would recommend the voluntary sterilization of people considered mentally or physically defective.[14] Lloyd George had opined that it was impossible to run an A1 empire with a C3 population, and he was not alone. In 1935, the BBC would broadcast a debate involving G. K. Chesterton, Bertrand Russell and the psychologist Cyril Burt, on the motion that: 'Parents are Unfitted by Nature to Bring up their own Children'. Burt explained that, in his opinion, many parents were unfit not merely to raise their children, but to have them in the first place.

These two enthusiasms, for psychoanalysis and for birth control, were combined in a series of lectures Stopes gave about sex education, and in particular about 'cleanliness, disinfection and chastity in the home'. The idea that children should be taught about sex was now beginning to grow, and was spelt out in two slim volumes published by the British Hygiene Council: *What Fathers Should Tell Their Sons*, and *What Mothers Must Tell Their Children*.[15] The first volume focused mainly on the risk of venereal disease: 'Alcohol diminishes control over the lower nature, so that it may safely be said that it is a large factor in the causation of venereal disease. Alcohol is not needed by the young, and they are much better without it. The best moral school is a good home, where high ideals are inculcated by example.' The second, illustrated with a reassuring line drawing of a mother reading to a well-groomed and clearly hygienic boy and girl, both with sensible knee-length socks and well-brushed, shiny hair, gave advice mainly on the evils of masturbation – for boys – and of sex outside marriage – for boys and girls: 'If very unfortunately a boy or a girl has attempted to live a married life before marriage, that is to say if they have prematurely and wrongly used the sacred powers of their body, it is only too likely that such young people may have injured themselves.'

At this time, widely held beliefs about heredity and biological determinism – which had been growing in the public consciousness since Darwin published his *On the Origin of Species* in 1859 – seemed to sit quite comfortably alongside the notion that a child could be formed, or its development distorted, by circumstance. Indeed, Freud had done a great deal to popularize the idea that the human personality was formed by an interaction between biology and nurture. And Truby King helped further in promoting the view that there could not only be good or bad nature, but also good or bad nurture. In 1909, he had given a lecture on 'Parenthood and Race Culture', part of which was reprinted in his classic baby-care book: 'The decadence of nations is threatening many lands. France, with its declining birth rate, has already become a second-class power ... the decay of Greece and Rome was not primarily due to a falling-off in the prowess of the phalanx and the legion, but to increasing luxury, lessened exertion, lessened contact with the open air, a growing cost in the standard of living, and an increasing selfishness, which expressed itself in a disinclination for the ties of marriage and parenthood ... if we lack noble mothers we lack the first element of racial success and national greatness.'

So the obsession with the degradation of the race, which had loomed so large in the public mind before the war, had not gone away. Indeed, it was gaining strength, thanks to the efforts of the eugenics movement, and also in part to the work of an ambitious young psychologist named Cyril Burt. Shortly after his death in 1971, Burt would be exposed and pilloried for having falsified some of his research data. He would come to be seen by the liberal classes of later years as a sort of neo-fascist hate figure whose work on intelligence and its determinist nature was racist and in need of dismantling. But much of his early work must have seemed liberal, if not radical, at the time. Before and after World War One, Burt conducted research which would have a profound effect.

In 1909, he had published a paper for which he had subjected a group of thirteen children at a prep school in Oxford to a series of tests. He then ran similar tests on a group of pupils at a council school in London. The prep school boys having scored more highly, Burt had concluded that the effect was hereditary.[16] The prep school boys were superior because their parents were superior, and their parents before them. Burt felt this knowledge could be put to good use. In 1918, Burt, by now the school psychologist for the London County Council, told an audience of social workers that it might be possible to develop a complete 'psychogram' of each child, which would help to determine what kind of work he or she might be fitted for. Every school leaver might be given a special dossier which would be passed to a juvenile advisory committee. Everyone would thus be categorized, indexed and correctly filed.

And while that never happened, the use of IQ testing became ever more widespread in British schools, and would later influence the 'eleven plus' exam on which entry to post-World War Two grammar schools would depend. Yet despite the centrality of the hereditary principle to Burt's thinking, he was also an early proponent of the idea that individual children had individual needs. He was one of the first to propose 'special' schools for children with disabilities – or 'defective children', as they were known at the time. And his work on young delinquents led to the opening of one of London's first child guidance clinics.

Burt's book, *The Young Delinquent*,[17] was published in 1925 and was a product of its time. Since the war had ended, the ongoing debate on childhood had come back to one of its perennial themes – concern about levels of crime among the young. There had been a growing number of juveniles charged with offences, with the total rising from 12,000 in 1910 to more than 29,000 in 1938.[18] Yet the focus, in this newly individualistic, child-focused world, was surprisingly liberal. In keeping with the new-found emphasis on psychology, the state had begun to focus not on punishment but on treatment. Indeed, it is significant that a book such as Burt's, written as it was by an educational psychologist rather than by someone from the criminal justice system, should have proved so influential.

In one sense it is not at all surprising that the book should have proved a hit, though. Burt's sense of drama and his ability to tell a good tale were striking. 'One sultry August afternoon, in a small and stuffy basement kitchen not far from King's Cross Station, I was introduced to a sobbing little urchin with the quaint alliterative name of Jeremiah Jones,' the book began. 'Jerry was a thief, a truant and a murderer. When first I saw him, he was just seven and a half years old, a scared and tattered bundle of grubbiness and grief, with his name still on the roll of a school for infants. Yet at this tender age, besides a long list of lesser faults, he had already taken another boy's life.'

Jerry, Burt confessed, was the only child murderer he had met during his researches. But he felt that in many ways his case, though extreme, could illustrate the common causes of child crime. The little lad had been the product of a chance encounter between his mother, then a chambermaid, and 'a quiet gentleman, well connected and seemingly well-to-do', who had been passing through and who had subsequently vanished without trace. Jerry's Welsh mother was 'in temperament somewhat dull and erratic'. She now worked as a packer in a warehouse and shared the subterranean bedsit room with Jerry and with her own elderly mother, who doted on the boy.

A fatal interplay between defective nature and inadequate nurture had been Jerry's undoing, Burt explained. Jerry was 'a weak, backward and excitable boy – just the type of youngster likely to dive into the first mischief that offered'. But he could only have come to commit such an appalling crime, he went on, because of the conditions in which he was placed – a lax, foolish grandmother, a school too far away from home and the daily absence of his mother had all played their parts.

At six, Jerry had fractured his skull while climbing on to a moving lorry. After a long spell away from school, first in hospital and later in a convalescent home, he had failed to settle, and had begun truanting – hanging around the station, which was near his home, as well as the nearby Regent's Canal. And it was during one of these illicit fishing trips that he had committed his crime. On a summer evening, he had been at the canal with two other little truants, one of whom had a little toy aeroplane. Jerry, coveting the toy, demanded he be given it. The other boy refused.

'Jerry, still cool and self-contained, announced that unless he "had that airyplane" he would "drahnd" the owner. The owner merely scoffed and pulled a face. So Jerry carried out his threat,' Burt reported. 'With a little skilful footwork, he threw the other off his balance; tipped him backwards into the water, well knowing (so he said) that "the water would choke him"; kicked away the child's fingers as he clutched the bank; and then watched him, with jibes and taunts, while his body went under.'

The crime initially went undetected. At the inquest, Jerry – still apparently emotionless in the face of his friend's death – maintained that the boy had fallen backwards into the canal. Indeed, he was congratulated by the coroner on his ultimately vain efforts to save his friend. Yet afterwards, his crime began to find him out: his behaviour became increasingly erratic – the sign, Burt suggested, of a guilty conscience. 'There were wild outbursts of inexplicable passion, half terror and half temper, such as in an adult would have been called hysteria or mild mania.' Burt was called in, and quickly obtained a full confession. Jerry had a longstanding resentment of the other boy, and had more than once threatened to 'take him to the cut and shove him in'.

The causes of Jerry's crime, Burt concluded, were as much social as they were congenital: 'Jerry, dimly conscious of a shadow on his birth, slowly framing to himself a notion of some social grievance, had grown fiercely resentful of the slurs that the neighbours cast upon his parentage. The very play-fellow, whose life he took, was wont to taunt him with an ugly name. This longstanding provocation, more than any passing whim for a twopenny toy, was the ulterior motive, though doubtless a half-unconscious motive, for his sudden violence.' Psychoanalysis, Burt thought, would have unearthed a deeper instinctive cause of Jerry's violent reaction to these slurs, and would also have cast light on how the boy's natural development had been twisted by his unfortunate circumstances.

The psychologist having detected the crime, the forces of the law might have been expected to take over. But what happened next was, to the modern eye, one of the most striking parts of the story. Burt made no mention at all of any police involvement in the case. His solution was not punishment, but treatment: 'The new device of mental testing, and particularly the measurement of intelligence, have entirely revolutionised the old methods of studying the criminal,' he wrote. Indeed, had the father of the dead boy not learned the truth and begun threatening both Jerry and his mother, he might have remained in the tenement basement where he had spent his early years. Even then, nothing seems to have happened, except that with Burt's help Jerry was removed to 'another home' outside London, presumably in the hope that immersion in a more desirable social setting would effect a cure for his criminal nature.

When the book was published in 1925, Burt wrote in its introductory section that Jerry had now been in three such 'homes', and that 'there evidently remains a great deal more that has yet to be learnt about his capabilities for good and evil'. It seems extraordinary, looking at this case now, that a child murderer should have gone unpunished in this way. Extraordinary, indeed, not just in the light of modern sensibilities but also in the light of the fact that the Victorians seemingly made little distinction between a child in the dock and an adult in the dock – in the late nineteenth century, the newspapers had often reported that a child had been punished for some minor offence by imprisonment or deportation.

Could Burt have made the whole story up? If it were true, then certainly it never made the papers. They did report several cases of drowning in the Regent's Canal in the early 1920s – indeed, at one point there was such a spate that the coroner issued a warning that it was dangerous for children to play near the water. Yet none quite fitted the tale the psychologist told. And, of course, Burt was later accused of fabricating research evidence. So it is indeed possible that the tale of little 'Jerry' was a fiction, or a half-truth.

Yet the fact that an eminent psychologist could report such an occurrence without attracting comment was surely indicative of something significant about attitudes at the time. If Burt did make it up, he was at least confident that he would not be discovered. No one, in any of the numerous reviews of the book – most of which recounted the story of Jerry's crime – raised the question. Who was Jerry? Why had the grieving family of his dead friend not had justice? And why had the boy not been punished?

The *Spectator* commented in its review of the book that it was hard, in these more liberal times, to imagine the way child criminals had been treated in the past: 'It is difficult to realise that less than a century ago children were liable to death or transportation for petty offences, and that there is, for instance, a case on record of a boy of eight who was convicted of arson "with malice, revenge, craft and cunning" . . . and duly hanged. Yet until the Childrens Act of 1908 [which established juvenile courts], several thousand children under the age of sixteen were annually consigned to prison.' Conversely, the *Daily News* did reflect that the 'common sense school' might have had Jerry flogged. But 'in the case of Jerry the psychologists won. He has been sent to three homes . . . and the experiences he has been through and the ways he has met them have been helpful both in forming his character and in shedding new light on his inner mental needs. It is hoped that in the end he may be trusted to go back to his own mother and behave like a normal schoolboy.'

Whatever the truth about Jerry, Burt certainly was in the habit of sending young 'delinquents' out of London – rather like the Swiss rest cure, to places where the air was more pure – to live with families which, he hoped, might be able to cure them. In his personal papers,[19] there was a letter from a woman in Melton Mowbray who had taken some of them in, apparently with little success: 'I am sorry to say that the boys have been behaving most disgracefully what with smashing doors, windows, crockery etc. We don't know what to do about it.'

There is, too, a sense that Burt was keeping a wary eye on the religious angle to this debate. 'The psychologist, the teacher, the harassed parent, know too well that moral perfection is no innate gift, but a hard and difficult acquirement,' he wrote. Darwin's notions of heredity were still very controversial, and the idea of 'original sin' had certainly not been completely banished. Burt strived, it seems, to tread a fine line between the belief that criminality could be innate and the conflicting notion that it could be learned, and unlearned.

The mobile child

Not every unwanted child was a bad child, of course. There was concern, too, about whether the children growing up in Britain were fit for purpose. And so in this age of fear about the future of the Empire, a neat solution came to mind. If Britain wanted quality children, and the Empire wanted just about any children it could get, why not export the quantity, and hang on to the quality?

The growth of child migration between the wars was not quite so simply conceived, of course. But the movement to send parentless or abandoned children to grow up in the colonies did mark the advent of an era in which children would become increasingly geographically mobile, for various reasons. In the 1930s, children would arrive unaccompanied from Spain, fleeing the civil war, and from Germany and central Europe – some of them via the Kindertransport. During the early part of World War Two, they would be shipped across the

Atlantic, parentless, to safety in Canada and the United States, as well as to New Zealand.

The transportation of children to Canada and the United States had actually begun in the 1870s, driven by the energies of two women called Maria Rye and Annie Macpherson. Maria Rye, having visited Canada in 1868, had concluded that its inhabitants were desperately short of farm labour and domestic servants. Meanwhile, the slums of Liverpool, Manchester and London were overflowing with what she described as 'gutter children'. She set up two houses, one at Niagara and one in Peckham, south London. Under her command, children would be shipped from one to the other, then farmed out to families on their arrival.[20] Rye's efforts were soon supplemented by those of Annie Macpherson, a Scottish evangelist who had opened a 'Home of Industry' in the East End of London, and who began taking parties of children to Canada in 1870. By the outbreak of World War One, the numbers being sent had reached around 80,000 a year. Thomas Barnardo also became involved, and sponsored the migration of 20,000 children to Canada by 1930.

But as so often happened, what started out as charitable exercises became government operations as the state gradually extended its reach into the realm of family life. In 1923, an Empire Settlement Act was passed, allowing the state to fund the migration of children via an Overseas Settlement Board. This funding went largely to Kingsley Fairbridge, who had devised a new method of settling the children into the colonies – the farm school. Fairbridge, who would die just a year later in 1924 of a lymphatic tumour at the age of thirty-nine, had by then set up his first such school at Pinjarra, Western Australia. Fairbridge had a dream: to fill the empty lands of the Empire with farmers.[21] Born in South Africa, he had visited England in 1903 and had been struck by how overpopulated it seemed. His theory was that town-dwellers would adapt much more quickly if they were transplanted young: 'Eight years' schooling would barely give a man a glimpse of the possibilities which lie before a farmer,' he wrote. 'This will not be charity, it will be an imperial investment.'

In the ensuing years, further farm schools would be established in two other locations within Australia, and the Roman Catholic church would also begin organizing migrations there too. Few of the children who were 'migrated' in this way between the wars were given any say at all in what happened to them. In many ways the scheme devised in the 1920s was a throwback to the Victorian days when the migrations of children had begun. And in fact the lives these children lived in the slums of British cities were little changed from those of their grandparents.

One of them was Flo Brown, who was put into a Barnardo's home with an older half-sister, Gwynneth, and a younger half-brother, Joe, by her stepfather after the death of their mother. Their family's tale was a familiar one of a cycle of poverty and dislocation. Flo's mother had also been raised in a home, in Liverpool, and had lost two husbands in the space of four years, one in a mine accident and the other in a factory explosion. Her third husband was a womanizer, a drinker and an abuser: 'He hit Gwynneth often, as well as my mother, and physical violence was not the only abuse he subjected my sister to.'[22] In 1925, after the birth of her fourth child, Flo's mother dropped dead during a violent argument with her husband. Her baby died later the same day of 'unsuitable feeding – infantile asthenia', meaning that it faded away for lack of nutrients. Later, Flo would discover that her stepfather, too, had been a Barnardo's boy. Her little brother, Joe, had rickets, and was separated from his sisters – something that never ceased to distress Flo: 'The rest of my life was to be dominated by this need to find Joey. I always knew where Gwynneth was but never Joey.'[23]

Flo was taken to Barnardo's, and spent more than a year at a home in London before setting sail for Australia with no joy at all in her heart. The voyage was presented as 'an exciting adventure', she said, but she felt only misery at the prospect: 'Apparently I cried for five days, so my guide lieutenant told me in a letter years later, and if I had cried for one more day they were going to put me off the ship and send me back.'[24]

They arrived at Fremantle on 28 May 1928, and settled into a home which Flo described as being not inhumane, but certainly harsh: the children's daily routine was ruled by a bugle and was militaristic in style. Her work included dusting and polishing, sweeping and scrubbing benches. Boys who transgressed – stealing fruit from the orchard, forgetting to do their work – were publicly thrashed in the dining hall.

Kingsley Fairbridge and his ilk had imagined they were giving slum children a fresh start or a clean slate. They were wrong, according to Flo. Even on the other side of the world, children such as her were second-class citizens. She had hoped to become a kindergarten teacher, but was told bluntly that she did not have the intelligence of the average Australian: 'Those words sank so deeply into my being that I was to be well into my fifties before I began to challenge the untruth and the handicap those words laid on me. I was offered no extra tuition, no alternative education. I was truly brought down a peg or two.'[25] Flo eventually found her brother, Joey, in 1991, living in Warrington. Her sister, Gwynneth, returned to Liverpool, where she married happily and had children, grandchildren and great-grandchildren.

Some of these migrant children did thrive, but few ever really managed to shake off their past. John Lane, who had been abandoned by his unmarried mother and then happily fostered to a family in the Cotswolds until the age of ten, wrote later that he always felt there was a void in his life, even though in his later years he was united with a family of half-brothers and sisters he had never known existed: 'Despite my apparent success, I found that at seventy years of age, the absence of a childhood relationship with any of them had left me with distinct feeling of remoteness – of a void in my subconscious like a deep well which yields no water.' His puzzlement at having been wrenched from the bosom of foster-parents whom he regarded as his real family never left him, he wrote.[26]

There were some positive experiences among the misery. But already there were concerns about the conditions in which these migrant children had to live – in 1924, the Overseas Settlement Board had sent Margaret Bondfield, MP, to Canada to investigate conditions there, and by the mid-1930s the clamour for change was such that the migration, shut down during World War Two, would take place only on a much smaller scale after 1945. In a sense, it was this new awareness of potential abuse, rather than the abuse itself, that was striking about attitudes to migration during this period. This was a movement that had gone on for years with little adverse comment. But now children were beginning to be seen as individuals, with needs. Soon, it would no longer be acceptable for the adult world to simply move them around like pieces on a chessboard. Soon, the children would have to be consulted.

The educational angle

Incrementally, all this new thinking was beginning to impact on the education system. For most children, the change would be imperceptible. But for a few, in particular the difficult, the socially awkward and the 'backward', it would blow into their childhood like a gale. Over the next decade, an extraordinarily motley, eccentric and inspiring group of people would assemble under the newly painted banner of 'progressive' education. For those who experienced their unique take on childhood, life would never be the same again.

Cyril Burt would certainly be regarded now as being among the more conservative proponents of this new style of education. 'Child study has done much to foster individual and differential teaching – the adaptation of education to individual children or at least to groups and types of different individuals,' he told an audience of educationists in 1927.[27] 'Already a better understanding of child nature has led to the substitution of "internal" for "external" discipline, and the predetermined routine demanded of entire classes is giving way to the growing recognition of the educational value of spontaneous efforts initiated by the individual, alone or in social co-operation with his fellows.' The most advanced 'educational experiments', Burt said, were being conducted by Maria Montessori, whose method of educating children through 'spontaneous self-development' was creating interest in the United States, Emile Jaques-Dalcroze, who had founded a school in Germany dedicated to teaching music through movement; and Homer Lane, who had started a community for juvenile delinquents in Dorset.

That Burt should have publicly praised Lane in this way in 1927, two years after his death, is significant because it indicated that those close to the heart of the education system were becoming aware of – and even approving of – this activity on its wilder fringes. Lane's colony, the Little Commonwealth, in fact existed only from 1913 until 1918, when it was abruptly closed down after two of its female 'citizens' accused Lane of having 'immoral relations' with them.[28] Lane, an American psychotherapist, was subsequently deported for failing to maintain his registration under the wartime 'Aliens Act'. But his ideas lived on for many decades. Lane believed real education was about 'the path of freedom instead of imposed authority, of self-expression instead of a pouring-in of knowledge, of evoking and exploiting the child's natural sense of wonder and curiosity instead of a repetitious hammering home of dull facts'.[29] In Dorset, he pioneered techniques such as group therapy, in particular with delinquents aged between thirteen and nineteen. Residents aged over fourteen became 'citizens', free to choose which of the colony's 'families' they would live in. The atmosphere could hardly have been more different from the regime at institutions such as Barnardo's and Fairbridge. Here, there was little or no adult discipline. The boys and girls developed their own 'judicial machinery' to deal with transgressions, and the adults studiously avoided giving the impression they were in charge. The 'citizens' drew wages for working to provide the commonwealth with food, clothing or recreation, and there was, Lane reported, little time left for them to take part in formal schooling.

Despite the sudden and ignominious closure of the Little Commonwealth, a host of other educational and psychological thinkers were ready to take on Lane's views. Among them were Alexander Sutherland Neill, a Scotsman who had met Lane during the war and who had hoped to join the Little Commonwealth. Instead, Neill undertook a course of psychotherapy with Lane in London before his deportation, and then went on, in 1924, to found a school along similar lines to the Little Commonwealth. Summerhill spent its first three years in Lyme Regis in Dorset before moving to Leiston in Suffolk. And a host of other little educational experiments were bursting out all over the country, often funded by wealthy enthusiasts who believed children should be allowed to regulate their own lives.

The parents of the children who went to the schools often tended to have sent them not so much in pursuit of radical ideals but in a spirit of desperation. In their early days, they catered mainly for society's juvenile misfits – those who had transgressed, or who had simply failed to thrive in the mainstream system. Parents usually had to be able to afford to pay fees, of course – though some of these early pupils later remembered protracted negotiations about the level of fees they would pay.

Peter Thomas, an only child whose father ran a small iron and steel foundry in south Wales, had only intermittently attended school before he was sent, aged eleven, to Dartington Hall, in Devon. There, Leonard Elmhirst, the heir to an estate in south Yorkshire, and his wealthy American wife, Dorothy, had begun what had originally been an experiment in rural regeneration. In 1926, they founded a progressive school where children could take part in agricultural activities as well as doing lessons. 'I'd been to a small fee-paying school for about two or three years – I didn't attend a great deal. I kept complaining about my stomach and eventually had my appendix out when I was eight, and that took time. I don't know that I had any particular friends,' he recalled.[30]

For Peter – who was told on his arrival at Dartington that as there was already a Peter on the roll he would henceforth be known as Stuart – a traumatic early experience of the school soon gave way to a whole new existence: 'I was miserable for six, seven, eight weeks – I don't know how long. We had to write letters home, one a week – I can't imagine what they were like. My mother said when I went back for the holiday they'd almost given up and gone to collect me. But suddenly my letters had started to get less tearful, I presume because I got into the swing of the school.

'It was such a friendly place – I was a single child and this was my family. I don't know when I felt it, but I thought, it's nice to have all these friends, they were very friendly and the staff were lovely. Because I hadn't really been to school consistently, I don't think really in my heart of hearts I knew it *was* a school. You were encouraged to go to classes, but I spent most of my time out on the estate. I got friendly with a local boy, Bobby Robson, who was my age. I just went to occasional classes.' The biology teacher, David Lack – a keen ornithologist who would later write a seminal work on Darwin's finches – roped in Peter and his friend Bobby to help with a study of the local bird population: 'We helped make great big wire fenced traps which we moved from place to place, catching robins. I'm still a member of the British Trust for Ornithology.'

The school, whose headmaster for many years was a charismatic man called Bill Curry, fast began to gain a somewhat scandalous reputation. Particular umbrage was taken at its lack of team games and at the fact that its pupils were in the habit of bathing nude in the River Dart, just at the point where it met the Ashburnham to Totnes railway line.

The experiences of children like Peter Thomas at schools such as Dartington Hall were rare exceptions, of course, in a system that was still largely dominated by routine and by rote. And the activities of the staff at Dartington were starting to attract attention that went beyond the perennial gossip about nude bathing. As the 1930s crept in and the air in Europe began to darken, the atmosphere around the school became more political. 'Curry', as he was universally known, became immersed in a pacifist campaign called the Federal Union, and the efforts of Dartington's staff were increasingly supplemented by those of liberal refugees from mainland Europe.

Such was the establishment alarm at these goings-on that the progressive schools gained their own security service file, entitled 'Dartington Hall School and other disturbances'.[31] The documents within it reveal that the security services became increasingly interested in what was going on at the schools during the years before World War Two: 'Dartington Hall has for some time been a matter of interest to us, and we have been able to reach some general conclusions about it ... presumably because it has never had to pay its way, the experimental purposes for which it was founded have tended to run riot. The most serious count against it is usually the lack of moral restraint consequent upon the general encouragement to "self expression" and this has attached an unsavoury reputation to the school,' read one note on the file. MI5 would have been monitoring all manner of subversives, most of them adult, but there is something particularly potent about the notion that children are being indoctrinated, that the enemy is getting in, as it were, through the basement window. Similar themes would emerge again during the 1970s, as the fear that the more socially degenerate elements on the political fringes might be finding ways of colouring the vision of the nation's youth. The fear, of course, is a very potent one and goes to the heart of the debate about who actually has charge of children's lives. As the education system took on an ever-greater role, and children consequently spent more time away from their home environment, the myth of a potent and mind-altering undercurrent in schools would become an ever-present one.

Not that the main complainants were parents, though. During the 1930s, MI5 would respond to a wide range of complaints about the schools and about the radicalization of children more generally – mostly, if the file is anything to go by, from a small group of conservatives who were concerned about moral standards. And while the security service would not find evidence of any major threat, it did feel the need to ask questions about what was going on. For instance, the Secretary of the International Law Society, Wyndham Bewes, wrote in great alarm to the Home Office about promiscuity at Neill's school at Leiston, and about another run by Countess Dora Russell in Sussex. He attached an article from a Norwegian magazine which gushed about Neill's liberal attitudes: 'Very often he was obliged to hide from parents what he knew about their children. As to young people of eighteen years of age, it had happened that he had been obliged to tell them that he could not allow them to sleep with each other because he knew that they could not afford preventatives ... In other cases he could well imagine that some of the young people slept together but he did not interfere because he knew that they had enough money.' Could anything be done, Mr Bewes wanted to know? The MI5 officer who responded thought not. If Neill had allowed a girl under the age of sixteen to have sex, there might be grounds for a prosecution: 'But there is no allegation of this. Quite frankly I feel unable to take the statements in this article at all seriously. It is typical left-wing eyewash. My personal feeling is that the article is quite unreliable and there is no evidence in it whatever that any sexual irregularity does in fact take place ... it would be difficult to justify any action on the strength of a tendentious foreign article.'

Why the Security Service would have been given the task of investigating illicit teenage sex is something of a mystery. However, its officers were tasked at the time with assessing all threats to the security of the UK, and some of the complaints about the progressive schools involved the political activities of their teachers – so the letters tended to find their way to the desks of MI5 officers, maybe for want of any other obvious recipient. Perhaps unsurprisingly, then, the responses of MI5 to these complaints became increasingly weary as the years went by. Yet as the international tension mounted, they continued to come in thick and fast – and during the 1930s this deep-rooted fear that young people were somehow being subverted grew ever stronger.

According to the right-wing press, children across the country were becoming increasingly radicalized, and the issue was fast becoming a head-on clash between the forces of conservatism and the those of the left. On 2 November 1932, the Winscombe Women's Conservative and Unionist Association sent an appeal to the government, asking it to take immediate steps to close down the Communist Sunday Schools which appeared, its members felt, to be springing up all around them. An enclosed resolution, proposed by Mrs Percival Wiseman, noted that these Sunday Schools were 'teaching children that there is no God, are deliberately making heathens in a professedly Christian country'. The resolution, the letter confirmed, had been passed unanimously. In evidence, the association sent a cutting from the previous day's *Daily Mail* about a new society called the League of Militant Godless, which had been founded by a

Communist named T. A. Jackson. 'The Reds of Moscow have thrown down their greatest challenge to the world. They have launched a campaign to dishonour God, defame the Bible, and eliminate religion from the life of mankind,' the paper had thundered. MI5's response was more measured: 'We have no information to indicate that there are in Cornwall churches in sympathy with the idea of substituting the cult of Lenin for that of divine worship. It seems hardly necessary to make further inquiries,' the agency's official noted dryly.

Despite this scepticism in official circles, there does seem to have been something of a proliferation of organizations for young radicals at the time: the Young Communist League was thought to have about 400 members, while the Young Pioneers of Great Britain, which had recently replaced the Young Comrades League, had claimed to be selling around 3,500 newspapers each month. This was sufficient to alarm the *Daily Telegraph* into running a series of articles on the menace in April 1933, including this parody of the Lord's Prayer, from the children's corner of the *Daily Worker*:

> Our fathers who fought in the last war
> They are still out of work
> Give them a gun
> They have been worse off on earth
> Than those that went to heaven
> They will take some day their daily bread
> And they'll use those guns
> Against those who have always trespassed against them
> They will not fight against the workers
> For theirs will be the cartridges,
> The power and the earth
> For ever and ever – Red Front!

And it was sufficient to inspire an admiral, Mark Kerr, to set up an Order of the Child, to campaign against such 'child corruption'. He wrote to the Home Office in March 1933 of 'sinister developments'. 'The communists are now attempting to get at the children by penetration into the ordinary state schools, and it is most significant that at the Special Conference of the Teachers Labour League in October 1930 it was decided by an overwhelming majority that this league should become affiliated to the National Minority Movement – the communist organisation active in this country and closely bound up with the Russian Soviet,' he wrote.

All of this passed the pupils of Dartington Hall by. But in the East End of London, a young boy from a very different background was soaking up the political atmosphere. Bernard Kops, the son of desperately poor Jewish migrants from Holland and later a playwright, was growing up in Stepney Green – a stone's throw, quite literally, from where Oswald Mosley's British Union of Fascists would hold its meetings.

'I joined the blue and white shirts,' he said. 'It was all shirts in those days. There were green shirts, red shirts. Our leader, Mr Pritchard, was killed in the Spanish Civil War. So we were quite organized.'[32]

Kops was born in Stepney Green Buildings, which overlooked a long strip of land where the Fascists would set up their soapboxes: 'The British Union of Fascists had this idea, they were going to take over the East End. So we children had a job to do – we had to stand on our balcony and throw stones over at the Fascist speakers,' he explained. When the BUF decided to send thousands of marchers into the East End on Sunday, 4 October 1936, Kops was among the ranks of children who were sent out to oppose the march.

'We didn't trust the police. We knew they had allowed the march to go ahead. I think the police didn't like any of the immigrant communities, anyone who wasn't English,' he said. 'We had to stand on the sidelines with our marbles, and throw them under the hooves of the police horses.' Kops, who was ten at the time, saw a police horse go down in the crowd: 'Though I don't think it was because of any of my marbles.' Afterwards, he said, his cousins tracked the policeman down and 'did him straight up – left him with two broken legs. He had been laying about him with his truncheon.'[33]

The Battle of Cable Street, as it became known, involved no fewer than 10,000 police and a massive 300,000 anti-fascist protesters. There were 150 arrests, 100 people were injured and several policemen were kidnapped. Afterwards, a law was passed requiring marchers to obtain a police permit before staging a demonstration, and the Fascists began to retreat from the East End.

Elsewhere, the news grew increasingly grim. In the Kops' crowded flat, the talk was of the Spanish Civil War, of Hitler, of whether the family should return to Holland. Fortunately for them, they could not scrape the money together to go: 'If it hadn't been for that, we would all have been killed.'

At Dartington, too, the mood was darkening. Bill Curry was often absent, up in London pushing the already lost cause of pacifism. Peter Thomas remembers unrest in the school as a result: 'There was quite a hoo-ha with the pupils – there was a sign, I think in the dining room: 'We want our headmaster back,' he recalled. The pupils became very involved with the Spanish Civil War, as teachers went away to fight. One of the Spanish teachers at the school was a refugee, and at one point the children knitted blankets for a group of Spanish children who were housed somewhere in the Hall.

During Curry's increasingly rare visits to the school, he would invite pupils up to his house for debates about pacifism. Yet despite all his efforts, by 1939 the children of Dartington, like so many others across the country, were preparing for war.

5   War Babies

'At 10.30 we heard from a radio news bulletin that hostilities had broken out between Poland and Germany. It seemed that war was inevitable. We listened to every news that we were able for the rest of the day. Mother and I went to the cinema in the evening, and we received a shock when we came out to find the town in a state of darkness.'[1]

To a fifteen-year-old boy, living in Hampshire and recording the outbreak of war for the Mass Observation organization, Hitler's invasion of Poland was an exciting development; one that would be bound to make life more interesting. Through a child's eyes, with so much in the world still unexplored, the events tended to be viewed with a sense of mounting excitement rather than with the knowing dread the adult world was feeling. The details this particular boy felt significant enough to record reveal a sort of banality about the preparations. Somehow, seen through this boy's eyes, the implementation of the civil defence plans which had been made over the preceding months and years come across as rather sedate, rather English and rather middle-class.

'I noticed while doing some shopping for my mother a large van outside an empty shop off one of the main streets. Gas masks, gum boots and steel helmets were being unloaded from it and taken into the shop. A few days later I learned that it was to be the ARP central store. Later in the morning I sat in the Princess Gardens and watched some raw recruits of a Scotch regiment being drilled. After dinner I went and sat in the municipal gardens with a book to read. I have got all this spare time owing to the fact that the school is closed for a holiday. As I got there a man and woman pushing a pram went by. "Well we shan't be gassed this time," said the man. "No," replied the woman, "I'm going to bed with my gas mask on tonight."'

Yet the war was to have profound effects on the children of Britain, some of which would only truly be recognized once the hostilities had ceased and the smoke had begun to clear. If the inter-war years had been years in which the Western world learned the importance of stability and parent–child relations in the life of a growing youngster, the war would throw all that knowledge in the air. The years of World War Two were, for many thousands of families, years in which parents and children experienced separation from one another. They experienced separation through evacuation and through displacement because of bombing and other disruption. But they also experienced separation because suddenly the workforce of Britain was largely female. In a way which was far better organized than it had been in World War One, day care was made available so that women could perform necessary war work. For many children, that meant daily contact with the state at a much earlier age than had previously been common.

In the past, a few children had been moved from one part of the country to another, some children had been separated from their parents, and some children had even had the opportunity to meet people of a different social status from themselves – but the numbers who had done so were tiny in comparison to what was about to happen. The war was to shake up the whole class system – not in a way which would cause it to be destroyed, but in a way which would allow the poor to see how the wealthy lived, and vice versa. After the war, no one would again be able to turn a blind eye – as the East End slum-owning Lord Alington, forced by Sonia Keppel's mother to confront the truth about his wealth, had done – to the reality of how the poor were living in Britain's inner cities. The net effect, then, would be a national eye-opening about the state of the population. The war would lay bare the nation's undergarments, and childhood would never really be the same again.

But all that was in the future as dawn broke on 1 September 1939. At 11.07 a.m. on the previous day an order had been issued from Whitehall: 'Evacuate forthwith.' And education authorities around the country, which had been making detailed preparations for such an event for some time, swung into action. The scale of the evacuation was breathtaking. In total, around three million people, most of them schoolchildren, would be parcelled up, labelled – quite literally, with brown tags and string – and shipped out from the cities to the 'reception areas' in the countryside. In practical terms, the organization of this unprecedented mass relocation of the population was astonishingly well executed: 'Party after party was marched to its proper train, safely bestowed in the carriages and dispatched without confusion and fuss,' noted the *Manchester Guardian*'s correspondent, who watched the scene at the city's Victoria Station as no fewer than 50,000 children were moved by train and bus. 'The early parties looked rather tired, as if they had been wakened too early. One marching column made the subway ring with the strains of the "Lambeth Walk". A coin-in-the-slot chocolate machine caused a little dislocation of one party, but discipline was easily restored.'

The scheme had been under development for years by this time. Discussions had been taking place since the early 1930s about the principle of removing vulnerable populations from areas where aerial bombing was likely to be intense, and in the summer of 1938 the Anderson Committee – which also introduced the Anderson shelter – set out the details. Evacuation would not be compulsory, though billeting would be, and schoolchildren would be moved with their schools. In London[2] and elsewhere, the need to prioritize the evacuation of children and pregnant women was quickly established. The phrase 'women and children first' had sprung from the sinking of HMS *Birkenhead* off South Africa in 1852 – as a result of an order from the captain, all the women and children on board were saved, while most of the men perished. And the notion that women and children were somehow uniquely delicate and precious went back much further. But in relation to children in particular this notion had gained a new poignancy, a new urgency, in the first few decades of the twentieth century, as the debate about the future of the nation – its health, its empire – had become more intense.

Some of the most shocking events of World War One, in particular the bombing of North Street School in Poplar, must have influenced the debate on how children should be made safe in the future, too. And while the worst horrors in the last war had been experienced abroad by adult men, there was a feeling that advances in military aviation were bound to bring the next one much closer to home. Yet while the plans made for children's physical safety were meticulous, no one even came close to predicting the social and psychological effect this mass movement of people would have. The evening of 1 September 1939 found the thirteen-year-old Bernard Kops, veteran of the battle of Cable Street, transplanted with his young sister Rose into an alien environment: 'I found myself in Buckinghamshire, in a church hall at that. I thought we had travelled to the other end of the earth. Friday night, when we should have been having *lockshen* soup, waiting to be billeted on a family who wanted us about as much as we wanted them.'[3]

The whole of the Stepney Green Jewish School had been grafted on to the small village of Denham. Both the village and its new residents were going to have to make major adjustments: 'Everything was so clean in the room. We were even given flannels, and toothbrushes. We'd never cleaned our teeth up till then. And hot water came from the tap. And there was a lavatory upstairs. And carpets. This was all very odd. And rather scaring.'

Yet from a growing boy's point of view, the upheaval was not all bad: 'We never had breakfast in Stepney Green, just a cup of tea and a slice of bread. There we were, in a shining little room that smelled of polish, and a table all set out with knives and forks and marmalade. And we were eating soft-boiled eggs. Well, if this was evacuation I was all for it.'

Everything here was unfamiliar. Bernard and his sister had never before eaten a real meal at a table laid with knives and forks. After a time, they did begin to settle in – though he said later that he never got used to the place. 'I was getting a little tired of all the gentility. And there was no life in the streets of Denham, people curled up and died at seven o'clock every evening.'[4]

Bernard Kops and his sister were lucky – the family that took them in were kind, and tried their best to help them feel at home. There were presents at Christmas: 'They didn't seem to understand that Christmas wasn't our festival. "Don't tell 'em," I said to my sister.' And an East End boy with an unfulfilled literary bent suddenly found himself with access to Shakespeare's sonnets and the poetry of Blake and Burns: 'There was one poem in particular: "My mother bore me in the southern wild and I am black but O my soul is white ..."'

Some children were not so lucky. Michael Bird had already had a disrupted childhood – he had been in care for several years before war broke out – but he remembered his time as an evacuee with particular distress.[5] Billeted with a family of cattle-slaughterers in Staffordshire, the seven-year-old found himself treated as little more than an unpaid servant: 'As a seven-year-old I had to fetch all our water requirements from an open spring well down the fields where the cows drank. Whether it was morning or night, you couldn't have a cup of tea until you'd chopped the sticks, broken and got the coal in, filled and lit the kerosene oil lamp, built and lit a fire, fetched the water from down the fields, and boiled the kettle.'

He was not alone. One local authority issued a memorandum about the work to which its evacuee children had been put: '19 June 1940. Following instructions, inquiries were made at the farms in the neighbourhood whether children can help with the work in the fields. One farmer accepted and a dozen older children went this morning to weed . . . 20 June 1940: 10 children worked in the garden of Buckland Vicarage weeding. . .'[6] Children were meant to be in school, but in fact many were not. In the cities, schools closed because their pupils had gone away, and in the countryside, many were without accommodation or had to share with existing local schools, working a 'double-shift' system. For the first year of the war, half the children in London did not receive full-time education. In April 1941, it was estimated that the total number not in school was almost 300,000.

Such concerns were mere logistical problems in the midst of a war which was threatening the country's very existence. But the response of the countryside to finding itself suddenly face to face with the social conditions that had existed for years in the towns was telling, and significant. Having seen children arriving, dirty, ragged and hungry, in their midst, it was hard to continue to feel that the problems of the inner city could stay in the inner city. The population of the slums had already begun to move out of the city centres just before the war, as outer-ring estates began to be built. But now evacuation brought the life of the slums right to the well-blacked hearthstones of Middle England.

Within weeks, the papers were full of complaint from those upon whom the children had been billeted. In Darwen, Lancashire, a third of the children shipped out from Manchester were found to be 'verminous', it was reported. And similar stories were to be heard all over the country. The Women's Institute, many of whose members were among the aggrieved, took up the cudgels in a report on the problems they had faced.[7]

'It was a real shock to them to find that many of the guests arrived in a condition and with modes of life or habits which were startlingly less civilized than those they had accepted for a life-time,' the report said, reproducing snippets of the responses it had received. 'In practically every batch of children there were some who suffered from head lice, skin diseases and bed-wetting . . . Some had never slept in beds, and had no training whatsoever . . . One boy, very thin, had never had a bath before, his ribs looked as if black-leaded, suffered from head lice . . . The school had to be fumigated after the reception . . . Except for a small number the children were filthy and in this district we have never seen so many verminous children lacking any knowledge of clean and hygienic habits. Furthermore, it appeared they were unbathed for months.'

Among the evacuees were children suffering from scabies, whooping cough, impetigo and chickenpox, the respondees complained. And their personal habits were terrible: 'The play meadow by the end of the first week was worse than any stock yard,' remarked one member whose village had received children from Bethnal Green, in London.

'A large number, even from apparently well-off homes, were quite unused to sitting down to table or to using knives and forks. They were used to having their food handed to them to take out, or eat anywhere. Some of the children had been sewn into their clothes, which were in such a state that they had to be burnt at once and fresh provided. There are some cases of the children being sent sweets and comics but no clothes, although the parents were quite well to-do. Clothing was often sent dirty and in need of repair.'

Children arriving in the countryside from Liverpool often had only the clothes they were wearing, held together by string and tape, with no soles at all on their boots. Not surprisingly, the children's parents came in for the worst opprobrium – especially in cases where they were accompanied by their mothers: 'A distressing proportion were feckless and ignorant ... The children simply sat down in the house anywhere to relieve themselves and actually one woman who was given the guest room always sat the baby in the bed for this purpose ... The appalling apathy of the mothers was terrible to see. "Pictures" and cheap novelettes were their one desire. Had no wish to knit, sew or cook.' The mothers fell into two groups, the WI reported: the 'frankly dirty and shiftless', and the 'indolent, bored or incompetent'.

One hostess from Westmorland wrote to the *Guardian* that the evacuees were so small and underdeveloped that they appeared eighteen months younger than local children their own age. But they had settled in quickly and begun to thrive. The main problem a few months on, she reported, was that their families had a tendency to want to visit them: 'The main curse has been the weekly motor trip from Tyneside, bringing hordes of assorted relatives every Sunday. These ... have invaded billets, expecting their meals but not to pay for them, stuffing the children with sweets all day, fomenting trouble between hosts and evacuated children. If the children were undisciplined and bad settlers to begin with, as children from such homes often are, the temporary parents got, and get, no chance to establish authority,' she wrote.[8]

To its credit, the Women's Institute did more than simply vent its anger against feckless parents and their dirty children before moving on. Its leadership and members recognized the gaping social chasm that had opened up before them. The message from its membership should be heard not so much during the war as after, it said: 'The material, it was felt, would be mainly useful not as regards the wartime aspect of evacuation, but in the solution of the long term social problems which have been so strikingly laid bare by recent events. It was in a constructive spirit and not with a sense of grievance that we set about the task.' Prompted by a resolution from the WI's annual conference, the Women's Group on Public Welfare set up a committee to investigate further, chaired by Margaret Bondfield, who had been Ramsay MacDonald's Minister of Labour and the first woman cabinet minister.

'The effect of the evacuation was to flood the dark places with light,' its report declared. The 'submerged tenth' of families described half a century earlier by Charles Booth – the family that lacked both the material and the spiritual resources to keep its head above water – was still with us, it added: 'Like a hidden sore, poor, dirty, and crude in its habits, an intolerable and degrading burden to decent people forced by poverty to neighbour with it.'[9]

This report became known for introducing the 'problem family' to the public arena: 'Always on the edge of pauperism and crime, riddled with mental and physical defects, in and out of court for child neglect, a menace to the community, of which the gravity is out of all proportion to their numbers.' But its message was broader than that. Its central theme was that the issue of poverty must be tackled on many fronts, and must be tackled as a matter of urgency once the war was over: 'The campaign for better education, academic, social and moral, must be waged side by side with the battle against poverty and bad material conditions,' it said. 'Character, especially if supported by the unmeasured and tremendous force of tradition, can and does triumph astonishingly over both poverty and squalor.' The report's recommendations read today like a prototype list for many of the social reforms introduced by the post-war Labour government: better housing, a national health service, family allowances, more parks and playgrounds in towns, a programme to alleviate the disgraceful condition of crumbling Victorian school building stocks.

Others saw the need for change in more drastic terms. A Mass Observation report on children and the war, published in June 1940,[10] remarked that while the women's organizations had tried to harness their shock to a movement for positive change, most simply felt anger and revulsion: 'The majority have turned their horror into fear and even hatred, seeing in this level of humanity an animal threat, that vague and horrid revolution which lurks in the dreams of so many supertax payers.' Whether urban poverty was a source of national shame or a threat to the established order, there was general agreement something had to be done.

For the children themselves, the experience of being evacuated was much more mixed. Some, like Michael Bird, were desperately unhappy. But for most, there was a strange confluence of emotions. For Bernard Kops, there was a strong sense of dislocation, of fear and of home-sickness: 'Over tea, I tried to tell them about my family in Amsterdam. Told them that to be Jewish meant to be persecuted. Mrs Thompson sliced up a tomato, put some salt on it and said: "Don't you worry your head about that."' On the other hand, the sight of open coun-tryside was revelatory: 'All at once I saw life in a different way. For now I realized that the world was an open place of light, air and clouds ... Doubt entered my mind that sunny day. Doubt and conflict ... I was part of that world, and I knew that I would soon tire of this one.'[11]

Ultimately, then, the experience of evacuation was bound to be a negative one for most children, even if they were well treated. The major revelation for many of them would be to recognize the strength of their family bonds, the importance of their familiar environments in forming their identities. 'The family came to visit us and brought us Yiddisher food. The Thompsons said, when the family had departed, that they were delighted to find they were nice people. We were very pleased,' Kops wrote later, acknowledging the sense of responsibility a child can feel when introducing his or her family to other acquaintances.

Kops, who left Denham in the early months of 1940 to take up a place at a catering college in Brighton, soon got homesick and took himself back to Stepney Green. And he was not alone. With not much happening in the early months of the war, thousands had made their way – alone, or accompanied by their parents – back home. The *Guardian* reported[12] that by January 1940, more than half the million or so children who had been evacuated were back home with their parents.

If Bernard Kops' account is typical, the feeling that families should stay together was mutual: 'When I got home my parents said: "What on earth are you doing here?" I said my school had been bombed, and two children had been killed. They just accepted that. I said Rose was fine,' he said.[13]

Across Britain, 43,000 people died in German bombings between September 1940 and May 1941, and it was estimated one in ten were children.[14] For Kops, the Blitz meant the discovery of a new world: the London Underground. The Kops family would spend night after night on the tube system, pushed along the Central Line from east to west until they could find a little bit of platform to call their own. Then Bernard would ride backwards and forwards on the trains, looking at the population of London sheltering from the bombs: 'The children of London were adapting themselves to the times, inventing new games, playing hopscotch while their mothers shyly suckled young babies on the concrete.'[15] Eventually, Bernard, his mother and sisters left London, first for East Anglia and later for Yorkshire, to get away from the bombing. Other families would stay in the cities, but increasingly children's lives would be dislocated from those of their parents.

From 1941, all women between the ages of eighteen and sixty had to register for war work, and although those with young children were exempted at first, by 1943 eight out of ten married women were engaged in work connected with the war effort. The Minister of Labour, Ernest Bevin, had promised to subsidize nursery places for their children, and as the war went on, tens of thousands of these places were taken up. Much has been said about the changing social attitudes brought about by the wartime opportunities for married women, yet less has been said about the corresponding effect of this policy on children. In 1940, there were just fourteen day nurseries in England and Wales; by 1943 there were more than 1,300.[16]

Again, this brought children – often younger children of families which lived in the inner city, where the demand for women to work in munitions factories was strong – into a different, more regulated environment. And again, those drafted in to look after them – often young women doing their own 'war work' – had their eyes opened to the different social conditions around them. Dorothy Brown and Eileen Adey both worked as teenagers at such a nursery on the Castlefield housing estate in High Wycombe, Buckinghamshire. They recalled later a life dominated by routine: 'Monday mornings were set aside for de-lousing – a row of basins, a row of children, the appropriate soap and comb of the time, and a competition (unknown to Matron) on the number of lice retrieved from a single head. We believe 40 was the highest score,' they would write later.[17]

The wide world comes to Britain

At Dartington Hall School, many of the staff had been dispersed – a few into the forces, some simply scattered, one living on a remote island to avoid being called up – and replaced by refugees from Germany, Spain and other parts of mainland Europe. Unsurprisingly, the presence of foreigners at the school soon began to attract attention. And this time, there was good reason – theoretically, at least – for the security service to be interested. In May 1940, MI5 filed a note from a C. A. Carrington,[18] who had been seized by outrage while attending a performance of Handel's *Rodelinda* at the Old Vic, staged by the Dartington Hall arts department. 'The great majority of the audience consisted of German-speaking people, who were conversing all the evening in German,' she wrote. 'Certainly the curriculum of the school of art was or is founded on Nazi or German methods.' A note was added by an officer of the security agency in August of that year: 'We have nothing to add to our previous minutes. A number of reports have reached us which appeared, on investigation, to have little foundation and it seems probable that these are no more than can be expected about a progressive institution in circles which are not perhaps very advanced politically.'

Scandalous gossip would continue to surround these progressive schools. As the war progressed and Dartington's headmaster, Bill Curry, continued to campaign for peace, there were even allegations of devil-worship in the school chapel: there had been, according to one anonymous letter-writer to the Home Office, 'certain rites of black magic' which 'have to be performed on sanctified ground . . . in this room certain boys of the school saw a ceremony conducted by men and women wearing masks of animals'.

And while MI5 seemed increasingly irritated by its correspondents' efforts, its officers were concerned enough by the political activities at the school to intercept wartime mail in which it was mentioned. Thus did a letter to a friend from an apparently dissatisfied parent, a Mrs Dorothy de Witt, find its way into the National Archives: 'The school was not very suitable . . . in fact the whole place was a perfect sink of a rather middle class immorality,' she wrote. 'The headmaster was running an irregular ménage and had a pornographic library famous throughout the district, and the whole place was a centre of some rather sinister form of politics. The instruction was very good but Dorian was turning into an unkempt young savage.'

Mrs de Witt recounted how, on boarding a boat to return home to Ireland, her son was searched by CID and relieved of two radical magazines named *Social Credit*: 'I thought we would miss the boat as they ... questioned us most closely about Dartington etc, and finally let us go but kept the papers.'

Dartington, with its rather cosmopolitan attitudes, had always been a place where different nationalities met, and where children came into contact with people they would never otherwise have encountered. But for the average child, it took a war to make this happen. Even for those children who were not evacuated, war brought a life populated by a much greater variety of people.

Michael Foreman, born in 1938 in Pakefield, near Lowestoft in Suffolk, barely knew in his early years that war was not the normal way for life to be. But looking back he could see his mother's village shop, situated by the bus terminus, filled with a rich cast of characters: 'What I remember is the bustle in the shop, from 7.30 a.m. until 7.45 p.m. I was in the shop all the time and that's the memory, of crawling in between the legs before I could walk and being surrounded by giants in uniforms,' he said.[19]

There were soldiers stationed near Lowestoft from all over Europe – the Free French, Czechs, Poles. And to a small boy who had never known peacetime, their presence seemed normal, even humdrum: they were billeted around the village; they went with the fishermen as they clambered past the mines and through the barbed wire on the beach to their boats. Even to a child growing up in a small village in Suffolk, the world was becoming a bigger place, with more possibilities. But it was the arrival of the Americans that really caught this boy's imagination: the GIs were different. They lived miles away on bases, and arrived in Jeeps bearing gifts of nylons and chewing gum. And they were utterly fascinating to a child.

'It was just the children who held them in that esteem,' Michael Foreman said. 'I think some of the older villagers would have thought they came in a bit late, as usual. But they were healthy-looking, and had well-cut uniforms. Things like baseball caps – we'd never seen such things. And they would wear them at a cocky, jaunty angle. They had wonderful flying jackets – everything was just better cut, and it fitted. Nice material, whereas the British Tommy had this old, kind of hairy uniform.'[20] Later, some of Michael's friends' older sisters would marry GIs and go away to the United States, and then exciting presents of silver six-shooters with fake cowhorn handles would arrive in the post. They seemed to be glimpses of a sunnier, more glamorous world: 'We just thought that was what it was like in America. Whereas in point of fact one or two of these GI girl brides had a very rough time of it. They found they weren't going to Hollywood, they were going to a trailer park in the back side of Texas somewhere.'[21]

The new faces arriving in Britain were not all adult ones, either. Many thousands of child refugees from Europe had settled in Britain just before the war, some of them with their parents but many un-accompanied. Most of this last group were the beneficiaries of a decision by the British government in November 1938, just after the 'Kristallnacht' series of attacks against Jews in Nazi Germany, to accept unaccompanied children arriving here. In the ten months before the outbreak of war, 10,000 such children were to be brought to Britain, most of them under the auspices of the Jewish Refugee Children Movement. Seven hundred were helped by a stockbroker called Nicholas Winton – and among them was a young Czech girl called Hana Kohn from Pilsen. Neither she nor her twin brother Hans were told the real purpose of their journey – instead, they were told it was an extended holiday, so they could learn English: 'Of course we were excited, we'd never seen the sea, never been on a boat,' she said.[22] 'We were very aware of the different atmosphere on the train from Prague which was a third class train with wooden seats and there were German soldiers. We were just told not to laugh or talk too much if they were around.'

Hana and Hans were sent on to south Yorkshire, she to a family in Sheffield and Hans to Rotherham. They only found out many years later that the later train carrying their elder sister had been turned back. Hana recalled settling in quickly with her new parents, a headmaster and his teacher wife, and learning English rapidly: 'You had to be prepared for making faux pas and people laughing. I never minded, because I felt people were laughing with me, not at me.' Within a year, she had won a place at grammar school: 'I think I was what they used to call a goody goody. I was a good learner and very happy and I eventually became deputy head girl for a couple of years.' Just as they learned from their contacts with English children, surely those English children must, too, have gained from them a sense of a wider world around them.

For boys, in particular, the war brought opportunities to learn about places they might never otherwise have heard of. A Mass Observation report on children and the war recorded the excitement with which many were watching the hostilities abroad:[23] 'There is an increased interest in the weekly periods devoted to current history in the senior forms. Maps are eagerly consulted . . . They will discuss eagerly the latest news as soon as they hear it,' the Headmaster of Bembridge grammar school on the Isle of Wight remarked. The Headmistress of a private school, evacuated to Devon, added that there was rejoicing when the Allies scored a victory – in particular, when the Navy rescued British prisoners from a German ship off Norway: 'The boys are much more topical than the girls. They have the *Daily Telegraph* map and always follow the movements of the troops in Norway. They were thrilled, of course, about the *Altmark*, and the sinking of the destroyers and everything like that. The girls aren't very interested, but the boys definitely, most of them, would love to be out there helping.'

Children in the world

The rest of the world was becoming much more real to a far greater number of children than before, and for a variety of reasons: 'The war had been going for nearly a year when my parents received the news that my sister Joyce and I had been selected with other children from Bristol to be evacuated to New Zealand,' Jim Porter would write later. 'I was not aware at the time that we had been chosen from "deprived" families. I knew that we were not rich but we did have our own shoes!'[24]

Ten-year-old Jim and his twelve-year-old sister had been selected by the Children's Overseas Reception Board, and were to be among around 2,700 children who would be evacuated to Britain's overseas territories – in particular, Australia, South Africa and New Zealand – between June and September 1940. Initially, the scheme was intended to go much further. The first wave of emigration alone was meant to take 20,000 children, and even before it was up and running, huge numbers of families had applied. At its height, the board had more than 200,000 children's names on its list.

For a boy from a poor area of Bristol, who had spent the early part of 1940 staring through cracked front windows at the remains of a neighbour's house, avoiding the bombs in a damp air-raid shelter on bad nights and sharing a bed with the lodger when it was quiet, the opportunity to escape was welcome. Jim had been used to twopence a week pocket money, but now he was given twelve shillings and sixpence to take with him, along with new – as opposed to second-hand – clothes, and his own toothbrush and toothpaste: 'I was up to date with the "Sea Vacs" serial in my weekly comic so I knew exactly what to expect. There would be fun and games and I would be the hero who sighted the U-boat periscope and saved the convoy!'

The CORB scheme, as it was known, would come to a tragic end in the early hours of 18 September 1940, when the SS *City of Benares*, a ship carrying ninety child evacuees and their escorts to Canada, was torpedoed and sunk 250 miles north-west of Rockall. In total, seventy-seven of the children were killed, along with 171 of the adults who were aboard. With the whole nation in shock, the overseas board was immediately disbanded. While some children did continue to be sent abroad privately – about 14,000 in total – the official programme was no more.

By then, though, Jim and Joyce Porter were in the Pacific and well on their way to New Zealand. Their ship, the *Rangitata*, had also come under torpedo fire in the Atlantic, and another ship in their convoy, the *Volendam*, was hit: 'I was suddenly woken to thumping noises and the sound of the alarm bells. We put on our lifebelts and stumbled our way to the boat stations on the first class deck, on the way sighting the *Volendam*, brightly lit and apparently on fire, falling astern of us. Someone said that a lookout on the front of the ship had actually seen the torpedo passing just a yard ahead of the *Rangitata* before it hit the unfortunate ship. We heard that the convoy had been ordered to scatter and felt the engines below vibrating as the ship picked up speed.'

As Jim Porter recognized, the experience was a terrifying one for the older children and the adults who were aboard. But for a boy of ten with an adventurous spirit, it was all part of the excitement: 'We lay on the deck just outside the lounge, wrapped in blankets. There was chatter, chaos, hot Bovril and biscuits to see us through until morning. Despite being summer, it was quite chilly and we were eventually taken under cover and fell asleep on the soft luxurious carpet of the first class lounge.' The passengers and crew of the *Volendam*, among them 320 child evacuees, were rescued and returned to Scotland. The children who did make it across the Atlantic were not told what had happened to them, and nor were they told about the sinking of the SS *City of Benares*.

Arriving at Auckland, Jim and Joyce were separated – Jim going to a wealthy family in one part of the city, Joyce to a working-class home in another part. They met once a fortnight: 'Looking back, I can understand the culture clash of a back-street boy from Bristol descending on a refined and respected local family. My table manners left a lot to be desired and it was hard being taught, quite severely at times, how to eat food and behave properly at the table.'

Yet despite all this, and despite having to move on because of illness in the family, Jim thrived in New Zealand, becoming a Scout troop leader, going to grammar school and eventually winning a scholarship to a college of art.

Preparing for peace

Jim Porter would write later that his world ended the day Germany surrendered. He had no desire at all to return to a United Kingdom which had suffered six years of war. Yet the overseas resettlement board which had sent him to New Zealand seemed very keen to send him back again – so keen, in fact, that he and his sister were already in the Pacific before Japan, too, was forced to surrender.

There was little to comfort them when they finally docked: 'We eventually arrived at a grey, subdued Liverpool, and stayed the night at a horrendous house where all there was to eat was dark bread and margarine. "There's been a war, you know!" The following day, we took a train through the most dull, overcrowded and dismal countryside I could ever remember.'[25]

Britain in 1945 did not seem a warm or a welcoming place to a boy who had grown used to bluer skies, a more affluent life and plenty of good food. Yet while Jim and Joyce were now almost grown up – Jim sixteen and Joyce eighteen – the next generation of children would reap benefits from the lessons learned through the experience of war children like them.

The war had barely run half its course before serious discussions started. The general tenor was this: that having had its eyes opened to the appalling conditions in which some of its population were living, the nation could not allow the situation to continue. Lord Airlie, speaking in a parliamentary debate in 1943, spoke for many: 'Who would have believed that it would have been possible that such bodily conditions and such insanitary behaviour could have existed in a country which calls itself a civilized nation as came to light after the evacuation took place in this country? The only hope is to deal with it as a national problem at the earliest moment . . . possibly the only solution will lie in trying to teach our children how to train their children to do those very things which used to be taught in the old days in the home and at the mother's knee.'

Lord Airlie spoke of cleanliness, discipline and religious adherence, and he spoke of the need to transmit these through family values. Others spoke of better education, better housing, better food. And the widely accepted solution was that the state should get involved, in a big way. As early as 1940, a committee named the Inter-Departmental Committee on Social Insurance and Allied Services had been set up, and within two years it had produced a report with a huge, all-embracing vision: for the building of a better Britain once peace had dawned. It seemed the time was right for grand designs and all-embracing visions, and the Beveridge Report, as it was known, provided both. There were 'five giants' of evil in Britain, it said: squalor, ignorance, want, idleness and disease. These should be combated through family allowances, a free health service and full employment, and benefits should be paid at subsistence level so that poverty could be abolished. The public reaction was so ecstatic that Churchill was forced to announce immediate plans for legislation.[26]

There were good reasons for making grand plans. First, signs of cynicism, even bitterness, about the future were being detected among troops who had by now been at war for four years. A failure now to commit to radical action that would lead to improvements in many of their lives might be detrimental to the course of the war, it was felt.[27] Second, if things continued as they had done, there would be serious concern about the future of the race. The press revelations about the state of the inner-city children who had arrived so badly clothed, filthy and generally unkempt on the doorsteps of their rural hosts bore many of the hallmarks of snobbery, of course. But there were real grounds for concern. Despite all the recent advances in public health, far too many children were still dying of preventable or curable diseases: in 1940, for example, more civilians died of tuberculosis in Britain than were killed by enemy action.[28] And far too few were being born. While the middle classes of the early twentieth century had worried that they would soon be outnumbered because they had discovered contraception while the poor had not, now all sections of the population were having smaller families. The nation desperately needed more of those children to survive, in all classes, Beveridge had warned: in 1901 there had been five children under fifteen for every pensioner. By 1961 there would be one child for every pensioner, and by 1971 there would be three pensioners for every schoolchild.[29] 'In the next thirty years, housewives as Mothers have vital work to do in ensuring the adequate continuance of the British race.'

All the political parties were in broad agreement: Britain needed more children. The Conservative election manifesto of 1945 would call for an increase in maternity beds, and for mothers to be given a special status. Churchill had even used a wartime broadcast in February 1943 to ram home the point: 'One of the most sombre anxieties which beset those who look thirty, or forty, or fifty years ahead ... is the dwindling birth-rate ... If this country is to keep its high place in the leadership of the world and to survive as a great power that can hold its own against external pressure, our people must be encouraged by every means to have larger families.'

Most of Beveridge's proposals were accepted in a 1944 White Paper. The National Health Service and Family Allowances were to come later, after Labour had swept to power in the 1945 election. There were other measures, too, aimed at building a stronger population: a national milk scheme, a vitamin welfare scheme for under-fives and nursing mothers, more maternity beds. In fact, the nutritional health of schoolchildren had already begun to improve before the war ended – by 1945 about a third of children were receiving free school meals, and they were also benefiting from the wartime diet – sweets were hard to come by, and the wartime meal tended to contain less fat, more vegetables and more wholemeal bread than its pre- or post-war equivalents.

Not that this was fully appreciated by the children of the day, of course. In November 1944, *Time and Tide* magazine printed a letter from a schoolgirl named Phillis Cannell, on the subject of the school meals which were supposed to be so beneficial to children: 'As one of these children I venture to protest. Being one of those who have rebelliously partaken of grey badly-peeled potatoes, an over-abundance of partially cooked parsnips and turnips, and thick cold gristly slabs of meat, I find myself incapable of enthusiasm for this payment in kind. At tea time ... one often remarks rather forcibly the conspicuous absence of the jam ration. Jam yesterday, jam tomorrow, but never jam today ...'

Schools, too, were set to change: an Education Act passed in 1944 raised the school leaving age to fifteen, introduced free secondary education for all and heralded the advent of the grammar school and the secondary modern. As the war came to an end, there was a strong feeling that education would provide one of the major keys to rebuilding the nation. 'Rab' Butler, the President of the Board of Education, was in an expansive mood as he introduced the Bill:[30] 'An educational system by itself cannot fashion the whole future structure of a country, but it can make better citizens ... Such is the modest aim of this Bill . . . We today have the responsibility for laying the foundation for the nation's future, and we dare not fail,' he said.

The war in Europe would end sixteen months later, with those high hopes for the future held firm in most people's hearts. In Pakefield, near Lowestoft, the young Michael Foreman would watch as residents built victory bonfires on the mined, barbed-wired beach. Later, a wrecked landing craft would become a pirate ship in which he and his friends could play. Others would return to peacetime with heavier hearts. Bernard Kops, in London when the war ended, found it hard to celebrate when most of his Dutch Jewish relatives were dead: 'Suddenly the bells were ringing and everybody was cheering and dancing and kissing and I went down to the Embankment with the crowd, but amongst them I thought of those other crowds, those of my family and people like them who had perished; who had suffocated, gone up in smoke. I thought of all the young men like me who no longer had dreams, who lay rotting under the earth.'

For many the victory would be tinged with regret, not just for those who had died but for what had been lost at home, as well. Jim Porter, arriving back from New Zealand with his sister, Joyce, had never had a very warm family life. But now his parents were virtually strangers: 'We met my mother and the lodger at Temple Meads Station. Dad was still somewhere overseas. Over five years had passed and we did not know each other. Mum had moved to Bath so we still had a bit further to travel, wondering at the immense bomb damage everywhere. Late that night, Joyce and I went to bed and the world was never the same.'

6   Born in the Ruins

It was with mixed feelings then, but primarily with a sense of relief and even optimism, that Britain's families began the job of reassembling the scattered jigsaw that war had made of their lives. Children returning from rural and foreign billets, fathers and even mothers returning from whence the war had flung them, refugees from elsewhere putting down roots in their new surroundings. For Hana Kohn, who had arrived in Britain on the eve of war on the Kindertransport, there was a slow realization that almost all her family were dead. Looking back, she found it strange that she had not asked more questions earlier.[1] 'I've often thought: "Well, when did I become aware of it?" I wonder why I didn't read the newspapers more. I seemed to have my nose to the grindstone with books and things I needed for study ... I don't think I was encouraged too much. But I think by about 1949 it became quite clear that there was no hope.'

It was to be many years before Hana would be able to piece together sketchy details of the fate that had befallen her parents, sister, grandparents, aunts and uncles. 'We have details of how some died horribly, like my uncle Arnold – because he was a slight hunchback he was one of the first. And Grandpa, who never hurt a fly ... Oh, I don't know. Treblinka, one of these places. They were just lined up and shot. In a way I'm glad I don't know the details.' Hana and her brother, Hans, who was later adopted by his English foster-family, threw themselves into preparations for university and for a life in which both would become pillars of their communities – Hans as a doctor, Hana as a teacher.

There were grim discoveries nearer home, too. Just three weeks after VE day, the government published an official report by Sir Walter Monckton on a boy called Dennis O'Neill who, like so many others, had been separated from his parents in wartime. For Dennis, though, the war had been merely incidental in this separation. His parents, Thomas and Mabel, had married in 1918 in the Welsh town of Newport and had nine children – one of whom died – before being convicted of child neglect in 1933. Dennis was finally removed from the family home in 1938, and spent the war years being shunted between a series of children's homes and foster-families. In June 1944, he was placed with a farming couple named Reginald and Esther Gough, at Minsterley in Shropshire. To the social workers who visited, the couple seemed ideal foster-parents. They were young and childless, and promised to bring Dennis and his brother Terry up as their own. And at first the boys seemed to be fine. In September 1944, Dennis wrote to another brother, Tommy, in an apparently cheerful mood: 'Dad and I will be off to the auction next week to take a bull. Terry and I have got two new rabbits . . . we have been blackberrying and kept the money for a new suit for best.' In January the following year, the Goughs called the doctor to say Dennis seemed to be having a fit. When the physician arrived at the remote farm, more than two hours later, Dennis was dead. He had died of heart failure after being struck repeatedly in the chest. His back bore the scars of beatings with a stick, he was painfully thin and he had septic ulcers on his feet. Both the Goughs were charged with manslaughter. Terry told the court he and his brother had lived mainly on bread, along with milk they could suck from the cows' teats. On the day before his death, Dennis had been beaten for taking a bite from a swede which was being kept for cattle fodder. Gough had thrown him out of the house, saying if he was going to eat the cows' food he could stand out in the field too. Even after the boy had finally been allowed to return to the house and go to bed, he had followed him to his room and beaten him again.

In the last days of the war, the papers were full of the case. The reports of the diminutive ten-year-old Terry, standing in the court-room recounting how he had seen his brother, stripped naked and freezing, being beaten with a stick by a stranger into whose care he had been delivered; how he had returned from school just before the boy's death to find him locked in a cupboard, brought tears to the eyes of thousands – particularly those who had been separated from their own children. There were numerous offers of adoption for Terry, who later wrote a book about his experiences.[2]

Reginald Gough was convicted of manslaughter and sentenced to six years; his wife Esther received a lesser sentence of six months for neglect. The court heard that in 1942, not long after their marriage, Esther had left her husband and had accused him of cruelty. But Newport Corporation, which had asked Shropshire County Council to check on the boys, had never discovered that fact before it placed them with the couple. The resulting Monckton inquiry led to tighter rules governing the fostering out of children. There was nothing new in child cruelty, of course, but the fate of Dennis O'Neill had touched a very raw nerve. 'Billeted Boy's Death', read one headline, reminding parents everywhere of how the imperceptible thread that bound them to their children had been stretched thin by war.

Dennis's death marked a sea-change in attitudes to child abuse. Earlier cases which came to the public's attention had usually involved cruelty by parents or employers. There had, until now, been a general assumption that if a child's home was less than perfect the best solution was to remove him from it. There had also been a view that it was always better for a child to live in the healthy, wholesome surroundings of rural England than amid the crowds and miasmas of the city. This case – along, perhaps, with tales told by returning evacuees – exploded those theories, and not just because it laid bare the depths of rural poverty and dysfunction.

But the fate of Dennis O'Neill, or rather the public reaction to it, had an even wider significance. It underlined a huge change in public attitudes to children and to family life, and it signalled the way to the next half-century of public policy.

In one sense, what set the death of Dennis O'Neill apart from the countless deaths of neglected, abused children that went before was the new sense of collective responsibility it demonstrated. There was somehow a feeling that it was not only Dennis's parents, nor even just his foster-parents, who had let him down. The central failure, in the eyes of the world, was not that of the individuals involved – though that had indeed been grievous – but of the state. Some of the most condemnatory reports were those of the evidence given in court by Newport Corporation, which had seemingly contracted out its duty of care to Shropshire, and of Shropshire County Council itself, which had failed to discover what was happening on that remote farm. By the time the Monckton inquiry reported in May 1945, most of the building blocks of the new Welfare State were in place, and huge policy changes were under way. In a broad sense, the case helped to cement the feeling that in future, the government would play a much greater part in the nation's life – and its involvement would not stop, as it had continued largely to do up till now, on the front doorstep of the family home.

In a specific sense, it gave rise to legislation that would radically change the lives of Britain's most vulnerable children over the next half-century. The 1948 Children Act,[3] brought about in large part through outrage over the O'Neill case, passed the power of the old Poor Law authorities to assume parental responsibility over a child to local authorities. The Act was followed by a series of further legislative measures which gave new powers to the state over children's lives: in 1952, the right to remove children from the family home even if their parents had not been prosecuted for cruelty; and, in 1958, the right for judges to order children to be taken into care in divorce disputes. Later, the tide would begin to turn and more emphasis would be placed on preventive work to help families stay together – but in some respects the broader effect was the same: when family life went awry, it was increasingly the state's job – in particular the job of social workers – to step in and sort out the mess.

But the O'Neill case also highlighted something more fundamental, something political with a small 'p' rather than a large one. Perhaps it was just the simple desire, held by so many, to return to a life with family at its heart after years of separation and war. Perhaps it was the coming to fruition of years of gradual change during which children had been handed the gift of individuality, a promise that they actually mattered. Perhaps it was that children were gaining scarcity value, as families continued to shrink. Perhaps it was just part of that wider post-war optimism – the feeling that now, if ever, things really would get better. But suddenly, the family was at the heart of the nation's consciousness in a way that it probably never had been before. The case reminded the nation that blood was, after all, thicker than water.

It helped, of course, that Britain had a newly married heir to the throne in Princess Elizabeth, who wed Philip Mountbatten in November 1947. The couple, along with their children – Charles was born a year later in November 1948 and Anne in 1950 – became a sort of national symbol of domestic and familial bliss, photographed often in poses which underlined the joy of family life.

'The central theme would be the same if wireless had never been invented,' gushed *The Times* in its preview of the King's Christmas message from Sandringham in 1950. 'It is of kinsmen and kins-women, grandparents, parents and children, assembled under their own roof to keep the Christian feast ... Sandringham, as is the way with homes in which children have been happy, has gone from strength to strength.'

Richard Cannon, born in Sevenoaks, Kent, in 1948, kept a scrap-book into which he pasted pictures of the young Prince Charles and Princess Anne, along with beautifully presented displays of food – which was, of course, still scarce – and sweets, which were rationed. The book contained a particularly striking picture of a little boy, not unlike the golden-haired child who illustrated the Frederick Truby King childcare book which had bestraddled the first half of the century. But in this picture the boy, shining-haired, gleaming and rosy-cheeked, is transplanted from his mother's Edwardian knee to a perfect suburban garden, where he sits playing happily alone with a bucket and spade. Instead of the formal shirt and shorts of Truby King's day, this boy has short dungarees, perfect for doing practical, boyish things. The picture speaks volumes about the joys of post-war family life, Mother presumably inside baking cakes and other delicacies in a shiny new cooker while Father commutes to a white-collar job in town, returning in the evening to a spick house and a wholesome meal.

It was all an illusion, of course, as Richard Cannon's own memo-ries of childhood demonstrated. The second of five children, he felt looking back that there had been a sort of national post-war dash for matrimony, of which his parents had been part: 'They married six or seven months after the war. I think there was a bit of a rush to find a wife or a husband,' he said. 'It was a time of relief at the soldiers coming home, and there was the need to marry and have children. That's often at the back of my mind, that it was a bit of a rush job.'4

Outwardly, the Cannon family home fitted perfectly into the 1950s image of domesticity. Richard's mother stayed at home in Kent while his father commuted to a job with British American Tobacco in London and was a member of the local cricket club. The house had flowerbeds in the front garden, a lawn and an allotment garden at the back, a bay window in the lounge. But Richard, who was one of five siblings, thought later that his father's bad wartime experience as a very young soldier under Montgomery in the desert – he had been eighteen in 1939 – must have left scars.

'I think the positive side he saw was that he was a part of something very big, that had achieved something . . . but I think a lot of the men of that age had six years of their lives stolen, really. I think it really affected the personality, and so it affected the household. When my father was at the cricket club, with all his mates around, it would be: "Oh yeah, what a great bloke." But at home he had a really violent temper. I have to say he was not a good father.'

That said, fathers were still quite remote figures in most families in the years after the war – as Mr Cannon's semi-residence in the bar of the local cricket club demonstrated. Most were out at work during the day, and the only adults the young Richard usually met when visiting friends after school were mothers. Yet in the public imagination of the day, the nuclear family – complete with father, of course – reigned supreme. The new Welfare State could be seen almost as a hymn to the nation's children – certainly to its hardworking, respectable families. Bohemianism was out, respectability was in. In short, the ideal child of the popular imagination had come in from the woodlands where he had spent the pre-war years building dens and climbing trees. In future, his natural habitat was to be a garden or a purpose-built playground in the suburbs.

The pressure to conform was enormous, especially on young women who had often experienced undreamed-of freedoms during the war, only to find themselves imprisoned by domesticity shortly afterwards. The papers were suddenly full of articles about children

– their winsomeness, how to ensure they ate properly, what to do with them in the holidays, the dangers of ill-fitting shoes. And the responsibility for ensuring these children were nourished, appropriately clothed and shod, and adequately entertained fell to this army of women who had married during or shortly after the war. An air of martyrdom hung around the new, full-on style of motherhood, as one correspondent – a full-time mother herself – confessed: 'It took time, as a mother, to acquire a sense of proportion. Nothing, I vowed, breast-feeding an undernourished infant for a full nine months, was to deprive my child of his birthright.' But this mother was absolutely sure she was doing the right thing – her own mother had worked, and she had been scarred by the experience: 'While we are tired and frustrated and hard up, other less conscientious women appear to be getting the best of both worlds ... Few of the children growing up today in homes where both parents follow full-time careers will consider as adults that their upbringing was ideal, no matter what their mothers may be saying now to the contrary.'

Guilt, then, lurked around every corner for the women of the 1950s. And to make matters worse, the psychologists of the day were starting to observe that children needed to bond with their mothers. This was the period, for instance, in which John Bowlby formulated his theory of attachment, which said children tended to form strong bonds with their main care-givers early in life. In an article for the *News Chronicle* in 1952, headed 'The Mother who stays at home gives her children a better chance', Bowlby wrote: 'Babies need mothers because a child's emotional development depends on his relationship with his mother in his very early years. If she neglects him when he is small there will be trouble afterwards. So the mother who stays at home is giving her children a surer foundation for mental health than costly equipment and an expensive education can provide.'[5]

So, this new emphasis on the family had its drawbacks, especially for children who were aware their own families were less than perfect. Yet there was a genuine sense of optimism, a real feeling that this was a good time to be a child. Family Allowance of eight shillings per week helped to stretch tight budgets, and despite the fact that post-war austerity stretched well into the 1950s, there was a new health service, a new school system, new housing, all of which had a direct effect on children's lives.

Some of this family-centredness might be seen as a sort of hard-headed attempt by the government to ensure necessary population growth. After all, Beveridge had warned during the war that a declining birth rate continued to be a threat to national prosperity. And in 1952 the Archbishop of Canterbury told the Mother's Union that two children did not represent a proper effort in this respect: 'Family only truly begins with three children.'[6] Yet it quickly became clear that the population was growing healthily as couples married and settled down to post-war life. However, the notion that Britain had a 'baby boom' generation, as America did, is something of a myth. Official statistics show the population of the UK grew by around two million between 1941 and 1951, as it had done in each decade since the early twentieth century – mainly because fewer people were dying. And while there was a spike in the birth rate just after the war ended, it was smaller than the one that followed the end of World War One. By the early 1950s, the birth rate had dropped again to wartime levels.

And in an age of growing prosperity, concerns about children's health began to turn in new directions. No longer would the newspapers worry aloud about the puny, underfed youths who might be the country's first line of defence in the event of another war. When sugar came off the ration in 1953, the papers greeted the event cheerfully: 'Nowadays, a child's pocket money is once again genuine currency, capable of conversion at any confectioner's into bull's eyes, humbugs, allsorts and chocolate; and the old joy that the young used to find in humouring their palates in their own way has returned. Already more sweets and chocolates are being eaten than before the war,' *The Times* reported in June 1953[7] – there had been an earlier attempt to de-ration sugar in 1949 but the resulting rush for the sweet shops had led to the decision being reversed. But the sense of unalloyed enjoyment would not last long. Before the decade was out, medical officers were seeing a worrying rise in obesity among the young. In the late Victorian era, workers had queued up on their days off to stare at Miss Ivy, the celebrated Lancashire Fat Girl. A century later, there would be no novelty in finding an over-weight adolescent female in Lancashire, or anywhere else. The UK's confectioners never looked back, and large swathes of the country-side were given over to the growing of sugar beet to feed the nation's new craving. Just as the old infectious diseases were being swept away by antibiotics and better housing conditions, they were begin-ning to be replaced by diseases of affluence – road traffic accidents, air pollution and, of course, over-eating.

Alan Briddock was born in 1934, in Sheffield, just as the old era was coming to an end. When he was four, his father died of pneu-monia – a not uncommon occurrence at the time. But even though he was not able to share the dream of a perfect nuclear family in a perfect semi-detached house, he did benefit from several of the huge changes brought about by the advent of the Welfare State. The Briddock family, which had lived in a two-up, two-down in the centre of town, were among the first to move when slum clearances brought the new council estates which would dominate housing policy during the post-war years. Their move came earlier than most – just on the eve of the war: 'The local authority were rehousing, to redevelop the area. Where we had lived, it was two up and two down, no bathroom, toilet in the yard ... my sister remembers it vividly. She said the new house was like a palace. The toilet was at the back, in the porch, but we had a bathroom upstairs. There was a garden. It was cleaner, there was more open space, the amenities were so much better than the old place. Nowadays it's talked about as a sink estate, but it's the people who make it what it is.'[8]

There was a new sense of possibility, too. Not only had families like the Briddocks moved out from the centre of Sheffield; the promise of a free secondary education – an academic education, for those who could pass the eleven plus – offered the possibility of social mobility, too. The 1944 Education Act had brought with it a free secondary education system with three types of schools – secondary moderns, technical schools and grammar schools. The last, of course, was for those who could pass the eleven plus exam. Alan Briddock worked steadily for it, and consequently found himself travelling across Sheffield every day – a walk, then a tram, then a bus – to Firth Park Grammar School, which had been recommended by the local vicar: 'None of my friends from primary school went there, but down the road there were a couple of guys. My mother couldn't afford the red coat and I just used to wear a red cap. I wasn't on my own in that respect.'

Alan's sister Lilian had passed, too, but their mother couldn't afford to send both of them. In general, Alan enjoyed it and did not feel he was different because he had not come from a well-off family. But one incident remained with him through his life: 'We were considered so poor we had vouchers for free boots. But once the head-teacher ... took me into his office and offered me a pair of shoes. They were women's cuban heeled shoes. He had no idea of the embarrassment a young person would feel at that! I could see they were women's shoes, and this silly old guy ... I was twelve or thirteen, and I was mortified. He thought he was giving me charity. If they'd been a decent pair of shoes I daresay I would have taken them – I think I just said they wouldn't fit me, and backed out of the room.'

Despite this, he was glad to have gone to Firth Park: 'It having been a fee-paying grammar school, the teachers were out of the top bracket, they really were. They were all graduates from university. There was a terrific English teacher – Doc Wood. I enjoyed it. Grammar school gave me the education that was required. Had I gone to a secondary modern school, I would have gone into the steel works as a labourer.'

Others, like Michael Foreman, who grew up near Lowestoft and who later became a well-known illustrator and author of children's books – was rather glad to have escaped the grammar school system. 'I used to cheat,' he explained. 'In the final year I sat next to Brenda Smith, who I thought was the bees' knees, and she was good at maths and I wasn't. And in examination conditions you get found out.'⁹

He remembers just one thing about the exam itself: 'The whole affair was a blur at the time, but I remember the spelling part. One by one we had to go to the front of the class and stand beside Oscar Outlaw, the teacher, as he sat at his desk. On the desk were several sheets of paper with columns of words. As he pointed to a word we had to read it. The only word I remember is the word I had never seen or heard before. "Antiku," I said. It was "antique". There couldn't have been many households in our village where antiques were part of tea-time conversation, but if there were, those were the children the grammar school wanted.'¹⁰

Michael Foreman's feeling that the grammar school system was not set up for village boys like himself was not universal. Elsewhere, middle-class parents were feeling the pain. For every working-class child who passed in through the gates of the grammar school, a middle-class child – whose parents would previously have paid fees – was left outside. A father calling himself 'Pater' wrote an anguished letter to *The Times* in July 1945 complaining that there were no fewer than 1,000 hopefuls applying to Manchester Grammar School: 'I am prepared for some sacrifice to give my boy a good education, and he in turn is anxious to learn, yet at the age of eleven his whole future is in jeopardy owing to rules and regulations of the education authority . . . The country is going to lose in the long run because the children and the parents who have the interest and the desire to send their children to a grammar school are not going to be able to, whereas children and parents who have not that interest are able to send their children on the result of an examination.'

There might even have been something in this view. Michael Foreman, having discerned that the eleven plus tended to favour boys who knew what antiques were, had no desire at all to pass it. Everyone he knew was going to the secondary modern: 'There were a few posh kids in the area but they went away to school, and they went away for holidays. They hardly existed for us at all. We were the "common boys" they shouldn't play with. We could spit further, pee higher.'[11]

Michael found himself in a borderline group, whose members had to undergo an interview. When his teacher told him the result he was overjoyed: 'I ran from the room, bounded down the stairs two at a time, which wasn't allowed, and burst out through the doors into the sunshine. I leapt and jumped and whooped down the road after my friends. I hadn't passed! I was going to the secondary modern school with my mates. What a relief!'

Childhood in a Cold War

'One day two strange boys arrived at school. One was very tall, the other had a very round face and startling white hair. We Pakefield boys had the usual very baggy British knee-length trousers which made the backs of your legs sore in cold, wet weather, and long grey socks which always slipped down around our ankles. These strange boys had tight trousers, hardly lower than their bums, and bright white ankle socks . . . But there was something about the two strange boys which excited me. They had come from somewhere else.'[12]

No sooner had one war ended, it seemed, than others were breaking out. At Michael Foreman's school in Lowestoft, the arrival of two strangers from Estonia made flesh of the news in the papers – the borders of the Soviet Union were closing, and families like those of Michael's friends, Rigo and Henno, were leaving before it was too late. There was trouble elsewhere, too: Michael's older brother, Ivan, was called up to go to Egypt during the Arab–Israeli war of 1948. The local station again became a place of sad goodbyes.[13]

There were major compensations, though. While Ivan was gone, his girlfriend Brenda would take the young Michael to the pictures every Thursday evening. If children had had their way, the Cold War would have been won before it had even started – by the Americans: 'We loved all things American. All our movie heroes – cowboys, Indians, even Robin Hood and his merry men – had American accents . . . I didn't like Saturday morning pictures with all the singing or the films made specially for kids. My mates and I went on Saturday afternoons to the real films. Hopalong Cassidy, who didn't sing, and best of all Gabby Hayes, like a Wild West Father Christmas. Roy Rogers and Gene Autry always burst into song and we booed them.'

This was the golden age of Americana, and the cinema was its king. Picture-houses had moved on from the days when they were unruly fleapits where the children of the poor could keep warm on a Saturday. Saturday-morning cinema was still a major event, but adults and children from all walks of life were now embracing the world of film. In 1946, eight out of ten people in Britain would attend at some point during the year, and the weekly audience would reach an all-time peak of around 1.6 million.[14] And a very large part of that audience consisted of children. A Mass Observation study in 1946[15] found that while one third of adults went to the cinema at least once a week, the proportion of children who did so was twice as high.

Despite the growing respectability of the cinema, it was still predominantly a working-class leisure activity, with the children of factory and clerical workers spending more time there than their middle-class contemporaries.

And there were comics, too. Again, Michael Foreman was among the lucky ones – his mother sold them in her shop, so he was able to read them first: *Film Fun*, the *Dandy*, the *Wizard*, the *Hotspur* and the *Rover*. 'Later a new comic, *Eagle*, appeared but I didn't like it. It was not daft enough.'[16] Most of these comics were perfectly innocent. But now, with the cultural dominance of America growing, there was a sense of unease about some of the material to which children were gaining access. A history teacher named Peter Mauger reported, for example, that he had been horrified by the sight of a young boy on a train far more engrossed in his comic than he would ever have been in a school book.[17]

Teachers were in the vanguard of this minor moral panic of the early 1950s. One early campaigner was George Pumphrey, a junior school headmaster from Horsham in Sussex, who would rail against this new habit children seemed to have formed of sneaking comics into school. His articles on the subject began appearing in *Teachers World* magazine, and the *Schoolmistress*, in 1948. Soon the unions were involved, too. At the 1952 conference of the National Union of Teachers, no fewer than fourteen motions on the subject were tabled for debate. The church had its concerns, as well. The *Eagle*, the comic so despised by Michael Foreman for not being 'daft' enough, was actually the brainchild of the Reverend Marcus Morris, who wrote: 'Morals of little girls in plaits and boys with marbles bulging in their pockets are being corrupted by a torrent of indecent coloured magazines that are flooding the bookstalls and newsagents.'[18]

Morris was talking about a strain of comic now being imported from the US, which would become universally known as the 'horror comic'. An infamous example, cited in a campaigning book on the subject entitled *The Seduction of the Innocent*, was the *Grim Fairy Tales*, which were parodies of the well-known stories which included Sleeping Beauty and Hansel and Gretel. The most controversial of these comics, *Foul Play*, featured a baseball player who was murdered and dismembered for some offence; his body parts were then used as bats and balls in a game.

A successful campaign was waged, leading to a ban under the Children and Young Persons (Harmful Publications) Act, 1955. And the interests that combined to make this happen were not just religious and educational. The Communists had an angle, too – Peter Mauger, the history teacher who was so shocked to see a boy enjoying a comic on a train, was in fact a member of the British Communist Party, which had seen an opportunity to exploit anti-American feeling. It, too, flung itself into a campaign against the comics and in so doing brought the Cold War into the world of children's literature. The left had not been slow to spot the growing dominance of the United States in the lives of the British populace, and it hoped to put a stop to it. In these years, the ideological struggle between left and right was not just about the big geopolitical blocks of the world, the US and USSR all-powerful with the smaller and less powerful countries lining up behind the protective barricades of either one or the other. The Cold War was fought, too, in the world of culture. And nowhere more so than in the world of children's culture. But there was never any contest, so far as the children were concerned. On the one side was Soviet-style austerity, the work ethic, a world in black and white. On the other was the unstoppable machine of American capitalism, in full colour, with music and lights.

To the young Michael Foreman, everything that came from America seemed strangely alluring – even the consumer goods that had little to do with childhood seemed bigger and shinier than the things post-war Britain could make: 'Magazines would have ads for the latest fridge, when nobody had fridges ... you'd see the ideal housewife, who would look very American. Also there were the B movies on Saturday mornings – there was one called *Blondie*, which was also a strip in the newspapers at the time. A typical American family, living in a typical American suburban street, with the front lawn and the picket fence. And the newspaper boy would cycle down the road and throw the newspaper into the front yard, because it never rained in these films, it was always perfectly sunny. Then you'd get to see what their kitchens were like.'[19]

Yet even the most pro-American youths knew it was OK to be anti-American on some fronts: 'I had a ban the bomb symbol in my window – but people thought it was a Mercedes sign,' Foreman recalled. 'And I painted "Ban the bomb" on the police station in the middle of Lowestoft in the night. My Auntie Lou, who lived in the north end of the town, came to the shop, saying: "Some fool painted 'Ban the Bomb' on the police station." I went on the second Aldermaston march.'

This was a generation whose parents and grandparents had all seen conflict, and during those post-war years there was never a time when peace looked certain. The 1940s brought the Arab-Israeli war; the 1950s the Cuban Missile Crisis, and the 1960s Vietnam. The young men of this age, in particular, could never be quite sure their national service would not lead them somewhere dangerous. Richard Cannon, growing up in Kent with a father who had fought in the desert under Montgomery, was always conscious of this: 'I'm the first of three generations that have had a peaceful life, really. I did grow up with a sense of that, but during the fifties you'd got Suez, the Korean War; and then that slowly led up to Cuba. Oh yes, there was a sense of fear. When I used to go to the cinema there'd be a Pathé newsreel and you'd see the build-up. I can recall that my father was expecting us to go back to war.'[20]

Was it this sense that the next generation might soon be plunged into another conflict that led the young to seek new ways of enjoying themselves, just as the flappers and bright young things of the 1920s had done? Was it perhaps that wages were rising, that part-time work for the school child was plentiful and that parents were allowing their offspring to hold on to an increasing proportion of their earnings? Was it perhaps just that the adult world was starting to take notice of children and young people in a way it had not really done before, and was disliking much of what it saw? Whatever the cause, there was little doubt about the effect: outrage.

Looking back, Michael Foreman couldn't remember whether teenage gangs were a new thing in 1950s Lowestoft, or whether they had always been there in one form or another. But he felt the war had changed things for this generation: 'Maybe because their dads had been away, and so there was this breeding ground for independence ... they were used to being amongst their own kind, and out of sight really.'[21]

'The dangerous people were the Teddy Boys,' he remembered. 'In Lowestoft, they were one tribe and the Fisher Boys were another. They were similar to the Teddy Boys, but they had wide trousers rather than pinstripes. The Fisher Boys would be off fishing for two or three weeks, and they'd come back with money and then they'd burn it. They'd spend a lot on clothes. Then there'd be fights in the jazz clubs.'

Michael would avoid becoming a Teddy Boy or a Fisher Boy because he would go to London, to art college, where to be working-class was a kind of youth identity in itself. Even before he left school, he and his friends would go on day trips to the capital: 'We'd go round the galleries, go to a jazz club, and seek out army surplus stores to buy jeans and work clothes,' he said. 'We did like to buy fisherman's outfits – they used to have really good sweaters and shirts. We liked to identify with work clothes, rather than clothes your dad would have. Working-class culture and your own identity, a bit stroppy and anti-establishment. Of course, posh people like John Osborne were doing that too – the kitchen sink dramas.'

The Teddy Boys have been credited with being the first distinct youth culture, which of course they were not. The myriad territorial gangs which had dotted the Victorian and Edwardian cities gave the lie to that theory. But perhaps they were the first national working-class youth culture – or at least, the first with such a strictly defined style and set of norms. The flapper, for example, or even the at-leisure public schoolboy, would have had a sort of uniform and language of his or her own – but they were not working-class. Certainly, the Teddy Boys were able to spend money on style to an extent no youth group had previously been able to match. Yet the Teddy Boys also carried shades of the Victorian gangs, particularly in terms of the violence with which they were associated. When the US film *Blackboard Jungle*, featuring Bill Haley and the Comets, was shown, there were riots. The Teddy Boys were present in large numbers, too, during the Notting Hill race riots of 1958.

It was not long before the newspapers began reflecting the opinions of the older generation on the subject of youth culture. *The Times'* arts critic, reviewing the film *Rebel Without a Cause*, directed by Nicholas Ray in 1956, took the opportunity to launch into a diatribe on the failings of the young: 'Modern fashion has promoted the routine of blaming the parents for the sins of the children to a fine art. The last person to be held responsible for delinquent behaviour is, of course, the delinquent himself. It is not necessary to be a bigoted reactionary, out of all sympathy with the emotional problems and difficulties of youth, to hold that Mr Ray's specimens deserve not commiseration but a visit to the headmaster's study – only the school they attend does not seem to have such an animal and discipline is not one of the subjects on the curriculum.'

Psychologists like John Bowlby, whose work suggested that persistent delinquents might be reacting to adverse events in their childhood, were commonly held to be responsible for new, liberal attitudes. And liberal attitudes were very commonly held to be responsible for a rise in juvenile delinquency. Leo Page, a barrister and JP who wrote widely on penal reform, wrote to *The Times* in 1950 imagining the speech a judge might give when passing sentence on a boy charged with persistently breaking windows: 'Your recent offences were due to the fact that during the first five years of your mother's life she was on two occasions, for some trivial fault, brutally struck upon her buttocks by your grandmother. The sentence of the court upon you, William Sikes, is that your mother be sent to prison for five years. Your grandmother will go to preventive detention for the remainder of her life; you will be bound over to be of good behaviour for one month.' The letter drew a hurt response from Bowlby himself, suggesting Mr Page should read his evidence – which, he said, was being replicated by other experimental psychologists all over the world – before resorting to satire: 'Their truth or falsity will not be settled by lampoon, polemic or appeal to authority. Nothing but well planned and painstaking research can decide the issue.' Yet Mr Page was one of many who would continue to believe psychologists and social workers were encouraging the young to misbehave: the issue even cropped up in *West Side Story*, which first ran on Broadway in 1957:

> Officer Krupke, you're really a square;
> This boy don't need a judge, he needs an analyst's care!
> It's just his neurosis that oughta be curbed.
> He's psychologic'ly disturbed!

There was general agreement that the young of the day lacked energy and direction. And it was a view that seemed to be backed by the evidence: in 1947, the sociologist Mark Abrams had asked sixteen-year-olds how they spent their spare time, and almost a quarter had replied that they spent it 'doing nothing'. Almost a third had been to a cinema or a dance hall the previous evening. And another piece of research at around the same time had found a striking lack of creative or constructive leisure pursuits among teenage boys – they just did not seem interested, for the most part, in contributing to community activities. The majority, according to this study from the Social Medical Research Unit, did not respect the institution of marriage, and many were emotionally disturbed. On the bright side, their physical health was good – which was more than might have been said for their fathers' generation at the same age.[22]

The perception that the young were going to the dogs was nigh-on universal. In January 1950, a film called *The Blue Lamp* was released – the precursor to the television series *Dixon of Dock Green*. Its theme was juvenile delinquency. In a voice-over, the film's central character, Jack Warner, reported that children were living in homes 'broken and demoralized by war', and went on: 'These restless and ill-adjusted youngsters have produced a type of delinquent which is partly responsible for the post-war increase in crime. Some are content with pilfering and petty theft. Others, with more bravado, graduate to serious offences. Youths with brain enough to plan and organize criminal adventures and yet who lack the code, experience and self-discipline of the professional thief – which sets them as a class apart, all the more dangerous because of their immaturity.' The film told the story of a young man named Tom Riley, played by Dirk Bogarde, and an accomplice. The pair were seen to gun down and kill PC Dixon during a robbery.

There was consternation in other quarters, too. In early 1950, the BBC felt the need to send a questionnaire to more than seventy child guidance clinics, to canvass their opinions on the possible deleterious effects of the radio crime series *Dick Barton*. Several of the replies expressed concern. The Portman Clinic in London warned that some children were having nightmares because of the programme's violent content. And its potential moral effect, even on children who were not frightened by it, was questionable: 'Many of them look on Barton as a fool who gets away with too much.' Subsequently, the programme gained a tailpiece in which a voice-over discussed the moral issues raised.[23]

But despite the widespread perception that delinquency was growing, the numbers of indictable offences actually fell during the first half of the 1950s. And in November 1955 *The Times* reported that numbers of delinquents had fallen so fast that no fewer than twenty 'Approved Schools' were being closed down. Between 1951 and 1954, the number of boys aged between eight and sixteen years who were convicted of an indictable offence had fallen from 47,000 to 31,000, the paper reported. The number of girl delinquents had also fallen, from 3,600 to 3,000. The causes of the decline were not known, the article said, but 'improvements in housing and other social services, and full employment together with the growing influence of the child care services ... have all contributed'.

So the 1950s were in many ways an age of plenty for children. They were better fed, better housed, healthier, better educated, than they had ever been before. Yet this was also an age in which the young were vilified, perhaps even more so than they had been in earlier eras. And the old, pre-enlightenment idea that children were born evil, needing strict discipline in order to drive out the devil from them, was having a resurgence.

A dream turning sour

Perhaps William Golding's *Lord of the Flies*, which was published in 1954, was not a novel about children at all. Perhaps it was really a novel about mankind as a whole, and the struggle between civilization and savagery. Certainly it was a commentary on the brutality of a world where one war had just ended and another – possibly nuclear – could begin at any time. Yet to the extent that it was about children, the picture it painted was not an optimistic one. The novel depicted a little group of boys stranded on an island, struggling to create a civilization for themselves and failing dismally. Lacking strong leadership, the novel suggested, children would fall quickly back into their corrupt and violent natural state. This bad spell was broken at the end of the novel by the arrival of a naval officer who behaved just as the 'civilized' adult world of the day would have expected: he remarked that British youngsters should have put up a 'better show'. And the boy Jack – who had come to personify evil and savagery as the novel reached a terrifying conclusion – was suddenly reduced to a small, unkempt young child, needing to be punished for bad behaviour. In some ways, *Lord of the Flies* was a novel about the importance of sustaining the post-war suburban dream. If the shiny carapace of the perfectly regulated family ever broke open, it suggested, the true – ugly – face of childhood would be revealed. The adult world, it suggested, should be vigilant at all times.

This generation of babies had a great deal to be grateful for – a childhood without war, the prospect of full employment as they grew up, a veritable army of health professionals on hand to check their teeth, eyes and general wellbeing. Rationing was at an end; swathes of new housing were being built and the austerity of the post-war years was largely in the past. For the child, there were many delights in this era – sweets freely available, more money for treats such as comics and trips to the cinema. Yet by the time the 1950s were out, the glossy veneer on that post-war dream was beginning to crack.

7   Children of the Social Revolution

While the magazines continued to print pictures of the perfect kitchen, the perfect home, the perfect family, their readers were becoming increasingly aware that life just was not like that. Boys like Richard Cannon, whose parents' marriage was marred by his father's violent temper and his drinking, knew the uncomfortable truth. And as the 1960s began, one uncomfortable truth could no longer be ignored: marriage was not necessarily all it was cracked up to be. Both men and women, emboldened by growing economic security, began grabbing the opportunity to escape unhappy domestic lives. Imperceptibly at first, the divorce rate began to rise. The perfect nuclear family would never be quite so perfect again.

Academics say the divorce rate is bound up with economics. When the relative cost of separation – both financial and social – falls, more couples separate.[1] If work is plentiful, the divorce rate is likely to rise because people can afford to live separate lives. And as divorce becomes more common, the stigma reduces and the social cost falls too. So the divorce rate continues to rise. Close up, of course, it rarely looks so simple. For Peter Popham, growing up in a middle-class family in West London, his parents' divorce was simply 'a terrible blow'.

Both Peter's parents had exciting wars: his father piloting a Hurricane and his mother serving as a catering officer in the

Women's Royal Air Force, which posted her to Egypt. Her marriage, to a man who had been married twice before, had been regarded by her family as a bad idea. And Peter's father had a tendency to disappear for long periods – once to work as a cook on a small boat sailing to the West Indies – yet like most children, Peter had assumed his parents' marriage was strong.

'The way children do, you get used to the fact that your parents quarrel a lot, or sometimes there are bad scenes or for some reason Dad's not sleeping in the bedroom any more. I think home's so important to children that they always discount the idea that it's going to go to the crunch. I certainly did,' he said.[2] 'I remember thinking when I was about fifteen, before my parents split up, how common it was becoming, looking round my friends and thinking: "Wow," how many parents had split. I was aware this was something new and rather strange, and in a sense sort of menacing in a way. When they actually did split up, it was awful. I think probably they'd decided in the classic way of the time to stay together for the sake of the children.'

After the millennium, women would be more likely than men to initiate divorce. But during the 1960s, the assumption among observers of the rising divorce rate was that the phenomenon was actually being driven by men. In 1971, the Conservative Political Centre published a pamphlet on the subject, regretting the terrible toll that divorce was taking on abandoned women:[3] 'The deserted wife and the unmarried mother may find themselves leading a life of total isolation, unable to leave the children, caught up in a situation of poverty and despair,' it said.

Indeed, the 'deserting father' became something of a hate-figure. Many disappeared without trace, according to the Conservative Political Centre, leaving their wives and children distraught: 'A health visitor in a middle-class suburb reported three attempted suicides in one week, by wives with children, deserted by their husbands.' But, in 1969, one such father did dare to put his head above the parapet and confess what he had done – in an article in the *Guardian*, headlined: 'I Left My Wife and Children'.

'I am a deserting father, the arch-villain of liberal humanists and social workers,' he wrote. 'Three years ago I left my wife and children and went to live with another woman. I last saw my children a year ago. Have I now, finally, to accept that we must become extinct for one another?' With perhaps painful honesty, this father confessed that he had stopped weeping for the loss of his children. In any case, they were apparently doing well now the tension of the break-up had ended: 'To tell the truth, I'm scared of the assault made by children on the emotions.' The reaction to the article was angry, and mainly from abandoned wives.

'My husband, unlike the writer, left me "out of the blue" with two toddlers and a third on the way ... He promised to see them once a week in order to establish some degree of security in their lives. This lasted all of two weeks,' one of them wrote. Others, including one deserted daughter, pointed out the terrible toll these break-ups were having on children. 'I cannot understand how he could hold me in his arms one day and say he loved me, then walk out of my life for ever the next. My heart was broken ... my emotions became more settled only after he had completely left, and I beg the author of the article ... PLEASE, PLEASE leave the children alone.'[4]

Others were beginning to notice the emotional effect all this was having on the children, too: 'Disturbed kids come from bad homes: There appears to be a greater number of educationally sub-normal children in one-parent families,' the Conservative Political Centre noted. 'There may be symptoms of lack of concentration, withdrawal, truancy, moving home and therefore change of school, or disruption in school attendance.'

These disturbed children were not just coming from homes where marriages had failed, either. There was a growing worry during the 1960s that the fabric of society could be under threat from the number of children who were now being born outside wedlock. Indeed, politicians and commentators were beginning to detect a trend that would accelerate in the next three decades. In the years just after the war, four out of every 100 babies had been born out of wedlock. By the latter half of the 1960s, this figure would double. By the millennium, four out of ten babies would be born outside of marriage. In the 60s, there was widespread agreement that this was a major social problem. Lord Derwent, speaking in a debate on the welfare of these children in 1967, told his fellow peers that the risks were great: 'It is now generally agreed that one of the important causes of juvenile delinquency is in fact illegitimacy,' he said. 'It is quite understandable. The child grows up feeling that it does not really belong and that it is rather different from other children. The child gets a grudge against society, and where this happens juvenile delinquency may well start.' The modern parlance was to call such children 'illegitimate', he went on, but 'I prefer the word "bastard".'

Nor was it just family life that was causing concern. The Welfare State, receptacle for so many of the nation's hopes and dreams during the fifteen years after the war, was starting to show its flaws, too. In October 1961, the *Observer* newspaper ran a series of articles entitled 'Gaps in the Welfare State'. They spelled out the extent to which poverty and inequality were still stalking the land, and the extent to which they penetrated every area of national life. And they helped to popularize a new term: the 'problem family'.

'Mrs A, the head of a problem family and herself a problem (she "can't cope"), would have no problem with definitions,' one article said. 'She is simply in a mess, and does not know where to turn. She has been deserted, the six children are under eight years old, she lives on National Assistance, far away from relatives who might help and four floors up. Although she is only 30 she has high blood pressure and ... is grossly overweight.'

The welfare state, the paper reported, was failing to join up the dots. It was dealing with the delinquent teenager, the neglected toddler and the rent arrears as three separate problems. And while local authorities were beginning to see the merit in employing family case workers, such preventive services were 'patchy to say the least'.

The underlying problem, the newspaper implied, was inequality. It also told the story of Alfred B, an unskilled worker saddled with £1,700 in debt from hire purchase agreements for consumer goods. 'The man is one of the have-nots, as we used to call them before we assumed that everybody had ... it is a sad fact that in the Welfare State it is more reprehensible not to have than it was in the days of Victorian charity.'

Of course, there were plenty of children with no reason to believe 'everybody had'. David Hughes, born in the late 1950s in Rhyl, north Wales, was aware from an early age that living on a council estate carried a stigma. 'I didn't realize it until someone unkindly pointed it out to me, but ... to those who lived in the posher areas of town, the drives and crescents and boulevards, we were considered "the savages from the reservation",' he wrote in his autobiography *The Reso*, named after the popular local name for the estate where he grew up.[5]

'I don't remember anyone saying directly, "You're off the estate," but it became clear later I wasn't welcome in certain houses. People would meet me in neutral venues. I remember a friend saying, "It's best not to meet at my house. Meet in town, or the football field." It didn't hurt – I didn't register it as a social snub – but at secondary school it became clear there was a form of apartheid, really, about those from the estate: "He'll be trouble. Don't bring him round the house."'

David, a bright boy whose bright father had been forced to leave school at fifteen during the depression of the 1930s and who worked in a chemical plant, was aware from an early age that there were things he could not have: 'I remember a shop called Hughes' in Rhyl where they had a model railway in the window. I was conscious of never being able to afford one, but there was a democracy about being able to stand outside and imagine, just like anyone else could . . . when I got married I bought a model engine every week,' he said.[6]

Britain was still a country of haves and have-nots, then. The National Child Development Study,[7] which was following the lives of 17,000 children born in a single week in 1958, uncovered what at the time may have seemed a striking fact – that some children were at a disadvantage from birth. 'Their disadvantages increase if they belong to large families, physically if they are male and across a broad spectrum if they are badly housed,' *The Times* reported.[8] 'Nearly half the children from unskilled families suffered from social, health and educational handicaps compared with those from professional families. They were on average 1.3 inches shorter. Working-class children were more likely to have a squint, a speech defect, poor physical coordination and to wet their beds after they were five years old. They were twice as likely to have hearing trouble. They were less likely to be immunized or vaccinated or to have been taken to clinics or health centres. Fewer working-class children had visited a dentist at all in their first seven years although more had bad teeth. In fact, the study shows that the children most in need of the health and welfare services were the least likely to have used them.'

There was a growing body of evidence that all the efforts of the post-war government had done little to make Britain a more equal society. One of the biggest disappointments – and one which was to remain controversial for generations to come – was the grammar school system. Here, too, things had not turned out quite as predicted. Working-class children like Alan Briddock from Sheffield, who won a place at grammar school, were still finding themselves at a disadvantage once they got there.

Alan, having come joint top of his year in the School Certificate exam, which all pupils then took at sixteen, progressed into the sixth form at Firth Park Grammar School. Yet there was little sense that the school was driving him on to greater things; no guiding angel, whispering in his ear of the better life to which he had been handed the key. A few months later, worried that he was not bringing money into the house and uncertain whether he could cope with further maths, he left.

'I don't think I had ideas about where it was taking me,' he said. 'I think I just ploughed on until I couldn't go any further. Nobody said anything. We didn't get any advice, nobody talked about when you left. They didn't say, "You're ripe for this or that." So I left school and on the Monday I went into the chemi lab at Arthur Balfour steelworks. I was sixteen.'[9]

For most working-class children, grammar school was never a realistic possibility at all. A study published in 1962 by a Liverpool University academic revealed that in one of that city's poorer areas only a quarter of the pupils even sat the eleven plus exam.[10] Just one in ten was destined to make it to grammar school. The *Observer*, reviewing the book, noted that teachers in deprived areas – most of whom were caring and well meaning – fed their pupils a standard academic curriculum, 'leavened by country dancing and songs about cuckoos'. In Liverpool 7, in sight of the docks and with racial intolerance and prostitution rife, the school experiences of these pupils seemed 'derisory', the paper's education correspondent felt.

One of the problems with the system was that while children like those from Liverpool 7 lived in homes where there was little interest in education, few books and nowhere to do homework, even if they should wish to do so; children in middle-class areas were being drilled for the eleven plus years in advance. In 1962, the president of the Manchester Teachers' Association felt inspired to warn parents against putting their children through private lessons in order to pass the test. 'Parents . . . may cause much misery in later years. They may be doing their child a grave disservice.' Children, said Miss Webster, Headmistress of the Styal Open Air School, would find the right niche only if they were left to progress naturally, without pressure.

Miss Webster's speech bore hints that schools were beginning to enter a new, more liberal age. Junior schools were relinquishing the formal approach to learning, taking on board the work of post-Freudian child psychologists. The Plowden Report into primary education, published in 1967 but commissioned by the government four years earlier, would be a sort of homage to the work of Jean Piaget. Piaget had developed four 'sequential stages' of intellectual development through which he believed all children must pass – albeit at a wide range of ages. These stages also embraced physical, motor and emotional development, and Piaget believed that it was pointless trying to teach a child something until he had reached the right stage along the continuum. Bridget Plowden's report went so far as to state, for example, that 'a child cannot read without having learned to discriminate shapes'.[11]

Despite this apparently biologically deterministic base, the report heralded in a new age of liberalism in education. It embraced, too, Piaget's theory that a child should be the master of his or her own destiny, in educational terms – sparking a wave of new, radical practices in primary schools. Learning became more flexible; play was placed at the heart of children's lessons, pupils were encouraged to use their environments and to learn by discovery: 'Teachers should not assume that only what is measurable is valuable.'[12] Typically, children in one of these newly liberalized primary schools might spend the morning learning the 'three Rs' and the afternoon doing 'discovery' – nature, music, literature, arts and crafts. An *Observer* journalist who visited one such school noted that the headmistress, a Miss Horsburgh, gave her pupils fine china cups to wash and then smiled benevolently when they broke them. 'The workbooks had no marks, only comments such as "good work", or "well tried".' Miss Horsburgh explained: 'I don't give my children marks, or grade them. They are individuals and I expect them to do the best they can.'

And secondary education was about to change, too. By the time the Plowden report was published, the Labour government, re-elected in 1964 under Harold Wilson after thirteen years out of office, had announced the abolition of the grammar school system. The period in which all children would – in theory at least – have access to a free, selective secondary education was destined to be a very short one.

In 1970, David Hughes, growing up in Rhyl, became one of his area's comprehensive school guinea pigs. He had greeted the news that his future would not rest on a single exam with a sense of relief. His new school would be an amalgamation of a secondary modern and a grammar. 'It was like the Hittites had arrived,' he remembered later.[13] 'At first it was a mixing pot – they developed a junior high school, which gave the grammar school time to prepare for the hordes, get the discipline right.'

At that stage, though, the ideas of educational psychologists such as Piaget had had little impact on the secondary school system in North Wales. The local authority's solution seemed to have been to divide pupils into ability groups and to carry on pretty much as before: 'Some of the nuances were lost on me. I was aware there were two streams in parallel – if you were in Glyndwr you did modern maths, while we had to do the standard stuff. The tutor groups were mixed ability, but the classes were segregated from day one. I think if you were top set, you were top set for everything. For the lower sets, the balance of the curriculum was more practical – using the assets from the secondary modern curriculum. If you weren't very good at maths, you did more woodwork and cookery.'

The teachers could be brutal, too: 'Once, a woodwork teacher got me to put both my hands in a vice. Then he walked away. It was a double period, eighty minutes, and I spent the whole time with my hands in this vice. It became psychological. I wasn't going to let on I was irritated. I thought afterwards it was a fair cop. He was an interesting guy. He showed us how to make a helicopter. I wouldn't have wanted to have crossed him.'

Schools may have been changing slowly, but changing they certainly were. Writing in the *Guardian*, Jill Tweedie lamented the loss of the orderly atmosphere of her old grammar school, and recalled her secret joy when one of her teachers, a Miss Needham – 'profile sharp as stalactites, great brown bun bowing the scraggy neck, feet two yards long in pointed button shoes' – had unfairly lost her temper with her for walking on the wrong side of the corridor: 'How super, how smashing, Miss Needham was being unfair . . . we judged all our teachers at some deep level by the standards of our parents' world. As girls we knew our looks and charm were all-important and so we applied the same criteria to our teachers. Did they have a man? Could they get a man? . . . Only the one or two rare birds, the cold clever women with sharp tongues and a deep cynicism, escaped our ultra-conventional net.'[14] Nowadays, Tweedie felt, the deep lines that had divided teachers from pupils were breaking down. Instead, teachers were being made to feel they must befriend their pupils. 'We ask for less exercise of authority and more equality, less parrot feeding and more understanding and involvement . . . Mothers who lam out quite happily at their own children condemn bitterly teachers who adopt, even once, the same methods . . . We demand liberal attitudes, but we give teachers very little extra help for the extra time liberal attitudes demand. The whole school structure today, combined with an appalling shortage of money, virtually demands an authoritarian approach to work at all.' Tweedie felt teachers were being driven to despair because they could no longer discipline their pupils.

The changes in the education system mirrored a broader change in social attitudes in which children were slowly being swept up. Eleanor Wintour, an American journalist living and bringing up a family in London, exhorted British parents in the *Observer*[15] to take a less buttoned-up approach to child-rearing than they had done in the past. The Brits were still making parenthood look far too much like hard work, she said: 'Americans, on the whole, aim at happy (some of them unfortunately prefer the term "well-adjusted") rather than good children ... In upper-class English circles it is common knowledge that American children are spoiled, whining, bad-mannered little creatures ... Americans have a vague idea that English children are quiet and well-behaved, but when they happen to run into any ... they find them quiet, unchildlike and repressed.'

Far from embracing this call to liberal arms, legions of British parents – most of them women – wrote in to the paper to complain about Mrs Wintour's attitudes.[16] 'Why must Mrs Wintour postulate such an extraordinary either-or? Cannot a good child be a happy one?' asked Claire Rayner, writing from North Wembley. 'We take it for granted that our children cannot live in an adult environment without learning a code of behaviour that makes them acceptable to adults.' Diane Hemingway from Birmingham asked: 'Happy or slaphappy upbringing? A look at American juvenile delinquency figures might give a pointer. We may have followed Americans in many fields, but let us stand firm on this and continue to bring up our children to be well-mannered, likeable people.' Jonathan Lewis, who had lived in the US for a year, wrote: 'The experience of myself and many European friends has been that American children are indeed spoiled, whining, bad-mannered little creatures – in a word, brats.' Not everyone agreed, though. Anne Spencer, from Chelmsford, wrote in to assure readers that there were indeed British families who were adopting the more child-friendly American style of parenting: 'There is perhaps an encouraging revolution going on.'

There was indeed. As early as 1961, there had been a feeling that children should be given their leisure time – as they had been given, in part, their educational time – and allowed to decide for themselves how to spend it. Peter and Iona Opie, who had been studying children's playground games, made a plea for more autonomy for children:[17] 'The qualities of self-organization, self-discipline and perseverance shown by most children of seven to eleven when they think they are on their own has to be seen to be believed. It is possible we too readily think of a child as a "good citizen" only when he is one of a school football team or a scout patrol . . . the more children have their free time organized for them . . . the more they lose the traditional art of self-entertainment.'

Increasingly, children were being seen in a wider social context as individuals, as social players in their own right. And as that change of attitude began to trickle into some of childhood's darker and more hidden corners, there would be radical change for some groups of children. In particular, campaigners for children's rights were beginning to ask why children who had disabilities, or who could not for some reason live with their parents, did not have a greater say in how they lived, or how they were educated. As the world began to wake up to the notion that all children had their own individual worth, it equally began to wake up to the fact that some children were not part of society at all. In 1971, Maureen Oswin published a book about the thousands of children who were hidden from view, spending their lives in institutions because they had disabilities or 'social problems'.[18] Writing in the *Guardian*, she described their lives:[19] 'I met children in locked hospital wards who never went on holidays, had not been outside the hospital for months, and had never been in a shop, children who had never seen food being prepared, or properly laid tables, because they always received their meals from a hospital trolley. Children whose lives were organized to suit the working hours of hospital staff, so they were got up too early in the morning, spent long, empty hours of boredom ... and were got ready for bed at three in the afternoon. I remember a dozen little limbless five year-olds, dressed in night clothes, bemused by boredom, sitting in a straight row, staring up at racing and football results.'

Oswin's reference to 'limbless children' underlined another dark news story of the time. In the late 1950s, increasing numbers of predominantly middle-class women had begun taking a new wonder-drug to counteract the effects of morning sickness. It was called thalidomide. Within a few years, more than 10,000 children across the developed world had been born with deformed limbs and other problems as a result of the drug – and many of them would spend their childhoods in institutions such as the ones Oswin described.

As the 1970s wore on, there was a gradual change of attitude towards these hidden children. But as David Hughes, growing up in north Wales, was to find, old taboos were slow to break down. David's older brother Graham was autistic: 'I was told it was oxygen star-vation at birth that caused it. That was easier to take than that there might have been something genetic,' he said.[20] Their mother had flatly rejected suggestions that Graham should go into an institu-tion, and throughout his childhood had fought for him to have as normal a life as possible. 'He was very thin and wiry, and he had a very limited range of subjects he'd converse on. I'm eight years younger – but I would set sums and he would struggle to do them, even though I was dumbing down: two and one, three and two. And yet on subjects he was interested in, he had an almost encyclopaedic knowledge. He was interested in electricity – from about the age of six he could wire a plug and knew exactly how it all worked. It was a bit like *Rain Man*[21] – I'd say I'd met someone born on the 13th April 1980, he'd say it was a Sunday, we went to so-and-so and it was raining, so we had to put on our coats. He was incredible, really.'

But when David was in his teens, Graham became increasingly

troubled. 'The first time was about 1972. He was pretty affable, but he seemed more and more agitated. We were in our living room and he was sitting there and rocking backwards and forwards. He started saying 'No, no!' – as if someone was talking in his head. He'd made a poker with a ram's head handle, and he picked it up and threatened me with it.'

For David, the stigma of having a brother who was mentally ill was hard to bear. As he studied for his A-levels, Graham became increasingly unwell and eventually was admitted to a hospital – an asylum – known locally as 'Denby Mental'. 'In Rhyl, if you did something daft, they'd say: "You're Denby Mental, you are." It was a place of horror. You didn't want anything to do with it. When I visited, it was incredibly distressing. It felt like the treatment was to sit in high-backed chairs and sit it out, with lots of male nurses coming every so often, and saying: "All right? Want a cup of tea, Gray?" Or, "Here's your medication – take this." My worry was he'd go in there and never come out. Some of the people there had clearly been institutionalized since they were children. It was like a vision of nineteenth-century Bedlam. I was really, really scared of that. Of him not coming out. Of knowing there were places like that. There was a whole group in society that basically nobody knew about.'

David found himself unable to talk to anyone at all about what had happened – even his girlfriend: 'Part of it was that mental illness was almost contagious, that we as a family might be tarred with the stigma. The closest I came was saying, "He's ill, he's in hospital." In no circumstances would I have told them which hospital. There was a lad who grew up on the estate with me – he lived with his Auntie because his Mum was in Denby Psychiatric Hospital. You could tell he had a really fractured life. He was talented but socially dislocated. "Your Mum's a nutter, so you're a partial nutter." The language associated with it was diabolical, really. There must have been thousands of people who went through that and said nothing. It's the first time I've talked about it.'

Gradually, these institutions would be swept away. In the mid-1970s a special committee on children's health, headed by the chair of the British Paediatric Association, Donald Court, would help to move the children's mental health system into the modern age and to prepare the way for their closure. Slowly, quietly, the pendulum was once again swinging away from the pre-enlightenment view of the child. Now, once again, children were born good rather than evil, and once again the adult world was beginning to be prepared to give children the benefit of the doubt.

Yet despite this new, warmer atmosphere, adult–child relations were very far from being perfectly harmonious. Across the Western world, children were beginning to act in new, sometimes alarming, ways. And the adult world often found itself scratching its collective head and wondering what on earth was going on. Strange, even hilarious, occurrences broke out. In Rochdale, in 1968, crockery was smashed and food thrown at the Newbold Infants' School after children who had been bullied out of their dinner tickets bit back and refused to watch their tormentors eating their food. The result was, quite literally, a riot. The *Guardian* reported[22] that 160 children had rampaged through the school, bean-bags had been thrown at dinner ladies and the school left strewn with twisted and broken cutlery. The following day, the chairman of the local education committee, Alderman Cyril Smith, watched sternly as the children filed, chastened and silent, into the hall for meat pie, potatoes and beetroot, declaring that all they needed was 'a bloody good hiding'.

Elsewhere, people were asking why children and young adults were indulging in similar outbreaks of baffling behaviour. So, why? Perhaps decades of changing thought about children, of increasing awareness of their need for individuality, was filtering through to their consciousness. Or perhaps the freedom offered by better education, better health and better housing had begun to embolden them. Certainly, greater prosperity was leading to children having more space, more time to themselves. Better housing meant more children having their own bedrooms; central heating meant they could spend more time in them rather than huddling round the fire downstairs. Now, teenagers used their own rooms to do homework, spend time with their friends, listen to music.[23] Freely available part-time work meant they had money to spend, and better adult wages meant their parents didn't necessarily need that money to go into the family purse. Children with money to spend could create and shape markets: for clothes, for records – and sometimes for leisure pursuits that were considered rather less than desirable.

In 1961, *The Times* reported that a young man named Jonathan Phillips from Surrey had been remanded in custody after being caught in possession of fifty 'cannabis cigarettes'. 'He had taken hemp cigarettes to parties instead of a bottle of drink, but sometimes took a bottle as well. The parties were mostly attended by teenagers and often one did not know who was giving the party.' Jonathan Phillips, it emerged, was considered very bright but had dropped out of school and had become 'a source of much distress to his parents'. His father, the paper reported, feared he was becoming part of the 'Beatnik fraternity'. The judge told Phillips his was one of the most serious cases of the kind that had come before him: 'Not only from your own point of view but from that of the young men and women who might have come under the influence of this drug which you were growing and manufacturing. The evidence here displays, in our view, that there are probably no depths of degradation to which the human personality in young people cannot sink when they come under the influence of something like this.'

There was bound to be a backlash against the more liberal atmosphere that was beginning to cling to the life of the young. And the new freedoms teenagers had gained were beginning to cause discomfort, not to say consternation, in some quarters. There would be plenty more for social conservatives to worry about as the decade wore on. A few years later, Peter Popham, at school in north London, would stop going to Sunday school and begin secretly smoking the occasional joint: 'Before long I was taking LSD with friends. Just sort of buying into the whole "underground", as we called it. But I was slightly too young to be part of what was going on, being conscious that I was on the fringes, peering in through the window.' At sixteen, he and a friend went up to town to the hippy-oriented Middle Earth Club, but felt their short hair marked them out as distinctly uncool.

Everywhere the less-than-liberal part of the adult world looked during the 1960s, it seemed to find young people doing things of which it could not approve. In February 1960, Lord Saltoun told the House with some consternation that sexual activity was now rife among teenagers. 'Fifty years ago when I was living in Hackney I do not remember that these fashions prevailed among children, although people were living far more on top of one another than today,' he said. The cause of the trouble was clear: sex education was being taught in schools: 'I do not think this kind of instruction is suitable for classes ... I am convinced that a lot of this misbehaviour among juveniles is due to this cause.'

Something was certainly going on. The teenage pregnancy rate was rising to an alarming level, doubling between 1955 and 1970 to fifty births for every 1,000 girls aged between fifteen and nineteen.[24] Yet most girls, if asked, would still express quite conventional views about sex. A *Guardian* journalist interviewing a group of schoolgirls in 1970[25] remarked that 'you can hear their mothers' voices behind them': 'Susan wouldn't get pregnant. That wouldn't be fair to her mum ... It's funny, she says. When she was younger she couldn't think how anyone could. Now if she's out with a boy she really likes. You know. The others don't say much. Lynne, in a small voice, says that those pictures in the biology room, of babies being born, put you off. They're all silent. "Still, it's fulfilling, having a baby, isn't it?" says Susan. They cheer you up. Oh, yes. They'd all like to get married and have babies one day. They don't know what they're going to do till then.'

But despite this conventional response, there were many places where the younger generation, having begun to form its own identities outside the classroom, was beginning to test the boundaries within schools as well. During the late 1960s and early 1970s, a whole series of episodes of radicalism, quickly squashed but widely discussed, were to break out. In April 1971, the Obscene Publications Squad moved in on the offices of a small publisher named Stage 1 Ltd, in Theobald's Road in London. Their target was *The Little Red School Book*, a slim volume which had sold 500,000 copies in mainland Europe and which was now being published in the United Kingdom with a print run of 20,000. The book, first published in Denmark, was written in a plain, informative style. It contained useful tips on how to complain about a teacher and how to organize a demonstration or a strike. It appeared to condone the use of illegal drugs, and advocated the sale of contraceptives in schools. The case would immediately send both liberals and conservatives running for the barricades: on the one side, a flamboyant Tory MP named Sir Gerald Nabarro and the anti-indecency campaigner Mary Whitehouse; on the other, the National Council for Civil Liberties and the eminent barrister John Mortimer. As the trial of the publisher, a twenty-seven-year-old named Richard Handyside, progressed, the papers were full of the story. Mrs Whitehouse railed that the book was 'a revolutionary primer': 'Children were constantly exhorted to collect evidence against teachers of alleged injustices or anything which was likely to enhance revolution.' Mrs Whitehouse declared herself 'very relieved' when Mr Handyside was fined £50, but the book continued to circulate.[26] Perhaps a partial clue to these episodes of apparent radicalism, though, was the reaction of more liberal adults. 'The crux of the matter is that the book encourages children to question the "system", and to organize themselves to fight it when it begins to crush and mould them,' a Mrs Stella Robinson from Surrey wrote to the *Guardian*.[27] 'I have read the Little Red School Book, and thought it absolutely first rate.' The truth was that liberal parents – and there were a growing number of them – rather liked having their children exposed to radical ideas. In fact, where the book did land among the young, it largely failed to inflame. In one conservative Manchester school, pupils were given the book to discuss in a lesson, the *Guardian* reported.[28] 'There was a great deal of laughter and a general agreement that it was naïve rubbish which would appeal only to middle-class revolutionaries.'

So, what was going on? Were books such as *The Little Red School Book*, or the sex education film *Growing Up*, which caused shock waves in May 1971 with its graphic portrayals of masturbation and orgasm, inspired by some new radicalism among children, some desire to shock? Or were they really aimed at adults who quite liked the idea that their children might be radicalized by such material? In December 1971, there was another row – this time over a magazine called *Children's Rights*. The magazine had published a communiqué from the Children's Angry Brigade, which exhorted the young to 'unscrew locks, smash tannoys, paint blackboards red, grind all the chalk to dust'. One of those who responded to a *Guardian* article on this development was A. S. Neill, founder of the progressive Summerhill school in Suffolk, who introduced himself as an editorial adviser to the new publication but confessed he had not read it 'owing to the small print'. Neill was eighty-eight years old at the time. 'I am all for children's rights: the right to reject the barbarous cane, the right to have some say in their studies, the right to wear what they like. But sabotage is not the answer,' he wrote.[29]

At around the same time, the National Council for Civil Liberties, founded in 1934 to promote human rights, decided to hold a conference to champion the rights of the child. Parents should run their homes in a way sympathetic to their children's lifestyles, the organization suggested, and should even allow their children to have a degree of sexual freedom. The very notion drew an angry response from some quarters. One correspondent to *The Times* felt the whole idea was ridiculous:[30] 'What are they trying to do? Destroy parental authority? . . . We can already see the results of lack of parental control in the troublesome youths and students of today . . . They should get their heads out of the clouds and start exercising some genuine responsibility to society as a whole.'

There certainly was radicalism among children, even though much of it was encouraged by adults. Peter Popham, attending a large, cosmopolitan school in north London, tended to avoid the small clique of Trotskyists who had a habit of cornering their fellow-pupils in corridors 'to preach rebellion'. These people were not regarded as cool by their peers. But Peter did begin reading alternative magazines – *International Times* and *Oz*. *Oz* had started out in 1963 as an Australian satirical magazine, but in England, where it was published from 1967, it quickly became essential reading for anyone who wanted to be associated with the hippy scene. Its brightly coloured psychedelic covers quickly became collectors' items. By 1970, though, the magazine was facing criticism that it was losing touch with the young. In response, its editors decided to invite 'school kids' to edit an issue. Peter Popham, who had been trying to inject 'a slightly hippy dippy thing' into his school magazine, took up the challenge. 'I thought this would be fantastic, but having got myself there, I didn't really know what I wanted to do,' he said. 'I ended up writing a couple of record reviews. I wasn't angry about anything. It was no good pretending I was. It was just a wonderful thing in its own right, to be part of the group that produced *Oz*.'[31] The issue, which was hammered out in a basement flat in Notting Hill and which contained a pornographic Rupert Bear cartoon, soon caught the eye of the Obscene Publications Squad. The law moved in – this was not the first such raid on the *Oz* office – and Richard Neville, Felix Dennis and Jim Anderson were all charged with corrupting public morals. The case became the longest obscenity trial in history, with John Mortimer, barrister and later author of *Rumpole of the Bailey*, defending, the comedian Marty Feldman giving evidence along with the jazz musician George Melly, and John Lennon marching in protest. The three were cleared but were convicted of lesser charges – later overturned on appeal.[32] By then, Peter Popham had left school and gone travelling in the Middle East, so he was not in London for the trial. 'I was in touch with them by post, and sent a long article on spec about hippy dystopia in Eilat, in southern Israel. I was just delighted and relieved when they decided not to call me as a witness.'

The *Oz* trial was sparked not by children's radicalism, but by the decisions of the adults who ran the magazine. And, inevitably, the ideological battle over childhood in 1970s Britain would be as polarized as the adult battles that were concurrently raging over class, race and gender. But as the decade drew to a close, one particular idea was gaining strength: children were, like immigrants, like women, like the workers, an oppressed minority. Their consciousness had not yet been raised; but once it was, they could be freed to fly in their own idiosyncratic ways to a brighter, better future. Writing in 1979, an academic called Martin Hoyles would argue that the popular image of the child had changed little since Victorian times: 'It is typified at Christmas in the image of the babe in the manger who grows into Charles Wesley's "Gentle Jesus, meek and mild" ... Particularly at Christmas, children are celebrated sentimentally as playthings.'[33] Yet the very fact that academics were beginning to examine the way in which children were viewed by the adult world was an indication that the wind of change was blowing. By now, a wealth of Marxist and feminist literature had built up around the notion that childhood was but an oppressive social construct, a tool of the capitalist or the patriarchal system. Hoyles' book included a chapter by the feminist writer Shulamith Firestone, entitled 'Down with Childhood': 'Women and children are always mentioned in the same breath ... The special tie women have with children is recognized by everyone. I submit, however, that the nature of this bond is no more than shared oppression. And that moreover this oppression is intertwined and mutually reinforcing in such complex ways that we will be unable to speak of the liberation of women without also discussing the liberation of children, and vice versa. We must include the oppression of children in any program for feminist revolution.' Firestone saw childhood as a kind of apartheid, invented by adults to bind children to the family unit, and claimed the use of animal terminology to describe children – mice, rabbits, kittens – was part of this machinery of oppression: 'The best way to raise a child is to LAY OFF ... Gone are the days of Huckleberry Finn: Today the malingerer or dropout has a full-time job just in warding off the swarm of specialists studying him, the proliferating government programs, the social workers on his tail.'

The current radical thinking, then, saw childhood not just as something invented by adults but as a tool they were using to keep their offspring in check. The idea that childhood was the happiest phase of life, for example, was a fantasy shared by adults who wanted to believe at least one part of their own lives had been free from drudgery, anxiety and ill-health. This view contrasted with the notion that sentimentality about children was actually becoming a sort of substitute for economic value, which had dwindled as the child's role had changed from that of wage-earner to that of scholar.

Meanwhile, the French philosopher Michel Foucault was drawing comparisons between schools, prisons and asylums:[34] 'Madness is childhood.' Hoyles added that the comparison was 'brought home forcefully' by the knowledge that the city of Omaha was dosing children with amphetamine-type substances in order to control their behaviour, and that hyperactive children in Britain were being similarly drugged.

At around the same time, an American schools reformer named John Holt argued that outdated notions had led to the young being made subservient and dependent upon adults:[35] 'The words "expect" and "expectation" are on the whole badly misunderstood and misused by most people who write about children. Most people use them as synonyms for "demand" or "insist" or "compel". When they say we should have higher expectations of children, they mean that we should demand that they do certain things and threaten to punish them if they do not.' The main function of compulsory universal education, he argued, was 'to control people's minds, what they thought and knew'.

Such views would always be contentious, but the notion that a child should have 'rights' had by now entered the mainstream. In 1973, Hillary Rodham, then a student at Yale Law School and soon to become Hillary Rodham Clinton, wrote that 'children's rights is a slogan in search of a definition'.[36] Soon, it would find one, as it solidified into the notion that the child should have distinct legal rights, separate from those of its parents. That would not happen overnight, but one major step along the way was the declaration by the United Nations that 1979 would be the International Year of the Child. In practical terms, it would have little effect. But it would get people talking about children, and childhood, in forums which had had little to say about them up till this point. 'Dare I say that I think some adults are tempted to spend a great deal of time telling children or other people what is good for them, rather than listening to children and learning from them of their needs?' asked the Bishop of Salisbury in a debate on the subject in the House of Lords that year.[37] 'If we are seriously listening to our children, then our sense of awe is heightened, and their ability to go to the heart of matters is constantly recognized.'

Suddenly, children were being credited with the possession of a special and unique perspective on the world; even a sort of elixir which the adult would wish to share: 'I think it was a Lebanese poet who said: "Your children are not your children. They are the sons and daughters of life's longing for itself,"' mused the Bishop, quoting Kahlil Gibran.

The sky turns dark

Such exaltation of the child as a unique being with a special perspective on the world had not been prevalent since before World War One. And so as the adult world once again began to idolize the notion of the innocent, the unspoiled and even the sagacious child in an era of rapid social change, perhaps it is hardly surprising that violations against childhood – events which had taken place with some regularity throughout history – would again begin to impact more strongly on the public imagination.

Maybe the trail of events had begun early in the morning of 7 October 1965, when a couple named David and Maureen Smith had made their way to a phone box near the flat where they lived, near Hyde, in Cheshire, armed with a screwdriver and a kitchen knife. The call they made, to Hyde police station, led to one of the most notorious murder inquiries of the century. The previous night, David Smith had been at the house that his wife's sister, Myra Hindley, shared with her boyfriend, Ian Brady. Smith had watched as Brady had murdered a seventeen-year-old apprentice named Edward Evans, first beating him with the flat of an axe and then throttling him with electrical cord. Brady had asked Smith to help him dispose of the body the following evening, but a terrified Smith had confessed all to his wife. A week later, with Brady and Hindley in custody, the police found a ticket to a left-luggage locker at a Manchester station in the back of Hindley's prayer book. Inside were suitcases containing pornographic photographs of a young girl along with tape recordings of her screaming and begging for help. The girl was ten-year-old Lesley Ann Downey, who had disappeared from a fairground the previous December. Her body was later found on nearby Saddleworth Moor, along with that of twelve-year-old John Kilbride, who had been abducted from a local market two years earlier. Brady and Hindley went on trial for all three murders. Years later, they would confess to two further killings – of sixteen-year-old Pauline Reade, whose body was eventually recovered from the moor, and of twelve-year-old Keith Bennett, whose remains were never found.

Child murder on this scale was, and always had been, sensational. The world's press was full of the story, and continued to follow its developments over the subsequent decades. Yet there was also a sense of propriety which surrounded such things in the 1960s. *The Times* did not run a leader on the subject until 1972, when it published a largely impenetrable piece about the rights and wrongs of Myra Hindley being allowed to go out for a walk – an event which had sparked public outrage. The first letter ever printed by the paper on the subject was in 1968, when a vicar named Kenneth Leech wrote to object to a proposal that a film might be made about the murders: 'I hope that I am not alone in finding the desire to make publicity and profit out of human suffering utterly disreputable and horrible . . . It is almost unspeakably cruel and nasty,' he wrote. Yet despite this reticence, maybe it was around this time that a sense of fear began to spread around the concept of childhood. Children, having become more precious to their parents as they became fewer and more expensive, were too valuable to lose. Parents began to gather their young a little closer to them – or at least to worry more about them when they were not close. The exhortation not to 'get into cars with strange men' became universal.

The next child murder case to hit the headlines during this period was in many ways even more disturbing, for this time the perpetrator and the victims were all children, and the perpetrator was a girl. One of the strangest aspects of the case, to the modern eye, is also one of the most mundane. It is the detail in a description of the last day of the first of two little boys who would become the victims of ten-year-old Mary Bell.[38] On the morning of Saturday, 25 May 1968, four-year-old Martin Brown, a solid boy with blond hair, blue eyes and a round face who called his father 'Georgie', woke up early in his home in Scotswood, Newcastle. As was his usual habit on a Saturday, when his parents had a lie-in while he babysat his one-year-old sister, Linda, he went downstairs to fetch a drink of milk and a piece of bread. He dressed Linda and took her into their mother's room before having a bowl of sugar pops in the kitchen. When he had finished the cereal he fetched his anorak and put it on. His mother, June, by now up and in the scullery, heard him call: 'I'm away, Mam. Tara, Georgie!' She never saw him again. Martin spent the day playing with other children around the streets of Scotswood, turning up variously at the local shop and at the house of an 'aunt' – a friend of his mother's – looking for food. At 3.30 p.m. he was found dead in a derelict house. The fact that a four-year-old boy should have spent his last day without adult supervision, being shooed out of his aunt's house when he did turn up there, excited no comment whatsoever. It seemed the adult world, which had begun to take much more notice of its children than previously, still saw them largely as independent – if vulnerable – beings.

Martin's death was initially thought to have been the result of a random accident, and even when Mary Bell and her friend Norma Bell – who was no relation – broke into a local nursery and left notes saying things like: 'We did murder Martain brown, fuckof you

BastArd,' and: 'YOU ArE micey y because we murdered Martain GO brown you BettER Look out THErE arE MurdErs about By FANNYAND and auld Faggot you screws,' no one took them seriously. Nine weeks later, three-year-old Brian Howe was found dead on a nearby piece of waste ground with a carpet of weeds and flowers covering his body and with scratches and pressure marks on his neck. The two deaths were then linked, and both Mary and Norma were charged with murder. Norma was eventually acquitted; Mary was convicted of manslaughter owing to diminished responsibility.

These murders, like the Moors murders, did not attract the kind of comment they might have provoked in later years. They certainly attracted widespread publicity, and Mary was dismissed as evil in true pre-enlightenment terms – the judge used the word 'wicked,' when sentencing her. In the media, she was described as a 'freak of nature', 'evil born' and 'a bad seed'. Such descriptions served a useful social purpose – they allowed these horrifying and seemingly inexplicable crimes to be neatly packaged up and put away – much as the Reverend Leech would have liked to have seen the Moors murders parked in a dark, inaccessible corner of the public mind. If Mary was somehow possessed by the devil, or if her twisted nature were the result of some freak genetic mutation, then no one was really responsible.

The truth was far more complicated, of course. And it is perhaps surprising, given the ongoing debate at the time about the links between criminality and bad childhood experiences, that Mary's own early life was not examined in more detail. It has since been suggested that her mother was a prostitute who exposed her child to sexual abuse by her clients, and who tried on several occasions to kill her. She did not know who her father was. In an account of the case written thirty years later, Gitta Sereny[39] – who befriended Mary in adulthood – argued that the girl should have been seen not as perpetrator but as victim. Sereny cited a case from 1861 in which two eight-year-olds beat a two-year-old called George Burgess to death in Stockport. There was never any question of the two older boys being tried for the crime, she wrote, quoting a *Times* leader on the 1861 case which said: 'Children of that age cannot be held legally accountable in the same way as adults. Conscience, like other natural faculties, admits of degrees: it is weak, and has not arrived at its proper growth in children.'[40]

If Mary's cries for help had been heeded, Sereny suggested, she would never have become a killer. Mary's probation officer told the author: 'In the public's justified horror about these events, and their ready acceptance of "evil" as an explanation, people tend to forget that they were children who carried around a baggage of childhood experiences unknown to or ignored by any responsible adult.'[41] But that was later. For now, child killers were, it seems, simply that – children who happened also to be killers.

It would be many years before anyone would take seriously the idea that the adults around Mary Bell could have prevented her from killing if only they had listened to her more. Indeed, the suggestion would always remain controversial – the feeling that such crimes must be born out of an evil which was in some way inhuman, even diabolical, rather than of a twisted and damaged childhood, ran very deep. But, even in the early 1970s, the notion that children in general should be heard, that their opinions should be taken into account, had begun to take hold.

This belief had not penetrated every corner, nor had it even penetrated very far into the system of social services which had grown up since the war. Ever since the death of Dennis O'Neill in 1945 had caused such outrage against the authorities who would foster out a little boy without making proper checks on his safety, the role of the state in children's lives, and particularly in the lives of children who came from families with problems, had been growing. Indeed, as a mother named Pauline Colwell gave birth in March 1965 to a daughter named Maria, moves were afoot to ensure that role would become even greater in years to come. The Seebohm Report, commissioned that year and published three years later, would bring social services departments into being within local councils, and would lead to a huge rise – 10 per cent a year for several years – in the resources available to social workers. Some social work departments ran to several thousand members of staff. And yet despite all this activity, and despite a growing awareness nationally of children's individual needs, it would be another twenty years before social workers would fully move on from generic work with families to putting the needs of individual children first. 'In the early 1970s there was a great sense of optimism about prevention to the point where some of the specifics of child protection were neglected,' one social services director would remark later.[42] 'Social workers were so focused on the family as a whole that they were forgetting about the child.'

And certainly, it must have been painfully, heartbreakingly clear to the Sussex social workers who handed little Maria Colwell over to her mother in November 1971 that they were not acting on the child's wishes. That morning, Maria had been taken to Middle Street School in Brighton by her uncle, Bob Cooper, who with his wife, Doris had been looking after her since she was a baby. Later, Mr Cooper had collected her and taken her to the social services office, where the handover was to take place. Maria screamed and clung to her uncle. Indeed, so hysterical was she at the prospect of being separated from her foster-parents that she could only be persuaded to go with her mother on the basis of a lie – that she would be allowed to return to the Coopers the following weekend. She never saw them again, and less than fourteen months later she was dead.

Maria was the fifth and last child of her mother's first marriage. Her father, Raymond Colwell, left just weeks after she was born and died a few months later. Pauline went to pieces, often leaving her children dirty and neglected and, according to an official report on the case, 'associating with numerous men'.[43] When Maria was five months old, Pauline gave her to the Coopers, both of whom became devoted to her. Her school reported that she was a nice girl, always polite and well dressed. They saw no particular problems with her health or behaviour. But relations between Maria's mother and the Coopers deteriorated, and Pauline wanted to end the arrangement. She had remarried, to Mr Kepple, and had two more children. Despite the fact that these children were sometimes left outside pubs in the evenings and that the older girl had been seen with bruising and a black eye, social services now felt Pauline's parenting skills were 'adequate'. And the rights of the parent took precedence, it seems, over the rights of the child. So if there were no good reasons to keep Maria in care other than that she wanted to stay there, she was expected to go back. For some time before the final separation, Maria had been going on visits to her mother's house, returning distressed and sometimes with bruises which, she said, Kepple had inflicted. Sometimes she would work herself into such a state at the prospect of a visit that she would be unable to go.

In the last year of her life, Maria would change, literally before the eyes of everyone who knew her, from a happy, healthy child into a thin, frightened shadow, depressed – according to her doctor – and often bruised. She was used by the Kepples as a drudge, dragging heavy bags of coal from the local shop. A neighbour would hear her mother slapping her and calling her a 'dirty little bitch' after she had apparently soiled herself. Yet the feeling that the authorities knew what they were doing seemed to prevail – her teacher, who had seen Maria hysterical at the prospect of having to go to her mother's, said later that although she had felt the procedures inhumane, she assumed they were for the best. Even when social workers saw Maria with a blackened face and an eye that was just 'a pool of blood', they accepted the Kepples' explanation that she had had an accident on her scooter. The neighbour who had reported these injuries then confronted Maria's social worker, demanding to know if she really believed the story. She allegedly replied: 'Well, knowing the family I would say that Maria has had a beating.' Yet still nothing was done. A few months later, in December 1972, Maria's social worker, Diana Lees, would see her, very thin and suffering from an infection and persistent diarrhoea, and soon after that would learn from a message left by the neighbour that Maria was now 'more or less like a skeleton', unkempt and dirty. Miss Lees did not return the call. On 7 January 1973, the Kepples arrived at the local hospital with Maria's limp body in a pram. The post mortem showed she had bruising all over her and a fractured rib which had begun to heal. She weighed just thirty-six pounds – ten pounds less than the normal weight for an eight-year-old. William Kepple was convicted of manslaughter and eventually served a four-year sentence.

It was the public, not the authorities, who were initially outraged when the details of Maria's death emerged. Neighbours and other locals queued to get into the public inquiry which was subsequently held, and many gave evidence of the abuse they had seen the girl suffer. Yet while the inquiry was swingeing in its criticisms of social workers – that they failed to communicate properly, or to draw properly the lines of responsibility for Maria's care – its final conclusion acknowledged that something new was happening – that although the state was at the sharp end of the public anger about Maria's death, it was not felt to be the only culprit: 'It is upon society as a whole that the ultimate blame must rest; indeed the highly emotional and angry reaction of the public in this case may indicate society's troubled conscience,' it said.[44] It was not enough for the state, representing society, to assume responsibility for those such as Maria. When Dennis O'Neill died at the hands of his foster-parents, social workers were held to have failed him. When Maria Colwell died at the hands of her stepfather, nearly twenty years later, society as a whole began to question how it treated its young. The case would spark decades of legislative reform, and yet the messages which came out of this inquiry would become depressingly familiar: childcare professionals needed to communicate better; they needed to be better trained. Each time another child died, the same failings would be found to be to blame.

And yet things *were* changing. Child abuse, as a concept, was at this time relatively new. Terrible abuse had always occurred, of course. But now the notion of child abuse as a 'syndrome', the abuser as someone suffering from a recognizable condition, began to grow. The term 'battered child syndrome' had in fact been coined some ten years before Maria's death, by a University of Colorado paediatrician named C. Henry Kempe. Kempe set out the symptoms of this condition – abusing parents would often bring their children to hospital with injuries, expressing apparently appropriate concern and saying they had occurred accidentally. Such parents were not incurable psychopaths, he believed, but were suffering from a form of psychological disturbance which could – by logical extension – be cured. In November 1969, a Home Office pathologist called Professor Francis Camps had told the Royal Medical Psychological Association that he expected the phenomenon to die out because it was essentially a social disease: 'Very nearly all injuries to children come in lower social class families. There is a high proportion of unemployed fathers amongst attackers,' he said.[45] Camps believed a lack of self-discipline could help to explain the rise in child injury.

The recognition of the problem would not stop it from happening. Over the next decade and more, every child death from abuse would lead to the same discussion: twenty-one-month-old Tyra Henry, battered and bitten by her father while in local authority care in 1984; three-year-old Heidi Koseda and four-year-old Jasmine Beckford, both starved and beaten by their stepfathers in the same year; four-year-old Kimberley Carlile, killed by her stepfather in 1986;

sixteen-month-old Doreen Mason, who died in similar circumstances in 1987. The list would go on. And every time, the same questions would be asked: why did the various agencies that dealt with
these children – for almost all were known to social services – not
talk to one another? How could warnings from neighbours and others
have gone unheeded?

It would seem, in many ways, as if each death demonstrated that
nothing had changed. It would seem, too, that the outrage engen-
dered by these deaths ran in a similar vein to the outrage which had
been sparked by the death of Mary Ellen Wilson in nineteenth-
century New York; that it had its roots in the notion that the child
was endlessly vulnerable and in need of adult protection. And yet
with each renewed outbreak of public revulsion and outrage, children
as a corporate body would garner a little strength. The radicalism
of the early 1970s was beginning to trickle down, and children would
never be seen in quite the same light again. From now on, a child
would be less and less an appendage of its parents; more and more
an individual in its own right. It would take another twenty years
or so before children would have those individual rights enshrined
in law, but the process had begun.

8   Eighties to ASBOs

Natalie Dowse, born on the south coast of England in 1970, would later recall little of this radicalism. Yet she would remember a childhood that was free from many of the cares her parents had faced: 'My mum played an important role with her own family. Her father died when she was fourteen, and she looked after her younger siblings. She helped her mother – from fourteen, she always cooked Sunday roast. When she was seventeen, she went to work full-time, as a secretary.'[1]

Natalie's parents had met through a rock band in which her mother's brother had played, and their world did not seem so far removed from her own world as maybe their parents' had to them: 'They lived in a council house and on a Sunday the kitchen was converted for band practice. Nan just let it happen, she was quite good like that – I think it was quite a noisy household.'

There was a sense, by the 1970s, that children were being brought up by parents who were somehow more youthful than the previous generation of parents. Parents who had experienced war only as children, and who had been afforded the opportunity to be young themselves before settling down. This was leading to a gradual narrowing in the generation gap, with some parents, at least, beginning to relate to their children at least partly in a way which betokened friendship rather than authority.

'We used to go out often as a family on Sunday, in the car,' Natalie recalled. 'I remember we'd listen to music and all four of us would sing along. My dad would play ELO, Doctor Hook, things like that. Even now – my parents still say they don't really want to grow up, they still buy music – my Mum will get a CD sometimes, and I'll copy it.'

For Natalie, there would be wider opportunities too. Unlike many teenagers of their parents' generation, she and her sister did not feel the need to work to earn pocket money. On the face of it, then, it might look as if the sky was lightening around childhood as the 1970s drew to a close. Yet in reality the opposite was the case. A combination of factors – the apparently growing incidence of abuse, fears that television, divorce and the modern world were corrupting children and drawing them to violence, a sense of uncertainty about where childhood was headed – were combining to create a sense of impending crisis in the world of the child. There was something in it, too: the 1970s were a more dangerous decade for children, in terms of vulnerability to crime, than any other before or since. The child murder rate rose to an all-time high of 200 a year in 1974 – about three times the level at which it would officially stand in the early years of the next millennium.[2] Natalie and her sister would follow strict rules about where they should and should not go when they left the house alone: 'When I went to comprehensive school, there was a short cut through the woods to get there. It took forty-five minutes to walk there by the road, but if you went through the woods it took twenty. We had to walk through together – never alone. We pestered our parents because we didn't want to walk the long way round. There had been incidents – someone I knew had been attacked. So I knew it could happen.'

For girls, the 1970s were a time of flux. Most had never read the works of Shulamith Firestone and her like, of course, and so were largely unaware that as female children they were thought to be living a life weighted by multiple oppressions. Yet there was a sense of a desire to grasp opportunities that were just out of reach; a sense that the role of the girl was changing. When Natalie told her school she wanted to study art, the response was not enthusiastic: 'I remember they were setting up work experience, and we had to go and see a teacher masquerading as careers adviser. I sat there and said I'd like to do something creative, or go to art college. And the teacher said: "What about hairdressing? That's creative." I had a friend who wanted to be a hairdresser, so I said: "OK, maybe I could be a hairdresser." I spent three weeks sweeping up and making coffee. I was probably quite timid, and I didn't have the strength to say it was really boring for me. I remember having this conversation with my dad while we were doing the washing up: "I'm really confused, I thought I wanted to go to art college but now I think maybe I should be a hairdresser." And he said: "Well, you've wanted to go to art college for a long time. So why don't you go to art college, and if you don't like it you can go into hairdressing?" He wasn't going to tell me what to do, but he was giving me the strength to do what I wanted.'

Natalie, who had always been artistic, would take A-levels, go to art college and spend her life creating extraordinary, intensely coloured pictures of sunlit childhoods that were perhaps not unlike her own. While the images her mother would have seen while growing up had been of perfect family lives, the young Natalie would be fascinated by strangely androgynous Soviet gymnasts such as Olga Korbut and Nadia Comăneci, who competed in the Olympics during the seventies, and by the tough, muscular girls who were pictured manhandling huge horses over fences. Later, her artist's studio would be full of her pictures of them – frozen images painted from television screen grabs, exuding a strangely alluring mix of glamour and sadness.

'I had a book with Nadia Comăneci's picture in. I was told they went to sport schools and I thought that was really exotic and special. I think a lot of girls wanted to be her – she was magical, doing amazing, dangerous things. I wonder if children associated them with being children – Olga Korbut was actually seventeen years old at the 1972 Olympics, but she looked pre-pubescent. And I used to beg and beg and beg to have a pony. My friend had a horse, and I couldn't understand why I couldn't have one. I remember putting little notes under my dad's pillow, so when he pulled it back it would say: "Please can I have a horse?"'[3]

The gymnasts were pure political propaganda, of course – a Cold War instrument designed to show the West how invincible the Soviets were. But something happened in the translation: the message that was being sent was quite different from the one that was being received by little girls in the Western world. To them, these were images of children exercising undreamed-of powers. These were girls who did things girls had not previously been seen so publicly to do; girls with superpowers. A gymnastics craze swept the United Kingdom, and tens of thousands of little girls queued to join, hoping they might be admitted to this newly empowered cadre of females.

The reading material available to girls at the time reflected this change, too. Now it was acceptable, maybe for the first time in many social strata, for girls to consider their future careers. Noel Streatfeild's *Ballet Shoes* – actually written before World War Two – was enduringly popular, telling the tale of three sisters who dream of a life on the stage or – in one case – of flying aeroplanes. By the end of the book, career glory appears to beckon for all three, and they vow to put their names in the history books. Similarly, *White Boots* told the tale of two girls striving to become champion ice-skaters – and underlined the message that hard work and determination were the keys to success. There was also a whole genre of 'career novels' in which girls became seamstresses, hat-makers, publishers' assistants. In most cases, though, the endings of these novels were just the same as the girls' mothers' endings – most of their heroines finished up marrying the boss – or better still, his handsome son – before settling down to a life of domesticity.[4]

While comprehensive schools were now throwing most girls into the company of boys, the private school system was still largely segregated. And it was struggling to chart an appropriate course in this newly ambitious atmosphere. The selective girls' schools had been founded, back in the late nineteenth century, by women who were closely linked to the suffrage movement, and so they had their roots in a kind of traditionalist feminism which had little to do with the separatist, angry brand which was now growing up. Heather Montgomery, born in 1969 and attending a private school run by the Girls' Public Day School Trust in Surrey, found that while she was encouraged to excel academically, the range of career options on offer still seemed strangely limited: 'If you were a scientist, then you should go and be a GP. If you were arty, you could join the BBC. You have to remember, the teachers at my school trained twenty or thirty years earlier – I don't think there was anything at my school that would have been unfamiliar to a visitor from the fifties.'[5] Heather would go on to Oxford, where she would meet a very particular breed of girl whose education had been similar to her own: 'We had been educated to compete with men in the workplace, and certainly to compete academically, but the downside was that I didn't meet boys until I went to university. The girls were all beautifully groomed and very socially competent – until you put them with men. They were really strong academically, but socially quite gauche. They found it very difficult to sit in tutorials and be taught with men. They tended to defer to them.'

And just as young women were beginning to wonder if there might be other options than a couple of years' office work followed by marriage and children, another major problem was creeping up on the young: unemployment. Since the war, children growing up in Britain had had no cause to worry about what they would do when they left school because there were always jobs available. In the 1970s, that began to change as the UK's manufacturing sector began to shrink. By the last years of the decade, youth unemployment had become a constant spectre, and a generation of children had begun to understand that their lives would lack some of the certainties their parents' generation had enjoyed. Between 1971 and 1979, 600,000 manual jobs disappeared from the British economy.[6] And at the same time, the number of children leaving school was growing. There had been an increase in births in the late 1950s and early 1960s, and migrant workers from the Caribbean and from southern Asia, arriving to take up vacant manual jobs in times of full employment, had brought their children too. The cohort which finished its compulsory education in 1980 would be the largest ever. About half that cohort – a much higher proportion than in other Western countries – would expect to go straight into work rather than continuing in education. The result: thousands of unemployed teenagers, many of them angry and dispossessed. The inner-city areas where immigrant communities lived were among those with the highest proportion of teenagers, and also among those where jobs were disappearing at the highest rate. *The Economist* pondered a question: was it more dangerous, in terms of social unrest, to tolerate unemployment among the young than among adults? The answer was already clear: In the summer of 1981, riots broke out in impoverished areas of London, Liverpool and Manchester. Four out of ten school leavers were able to find work; but for the black youth of the inner cities the chances were virtually nil.[7]

Nor was it just the unemployed and impoverished young who were feeling alienated. The sense of grievance ran right through every stratum of society. Heather Montgomery, at her private girls' school in Surrey, picked up on it: 'I got very interested in politics, which wasn't considered very respectable. I certainly had a strong sense of injustice about being a child, and being a teenager and not being listened to and having very limited choices about what I wanted to do. It was a very academic school – the only choice was about which university you went to. Polytechnics were not an option. I just did have the sense that I had absolutely no agency at all, and I pushed very hard to go to a sixth-form college – but that wasn't allowed. I did have this sense of unfairness, of always being told what to do, having no say over anything, having to wear a boater in the sixth form, those sorts of stupid things.'

Life in the early eighties was political – and mostly it was political with a capital 'P'. Heather Montgomery found herself caught up in it: 'You had all the last great causes. You had apartheid, you had Thatcher, you had pit strikes. I wanted to feel connected with those sorts of things even though I was a middle-class schoolgirl in Surrey. My crowning moment was appearing on *Question Time* with Robin Day, asking about secondary picketing. I was interested in party politics and big issues. I wouldn't have known a miner if one had bitten me on the nose, but it was a cause I cared about.'[8]

The older generation had failed to see this new politicization coming. 'Youth have traditionally been seen but not heard,' wrote Simon Frith in *Marxism Today* in 1981.[9] 'As the media's bewildered response to the riots made clear, no one had been listening to youth's rough music except the young themselves. The young had been talked about more than ever in the last decade, but they had not been heard.' While earlier generations of rebellious youth had been kicking against their parents' safe, comfortable lifestyles, this generation felt angry and let down. And the adult world began to feel a rising sense of panic.

Everywhere there seemed to be a sense of dislocation, a sense that old orders were breaking down and without any clear sense of what was to replace them. In his 1983 book, *The Disappearance of*

Childhood, Neil Postman,[10] an American cultural critic, argued that television was largely to blame. In the past, he said, children's lives had a sort of hierarchy to them: learning to read was a process which could only be achieved, for example, by progressing from one stage to the next: 'The literate person must learn to be reflective and analytical, patient and assertive, always poised, after due consideration, to say "no" to a text. But with television, the basis of this information hierarchy collapses. Television erodes the dividing line between childhood and adulthood ... first because it requires no instruction to grasp its form, second because it does not make complex demands on either mind or behaviour, and third because it does not segregate its audience ... The new media environment that is emerging provides everyone, simultaneously, with the same information ... electric media find it impossible to withhold any secrets. Without secrets, of course, there can be no such thing as childhood.'

Others were noticing similar phenomena. Adults were even beginning to ask a new and shocking question: what were children actually for? 'At a time when we were confident that our work was making their future brighter, it was easy to think of children as innocent and refreshing,' wrote an American academic, John Sommerville.[11] 'But we have always known that they could also be messy, tiresome and cruel ... children are more obviously a liability nowadays.' He quoted an American columnist, Ann Landers, who found seven out of ten readers answering a poll had responded that if they had their time again they would not have children. 'Our children now represent a time that will only have bigger problems and not a better life ... we may resent the fact that these little citizens of the future are already compounding all our problems – energy, food, employment, pollution, crowding.'

After a century in which successive governments had urged the populace to reproduce, suddenly the accompanying sentimentality about children and childhood was beginning to break down. Women began, in growing numbers, to confess that they were not in fact maternal: 'Finally, we non child-oriented types are coming out of the closet,' wrote Tricia Stallings.[12] 'There is nothing wrong with not having children. The only wrong is when we, feeling as we do, have children as a result of society's pressures. Then we become unhappy parents producing unhappy children.' Parenthood, she wrote with a sense of revelation, was a choice.

And yet in place of the old, sententious attitudes about children and their preciousness, a new feeling was beginning to grow. In the coming decades, parents would find themselves unable to admit the truth about their situation – some of them weren't even sure whether they wanted their children at all. This unease, underpinned by a deeply buried sense of guilt, would begin to manifest itself in diverse and unpredictable ways – renewed waves of moral panic; exaggerated concerns about children's health and wellbeing; increasingly strange stories about danger and jeopardy surrounding children. And, as ever, regular outbreaks of opprobrium over the failings of the young. The problem was always in someone else's home, someone else's neighbourhood. But there was little doubt, now, that there *was* a problem.

'Babies are the enemy. Not your baby or mine, of course. Individually they are all cute. But together they are a menace,' Sommerville wrote.[13] Child-rearing was about to become an increasingly uneasy, defensive business. Women would be unsure whether they should be at home, baking, or out at work, using their education. Fathers would be unsure of the same thing, too. Having had children, and not being entirely sure why they had done so, parents would feel increasing pressure to share their company. If children were to have no monetary value in the home, if the wider economy were to have little use for them once they had finished their increasingly pressured and expensive education, and if they were to represent an increasingly unsustainable burden on the planet, then what was the point of them? The answer which parents increasingly gave was that children would have to be enjoyed for themselves. The next age of the child would be an age of over-enthusiastic parent–child relations. It would be an age, too, in which children would come under increasing pressure to please their parents – to please them by succeeding at school; to please them by being amusing company; to please them by being more attractive, more successful, better at everything than their parents' friends' children. The age in which children were a distinct grouping, left largely free to develop in one another's company, was passing. In the coming decades, intensity and pressure would be the bywords of the Western childhood.

Sex and scares

To the children of the 1970s and before, sex was generally still something rather remote and frightening. Mary Hudson, writing in the *Guardian*,[14] had described her discomfort, on arriving at university during the 1960s, at the discovery that there were young men there who wanted to sleep with her. 'Only men who really knew me realised that I was still a terrified virgin who would go to any lengths to avoid seduction. I would carry a well-thumbed copy of *Winnie the Pooh* to parties and produce it in times of stress. I found a heartfelt rendition of Eeyore's Birthday would cool the ardour of most young men.'

By the early 1980s, though, things were beginning to change. Access to contraception had become easier for teenagers, and although the number of teenage pregnancies had fallen, the number of abortions – legalized in 1967 – was continuing to rise. So it was hardly surprising, in an era of uncertainty, alienation and rapid social change, that promiscuity would be blamed for many of society's ills. There was some confusion, though, about the precise

nature of the problem. Were young girls becoming too promis-
cuous, even leading vulnerable young boys into temptation? Or
were they, themselves, the victims of a new world which was
propelling them too fast into adulthood? In a parliamentary debate
on the subject in the mid-1980s,[15] Viscount Buckmaster argued that
the latter was the case: 'For many young girls, early sex is more
than mere physical gratification. It often leads to the awakening
of the homemaking instinct; the longing for a child and for a
fulfilling and permanent relationship. When those desires cannot
be realised, depression often sets in—leading in some cases even
to attempted suicide.'

While early sexual activity could be dangerous for the individual
girl, he went on, it was also dangerous for society as a whole. After
all, rising divorce rates and increased levels of single parenthood
were already posing a threat to the social fabric. What hope was
there if young girls – who, for the most part, had previously been
relied upon to remain pure – were to be damaged in this way? It
seemed the Viscount, having worried aloud that early sex could
plunge girls into disappointment and despair when marriage did
not follow, was also worried that it might lead them to stop worrying
about getting married altogether: 'The irresponsible attitude of many
children today towards such conduct can hardly be the best preparation for marital fidelity. How can those hasty, furtive fumblings
in cars or in bedrooms, with an ear cocked for the parents' return,
help towards a stable marriage? For many young people today,
hopping into bed with anyone, at any time, is just as normal as
turning on a tap. We are indeed paying a terrible price for our failure
to give children proper guidance.'

Most conservatives agreed, though, that the liberal attitudes imbued
into the young in the 1960s, and still allegedly being promoted in
schools, were to blame. In the same debate, Baroness Masham of Ilton
added her voice to the rising chorus of alarm: 'We have heard of a girl

aged eight years being involved with prostitution. I have asked many young people why there is so much promiscuity. They blame the 1960s. What happened in the 1960s? The Abortion Act, among other things. There is now the escape from being pregnant ... with the risk gone, many young people seem to think that they should sleep around. They go along with the idea that it is the done thing to do.' Both schools and the Church of England were blamed – schools for promoting liberal attitudes; the church for failing to speak out more loudly about the collapse in the morals of the young.

The feeling was abroad that teenagers were too often busy having sex with one another – and that this was a dangerous new development. A rash of organizations grew up aimed at trying to shore up the allegedly fast-collapsing traditional family: the Parliamentary Family and Child Protection Group, Family and Youth Concern – otherwise known as the Responsible Society, Christian Action Research Education Campaigns, Moral Rearmament, the Christian Broadcasting Council, the National Council for Christian Standards in Society, the Conservative Family Campaign – the list went on. Some campaigners, however, preferred to fight their battles alone. By the mid-1980s one woman in particular would come to personify the rising sense of panic on the Christian right about the morals of the nation's youth: Victoria Gillick. A mother of ten, Mrs Gillick had demanded an assurance of her local health authority in Cambridgeshire that it would not offer contraception to any of her daughters without first asking her permission. When the health authority refused to give any such assurance, she took it to court. The case went all the way to the House of Lords.

The liberal *Guardian* newspaper's leader-writer conceded, in the face of an appeal court's decision in Mrs Gillick's favour, that many young people were indeed having sex: as many as one in twenty, the paper said. Some might even stop doing so rather than have their doctor ask their parents whether or not they should be allowed contraception. Many more would simply take risks and end up pregnant. The paper went on to point out that a majority of mothers actually believed in sex before marriage, and so might well allow their daughters to go on the pill. And then it hit the nail on the head. In effect, this was not a case about teenage sex at all: 'The court's judgement is a searching exposition of the legal rights of parents ... in effect, Mummy knows best.'[16] The Law Lords did not agree, and finally in 1985 they ruled that it would indeed be lawful for a doctor to prescribe contraception for a child under sixteen without consulting her parents.

The case would have far-reaching implications. Victoria Gillick was a campaigner for old-fashioned moral standards, certainly, but she was much more than that. She was a campaigner for the rights of the parent; a campaigner for the notion that the child was, essentially, the property of its parents until it reached adulthood. The House of Lords had ruled, in effect, that parents did not have the right to a say over their daughters' lives, even if they were still children. The Children's Legal Centre was quick to point out that as of now, children had the right to make their own decisions. Writing in the *Sunday Times*, Polly Toynbee concurred: 'The Law Lords concluded that parents may not always know best.'[17] And there was a corollary to this – if children had the right under the law to determine their own lives, then where should it all stop? Was it practicable or even desirable for the state to prosecute parents who allowed their children to drink, smoke, read porn or watch violent films? Evidently not, if they had no legal right to prevent their children from doing so.

Toynbee had been a member of a committee set up to look into obscenity and film censorship, which had concluded that ultimately children had to be allowed to make their own mistakes: 'When my own daughter was twelve, she and her friends went through a craze for huddling together in a screaming bundle, watching horror X movies in one or other of their houses. Much as we disapproved, were we to ban her from visiting friends?'

But while liberal parents welcomed the outcome of the Gillick case – and had probably always given their children a degree of freedom anyway – concern was still growing on a number of fronts about children's vulnerability. Gitta Sereny, who had written eloquently and sympathetically about Mary Bell's crimes against two little boys, had now written a book about runaway children. As the Thatcher era wore to a close, growing numbers of young people were living on the streets of major cities, having fled from unemployment, abuse or family strife. Sereny's book[18] would document how some, both girls and boys, were working as prostitutes in order to stay alive. Some children could not live with their parents, she said, and some parents could not live with their children – the feeling that family life was in its very nature less than perfect was increasingly entering the fabric of social discourse. But these children still needed places of sanctuary. Children like thirteen-year-old Alan, picked up in Mayfair by a man with an upper-class accent and a 'super' car: 'He gave me this ten pound note and told me to wank him off. Well, it was sort of good fun, getting paid doing just that. Half an hour later I got someone else and I asked him for £15.' Sereny had a stark analysis of who was responsible: 'The blame lies squarely on me and you. I, who am writing, and you, old or young, who are reading. It is we who in this last quarter of our rich twentieth century, in our enlightened Western world, have unthinkingly, recklessly and greedily created and supported an atmosphere of life which, it would appear, is intolerable to many of our children.'

The feeling that the world at large, the adult world, was to blame for a malaise in the world of the child was growing apace. During the late 1980s, this was accentuated by an ongoing debate about plans for a United Nations Convention on the Rights of the Child – a debate writ large on the international stage, and in smaller print across issues such as Victoria Gillick's campaign. Now children were not only believed to have some autonomy within the home – once the convention was passed in 1989 and ratified by the various UN member states, they would have their rights spelled out in detail and underpinned by statute. Running to more than 7,000 words and fifty-four separate articles, it would 'give' children the right to know and be cared for by their parents, the right not to be discriminated against, the right to express their views, the right to associate freely. Perhaps most significantly, it said that their interests must be foremost in any transaction concerning them. Henceforth, parents' rights would be very firmly relegated to second place.

And yet this unease persisted: this feeling that all was not well in the world of the child, this nagging sense of guilt. As the 1980s progressed, new evidence was emerging all the time of the levels of abuse to which children were subjected. And it was increasingly being recognized that this abuse was not just confined to beating and starving children, as it had been in most of the high-profile cases up to this time. For the first time, it was being said aloud that children were sexually abused, too – not by strangers, but by their own parents. Caroline Coon, writing on the subject in the *Guardian*, suggested that until this point it had simply been impossible for anyone to talk about it: 'Looking back it seems to me that the fierce debates about abortion, birth control, battered women, rape, have all been a rehearsal for incest – as if to tackle incest before we were expertly practised in sexual controversy generally, as if this most disturbing issue had to wait until now because it was finally the most important to the individual, the family and society as a whole.'

A whole body of literature was appearing, underlining the feeling that sexual abuse within families was much more common than had previously been thought. One academic, Jean Renvoize, had estimated that one woman in ten had been a victim of incest – and yet the number of convictions stood at not much more than 100 per year.[19] Numerous stories were beginning to emerge from children's homes, too – it was, as Coon implied, almost as if once the floodgates had been opened, a huge, untold story had come flooding out. This was a problem which had been largely hidden up until now. Until the mid-1980s, the government did not even have a policy or guidelines for dealing with child sexual abuse within families. Now, suddenly, it seemed to be everywhere. The first national survey on the issue, conducted in 1984 for a television documentary,[20] suggested that thousands of children were being abused in this way every year. Children were being abused, too, it now emerged, by adults who were being paid to protect and care for them – in 1985, the Association of County Councils produced examples: a man with convictions for sexual offences against children employed in a local authority hostel and abusing children again; a teacher dismissed for sexual malpractices moving to a private school; a driver convicted of acts of gross indecency with mentally handicapped children continuing to offend; people with convictions for sexual offences volunteering to work with children.[21]

Professionals working with children were beginning to come alive to the issue. Increasingly, they felt exposed, uncertain whether they were missing cases of abuse. It was in the midst of this anxiety-ridden atmosphere that a new paediatrician named Marietta Higgs arrived, in early 1987, to take up a post at the South Tees health district, in Cleveland. The previous year, she had learned from a consultant in Leeds about a new technique for detecting child sexual abuse – it was called Reflex Relaxation and Anal Dilation. Using this technique, Dr Higgs began testing children who came into her care to check for signs of abuse. And the cases began mounting up at an alarming rate. In response, the local authority, which had recently appointed its own child abuse consultant, began removing the children from their homes. By April that year, the local police were beginning to question the use of the technique. By May, Cleveland's new sexual abuse consultant was calling for more resources to deal with what had fast become a crisis. In just five months, Dr Higgs and a fellow paediatrician diagnosed no fewer than 121 cases of child abuse. By June, the case had reached the ears of the local MPs, who were demanding to know what was going on. Because there were no more foster-families with which to place the children, a special ward had to be set up at the hospital. Outside, the children's furious parents gave interviews to journalists who flocked to the industrial town to cover the story. The situation was reaching fever pitch. Children were being dragged from their beds at two in the morning, one local MP alleged.[22] Why? Suddenly social workers, hitherto seen mainly as an over-stretched workforce which sometimes missed cases of abuse, were in the frame for pursuing a witch hunt against innocent parents.

Twenty-five years on, the Cleveland case continues to divide public opinion. Dr Higgs continued to practise, despite the finding of a 1988 official report that she and her colleagues had failed adequately to consider whether they were acting in the best interests of the children concerned, and of their parents. In 2007, one of the victims would describe her experience in an interview with the BBC. Even after twenty years her stark description would speak volumes about a six-year-old's bafflement at being removed from her home without explanation.[23] She had been at school, she said, painting a vase of red flowers, when her mother had arrived with a social worker and a policeman.

'When we got to the hospital Dr Higgs took me into a room. Mum had to wait outside. I was told to take my clothes off, she looked at my bottom and my front, I got dressed and went into the playroom while the doctor talked to my mum. Some social workers gave me two dolls to play with; the dolls had no clothes on. They asked me if I knew what private places were, and could I show them the dolls' private places? They asked me if I knew what a secret was, and did

I have any secrets? I said yes to both questions, they wanted to know my secret. I looked at Mum. I told them how my dad was in prison, and had been since I was a baby – that was my secret. I was taken away.' Kerry did not say how long she was on the ward, but she did say she still suffered from the nightmares she had had while she was there: 'Dr Higgs made a mistake – a huge mistake. I was safe at home.'

Increasingly, confusion and anger rained down on the field of humanity in which children sat. For most children, the details of cases like this one were supremely irrelevant. And yet the sense of fear, of uncertainty that surrounded childhood continued to grow. It was to get worse yet. In February 1989, in the aftermath of the official report into what had happened in Cleveland, the *Guardian* ran a letter from a Judith Dawson, a child abuse consultant in Nottingham. She had recently investigated a case in which no fewer than twenty-three children from a single family had been abused, and in which eleven adults had been convicted, she said: 'Torture and ritualistic sex was a daily occurrence for some of these children. These children within this family were only ever able to tell of their abuse after they had come into care.'

Who to believe? Were there abusers in every street, threatening children with violence if they told of their experiences? How common were these networks of abusers, working together? Was there ritual, even satanic, worship involved? The public imagination began working overtime. Dozens of 'victims' came forward to disclose that they had been subjected to satanic rituals in which sexual and other types of abuse were perpetrated. In Rochdale, Lancashire, a grim joke was told: 'What's the difference between a rottweiler and a social worker? Answer: there's an outside chance you might get your children back from a rottweiler.'[24] By now it was 1990, and no fewer than twenty children from the Lancashire town were in care. Police investigating allegations that satanism had been involved found no evidence; the local authority said later it had never made the allegation. In Orkney, the following year, nine children were taken into care in similar circumstances. Two months later, all were allowed to go home.

Why did all this arise when it did? Certainly there were claims, coming from the United States, that satanic abuse was going to be the next big thing. And the trauma of the discovery that widespread sexual abuse of children by male relatives had been going on for years, barely even detected, was heightening everyone's awareness. Several factors came together in a sort of unholy confluence, maybe: there was a vogue for the occult at the time, and the suggestion that countless children were being swept up by Satanic circles was an easy one to make. Evangelical Christians were hotly pursuing the issue, too. One such group, named Reachout, had collected hundreds of occult books and magazines, all widely available, according to the *Sunday Times*,[25] and was presenting them as evidence that there was a network of Satanic groups operating in Britain. 'They prey on the minds of teenagers, especially those craving power and control, or those lacking self-esteem. I'm not saying everyone in witchcraft is molesting children, but there are groups who do,' the group's founder, Maureen Davies, told the newspaper.

In the end, the phenomenon went away more quietly than it had arisen. But not before an inquiry had been commissioned by the Department of Health to examine the evidence. It was conducted by Professor Jean La Fontaine from the London School of Economics, and after examining eighty-four cases in detail she pronounced all but three unsubstantiated – and those three free from any evidence of actual Satanism. 'My own view is that it is a modern phenomenon which is comparable to the witch-hunts of early modern Europe,' Professor La Fontaine said.[26]

Yet witch-hunts happened for a reason – because there was a perceived threat. And the threat around children and childhood seemed very real indeed at that time. It was a threat born of uncertainty, and guilt. What were adults' responsibilities towards children? To protect and nurture them, or to set them free to make their own decisions, their own mistakes? To shelter them from the harsh realities of the adult world, or to initiate them so that they might be stronger? And – what were they here for? What were they to be in the future? Why did their parents even want them? More than ever before, as the 1990s began, these questions hung heavy in the air.

Murder and moral panic

In the late sixties and early seventies, there had been a small rash of films featuring Satanic children. These films left disturbing images etched on to the popular imagination: the possessed boy, Damien, in *The Omen*, frantically pedalling his red tricycle towards the little table on which his pregnant mother stood, watering plants; Mia Farrow, gently rocking the cradle of her devil-spawned son in *Rosemary's Baby*. It seemed that in those years, the public mind was easily caught up with the notion that children could be possessed in some way by evil; that they could become twisted, violent aberrations in an otherwise sane and humane world. When Mary Bell was convicted of murdering four-year-old Martin Brown and three-year-old Brian Howe in 1968, the response was that she was evil, a 'bad seed'.

It is a mark of how fast the world can move on, then, that on Saturday, 13 February 1993, when grainy images began playing on news bulletins of two young boys leading two-year-old James Bulger by the hand from the Strand shopping centre in Bootle on Merseyside, only a few such comparisons were evoked. The two ten-year-olds, Jon Thompson and Robert Venables, beat James to death and left his body on a railway line, where it was found two days later. In the days and months that followed, the public mood would be one of grief, anger, bewilderment even. But the devil child, the epitome of the notion of original sin, had largely been banished from the public mind. As the details emerged of the crime that Thompson and Venables had committed, there was no such simple explanation. Even though it was widely reported that the boys had been watching a video called *Child's Play 3*, in which a doll is possessed by the soul of a serial killer, it was the social phenomenon of the 'video nasty' that was blamed for the crime, rather than the sort of evil spirit it depicted.

Events such as violent deaths can often come to define an age – or rather, to define how that age differs from the previous one; how the world has moved on. Extreme occurrences in which the entire nation joins in shared and powerful emotion are bound to shake out something fundamental about the way in which a society is operating, and the death of James Bulger was no exception. In an age characterized by adults' guilt over their conflicted emotions about children, about child-rearing and about the place of the child in the wider world, the question that was asked was not really a question about what Thompson and Venables had done. It was: what have *we* done? It was a question asked loudly, repeatedly and with real anguish. The trial of Mary Bell, a quarter of a century earlier, had passed decorously, accompanied by fairly prominent news reports but very little comment. The Bulger case led to a national orgy of self-examination.

Within four days of James's murder, the *Daily Mail* had engaged William Golding, author of the classic 1950s novel about savagery, *Lord of the Flies*, to write about it. 'A Haunting Indictment of the Society in Which Two-Year-Old James Bulger was Murdered', it was headed. The headline summed up the tone, not just of the *Mail's* coverage but of the major reaction to the crime. Published the day before Thompson and Venables were arrested, the piece gave voice to a fear which lurked in many hearts – that somehow we were *all* to blame. 'Where the orders and patterns of society cease to matter, gangs begin to find cohesion merely in the joint fulfilment of their darkest instincts . . . If parents are absent, if fathers do not provide strength and mothers do not provide love, then children will plumb the depths of their nature.' Golding acknowledged, as he had in his novel, that he believed boys had some innate ability to behave in uncivilized ways. But the mood of the time was this: society was to blame. And before the perpetrators had even been identified, the verdict had been passed: the fabric of civilization was perishing, and children – all children – were the victims.

A host of other prominent writers joined the chorus. Beryl Bainbridge, a Liverpudlian by birth, confessed to an angry reaction on meeting a group of shabby, pale-faced boys during a visit to the city:[27] 'The shameful thing is, I wanted to verbally abuse them; I wanted to tell them they were scum, that they disgusted me. There was a woman passing who saw the shock on my face. She said: "There's more of them than there used to be. They should have been drowned at birth." I found myself nodding, as though we were discussing kittens. Seconds later, of course, I felt ashamed . . . they were nothing more than little lost boys damaged beyond repair by ignorant parenting, drugs, video nasties. It was easier in the past – it always is – to know what was right and what was wrong.'

'Most of all,' Bainbridge concluded, 'we must take on board that this latest manifestation of wickedness is not a sign from an angry God or the work of the Devil but rather something for which we ourselves must take responsibility.'

Politicians, too, took up this baton. Tony Blair, then shadow Home Secretary, made a speech in which he said the crime had provoked anger and disbelief in equal proportions: 'These are the ugly manifestations of a society that is becoming unworthy of that name.'[28]

It was inevitable, of course, that the family would come under scrutiny – that was happening long before it emerged that both Thompson and Venables had had early lives punctuated by marital breakdown and violence. In the *Independent*,[29] Gitta Sereny argued that these factors had become the norm: 'Under modern-day pressures family discord is almost the rule rather than exception. This does not, of course, mean that most are without a sense of right and wrong, but that their moral priorities have been unbalanced.' A little while later, the Bishop of Worcester told peers that in 1993 no fewer than 76,000 children under sixteen had witnessed their parents' divorces:[30] 'It was Richard Baxter, a luminary of my own diocese, who said that when marriage and the family fail, all else miscarries,' he said. 'We are letting down our children and thereby placing a time-bomb under our society. We have tolerated the breakdown of marriage and the family in the name of self-fulfilment and sexual liberty, and this in a country shaped in the Christian tradition, which values children so highly.'

There was a consensus around the Bulger case in both liberal and conservative media: 'There's a major failure of parenting,' psychologist David Pithers told Melanie Phillips, who was writing in the *Observer*.[31] 'But it's not the neglectful lack of care that people think it is. Parents are getting to the point where they just don't know how to look after their children any more. They have these worldly-wise children who are searching for power in a world that rejects them. Parents are under pressure as never before. Children's distress and disorder and violence are rising. Families increasingly cannot cope.'

For several years, there had been a growing sense of crisis surrounding children and childhood, and now it was being voiced and made real. Parents were no longer sure whether the major cause of the crisis was neglect, or over-attentiveness. There seemed to be no certainty over whether children were the charges of adults, in need of their protection at all times, or whether they were independent beings with independent human rights. In the year James Bulger was murdered, other major media stories about children included that of a mother, Yasmin Gibson, who left her eleven-year-old 'home alone' while she went on holiday to Spain; a nurse, Beverley Allitt, who received thirteen life sentences for murdering children in her care; and a fifteen-year-old boy fined £500 for rape. Children were concurrently, it seemed, both the perpetrators of terrible crimes and the vulnerable victims of them. Both these phenomena were increasingly disturbing.

'As a baby I was weighed weekly, inspected and injected and pronounced satisfactory,' wrote Penny Fox in the *Scotsman*.[32] 'This is what happened to all children born soon after the end of the Second World War. We were a precious commodity, we were considered worth investing in. In this and other ways, children were "put first" in our social policy. But is this the case now? There is little evidence, I believe, that we are doing more than fiddling while Rome, Edinburgh, any other city, any other rural area, is burning up our children's freedom.'

The problem seemed to have many causes, many symptoms. A major one – highlighted by Penny Fox – was fear itself. Adults had begun to feel that fear of abduction, fear that if children were allowed to stray, some unspeakable fate might befall them, was turning them into a nation of stay-at-homes, with sedentary lives. Yet the dangers to children from strangers who might abuse or murder them had not changed. Bournemouth University estimated there were around 900 such men in the population at any one time, fewer than 2 per cent of whom would go on to kill.[33] The risk to each individual child in any given year was less than one in a million. So, why now? Parents had always had fears about their children's safety; and the feeling that children could do evil had long lurked in the depths of the nation's soul. But, now, in an age of uncertainty and guilt, these terrors seemed more real than ever. Perhaps William Golding, writing in the week James Bulger was killed, had pointed the way to an

answer: society had lost its grip on the certainties of life: 'There are
... conditions in which cruelty seems to flourish, which is different
from saying that it has clear causes. What are these conditions? Chaos
is one, fear is another. In Russia after the First World War, there were,
I believe, gangs of children who had lost their parents. Dispossessed,
without anywhere to live or anything to live on, they roamed the
country attacking and killing out of sheer cruelty. There was, at that
time, social chaos in many countries, and, left to themselves, these
children found a kind of elemental cohesion in their viciousness.'[34]
Golding's point, which was an attempt to explain the causes of
extreme cruelty such as that inflicted on James Bulger, had a wider
resonance. Since time immemorial, children had been the recepta-
cles for adult fears about moral decay and decline: now they were
becoming the focus of a deeper malaise, an uncertainty about the
very ways in which societies were organized.

Fears about children were soon popping up in every sphere: their
education, their health, their leisure – even their means of being
conveyed into the world. The new possibility of testing for genetic
conditions or even gender during pregnancy, coupled with the
widening availability of IVF, was giving parents greater and greater
choice not just about when to have children, but about which type
of children they might choose to have. Gill and Neil Clark confessed
– to the *Daily Mail* – that they had paid £650 to a private clinic to
ensure that their third child would be a girl:[35] 'From my point of
view it felt unnatural,' Neil confessed. 'I didn't feel as though I was
so much a part of it as I had been with the boys. Gill's got a T-shirt
with the words "It started with a kiss", and I look at that and I think:
"Well, it didn't."' In the *Mail*'s view, the couple's action had in some
way potentially left humanity vulnerable to some hidden danger –
the threat, perhaps, of biological engineering on a grand scale. They
had, it said, 'led the human race on to a path which, some argue,
could upset the natural balance of the sexes for ever'.

Since the war, virtually all adults in the UK had been able to make choices about whether they should become parents, and when. But those choices had been largely negative ones: thanks to free contraception, one could decide not to do it. But what was happening now smacked of something that was increasingly feared: children were becoming a 'lifestyle choice'. The phrase seemed to strike fear into conservative hearts. Lifestyle choices, it seemed, were a bad thing when it came to having children. The reasons for this were unclear, but seemed to speak to a deep-rooted feeling that childbirth and child-rearing should be closer to nature than they had now become; maybe that they should be not in the hands of mankind, but in those of the Almighty. In an increasingly secular society, this might have seemed strange, yet the attitudes were strikingly persistent. They spoke to many fears – not only did man seem now to be meddling with nature – or God's will – but the developments seemed to place the nuclear family in even greater jeopardy than before. Now, children would not only be at risk of growing up without the experience of two parents because of separation and divorce – now single parenthood was becoming a positive choice. The Lord Chancellor, Lord Mackay of Clashfern, felt the need to reassure peers, during the passage of a bill which would make it easier for single women to conceive via IVF,[36] that the values of the nuclear family were still the only socially acceptable values: 'The sanctity of the family unit should not be lost sight of in the wish to help childless couples have the children they can so fervently desire, it would clearly be unfortunate if this Bill was seen in any way to be conflicting with the importance we attach to family values.'

In a sense, many of the social diseases that were now felt to ail children were diseases of affluence. Even the rise in divorce, of course, had an economic angle – couples could now afford to separate, where in the past they might have been forced to stay together. But children were now being sucked into economic activity which was more overt than it had ever been before. A selection of headlines from the 1990s underlines the point: 'The Targeting of Food Ads on Children's Television Can Do More than Just Harm their Pockets', 'Born to Buy.' At least a part of the fear surrounding childhood now was about the fact that while children were able to exercise less and less freedom of movement, they were exercising ever more financial muscle.

As children were increasingly seen as a distinct market, they came under increased pressure to consume. One of the biggest fears around children – as ever – was their diet. But now, instead of worrying about the lack of nutritional value in an endless succession of meals consisting of tea and bread, the medical profession was worrying about the pressures on children to eat certain unhealthy foods – or, conversely, to stay thin. And while some children were eating the wrong foods, and some were not eating enough, one adolescent in six was now considered to be obese. It was almost as if affluence itself was eating into the fears around children. Food additives, vitamins, junk food … somehow, child consumerism seemed to be running away with itself. There was a feeling that the nation had put a ticking time-bomb under itself, which one day would explode with the after-effects of obesity and other indulgence-related conditions.

Everywhere, children were under pressure. There was pressure to achieve at school, as a new government elected in 1997 set targets for literacy, numeracy and GCSE results. There was pressure to be slim, in order to be able to look good in fashionable clothes. There was pressure to have the right stuff, the right audio equipment. Pressure to have seen the right films, to be able to achieve the right levels in the right computer games. Pressure, maybe, to grow up too soon. Somehow, it all seemed to be one big rush. And parents were feeling a sense of loss.

'Where did all the innocence go?' asked one writer in the *Scotsman*,[37] wondering aloud what had happened to the magical sunny days, picnics and sand-pies of the Enid Blyton novel. Fear seemed to be everywhere, the author suggested. She quoted a woman whose eleven-year-old son, needing to take a taxi to ice hockey practice because his mother's car was off the road and – presumably – because public transport was considered too dangerous, had panicked, fearing the taxi driver might abduct him. His mother, far from telling him to buck up and be grateful that she was forking out for a taxi, as a mother from an earlier age might have done, were she able to fund such a thing, insisted he phone her the minute he arrived.

The answer to her question was that the 'innocence' and the magic had been swept away by a new desire abroad in the adult world – the desire to extract added value from children. Having lost their old traditional economic value, children had gone through a phase in which their parents sometimes struggled to work out what they were getting from their relationships with them. Now the future was becoming clearer. The ideal child of the 1960s, like the ideal child of the 1930s, had spent his life – even her life, sometimes – roaming free in the idyllic English countryside, picking blackberries, fishing, occasionally getting into a scrape or two. The ideal child of the 1990s had no time for such japes, even if he or she were allowed to go on them. Because now the child had to earn his or her keep in new and more complex ways. Take sixteen-year-old Zita Lusack, for example, interviewed by the *Mail on Sunday* in 1994, with her mother looking on proudly, about her ambition to be a top gymnast. Zita weighed seven stone, but was still trying to lose weight in order to achieve the childlike physique demanded by her sport, the newspaper reported: 'Dinner has become a portion-controlled ready meal she eats in the car during the hour-long ride to her training base at Heathrow. "I work out for four hours every night except Mondays and Thursdays, most of the weekend, and, before competitions, Thursdays, too. Sometimes I think it's worth the sacrifice, but there are times when I don't. I've been training for ten years now. But when I turn eighteen, it will be all over.'" Or fifteen-year-old Juanita Rosenior, who in 1999 was working in her spare time as an editor for *Children's Express*: 'My day consists of seven 45-minute lessons. I spend my time swapping career ideas with my friend, Ebony, who encourages me, and we work together as a mini study group. We do this through phone calls, meetings, shopping and general social-ising. Being a child of the technology era, my prized possession at the moment is my new mobile phone which comes in handy at lunch times.'[38] Or three-year-old 'Ella from the West Country', described in the *Observer*, winning a Miss Pears competition: 'The nine other finalists milled around, being brave and confused, the organisers tried to clear the stage, cameramen stood on chairs to get a glimpse of the triumphant winner. She was crying. She didn't want to be Miss Pears 1997. She didn't want to be here, in a big hall surrounded by strangers who were calling out her name and asking her to look their way, smile please and look cute. She didn't want to sit on the plush throne and wear a spiky crown and smile prettily and toss her locks. "Mummy," she sobbed. The photographer ... sighed as he clicked. "Beware ambitious parents," he said, then, "Come on, Ella, smile." ... Later she crouched in a corner, knees up in her red dungarees, while her dad answered questions (yes, he was pleased; yes, their prize was a trip to Florida and Disneyland; yes, Ella was only three years old; yes, it was all wonderful) and pushed melting chocolate biscuits into her rosebud mouth.'

The child of the nineties was beginning to realize that achieve-ment – achievement which would require tough, focused, hard, nose-to-the-grindstone labour – was the route to a parent's heart. This state of grace usually needed to be attained through academic excel-lence, but it could alternatively be reached through sporting prowess, through beauty or even through stardom. The key to becoming the ideal child of the nineties was to be better – or preferably, best.

Feeling the strain

Stanley Kasumba had lots to say about his life that was positive – he got on very well with his parents, for example. And he had a strong sense that each generation had to be better, to achieve more than the one that went before. Born in 1990 and growing up in north London, he felt he had seen quite a bit of life. But at the same time, things seemed to have been well mapped out for him.

'When I was younger I was in football clubs, small teams within the area. And there would be reading workshops from the library. Everything was really set. It wasn't really your freedom. It would be like your mother telling you, there's this thing you should do,' he said.[39] 'My parents are very ambitious for me. I think now that's what parenting is about – they put everything they have into their children. They want them to do the best. Maybe that wasn't really the case in the past. In the past parents would be preoccupied with so many things that they wouldn't channel everything into their children.'

Stanley was doing A-levels and hoping to go on to university, and he was aware of competing pressures upon him. Parents, wanting him to do as well as he possibly could. Friends, whispering in his ear suggestions on this or that way to break the rules – at thirteen or fourteen, a spot of vandalism; at fifteen or sixteen, some illegal drugs. In many ways, Stanley's teenage years could be characterized as a delicate juggling act – which, it had to be said, he appeared to have carried off with aplomb. And yet at seventeen he looked back with a kind of envy on his younger self: 'As I grow older, I think back and I think: "Oh, man! Look how old I am." I'm not that old, but I remember when I was eleven and we used to play in the park, and when I was twelve, and the first day I walked to school. I don't feel as joyful. There's always that thought – what am I going to do, why am I feeling this way? I'm so much in control of my life. Then, I didn't have to think about anything. I could just be free and happy.'

One of the striking things about Stanley was his tendency to reflect in this way about his circumstances, his past, his future, his state of emotional equilibrium, or otherwise. The 1990s child, it seemed, was a child in touch with his own feelings and able to express them, perhaps in a way which few earlier-born children would have been. Perhaps it was not so surprising, then, that when the United Nations Children's Fund, Unicef, published a report on child 'wellbeing' in a range of rich countries based on statistics from just before and just after the millennium, it found the United Kingdom and the United States in the bottom third of the table on five of the six measures they used. The United Kingdom's children were found to be the worst behaved; the least content in their family lives. Overall, their levels of personal happiness and wellbeing were found to be the worst of any of the twenty-one developed countries included in the study. The only measure on which the UK's youth scored well – in the middle of the table – was health and safety. These findings quickly became the subject of controversy, with academics disputing the comparability of the data. But they did provide an interesting picture of how British children were feeling – not so much, perhaps, of whether they were *actually* safe, healthy and getting a reasonable education, but of whether they and their parents thought they were. So, for instance, British children tended to rate their health as being quite poor, while in fact their chances of dying young were low – in case of accidents – or average – in the case of disease. Similarly, the British fifteen-year-old achieved above-average scores in English, maths and science, and at the same time were more likely than the average to expect only low-skilled work on leaving school.

Was the British child now just better at expressing his or her feelings than his Czech or Dutch counterpart? If so, why would he or she choose to express negative emotions, while the Dutch child –

who was judged the most well-appointed of all – expressed positive ones? Certainly, the British child was more likely to live in a single-parent or a step-family than any other apart from the American child, and less likely to sit down to eat a family meal on a regular basis. He was, though, likely to say that his parents spent a good deal of time talking to him. Whatever the reasons, it certainly seemed the British child, around the time of the millennium, was not a particularly happy child. Which was, in historical terms, surprising. After all, the British child was more likely than ever to live to adulthood; more likely than ever to receive a university or a college education, more likely to have plentiful food, a warm home, a family car.

Somehow, it seemed, the nation's children had become all mixed up. And not just 'mixed up', in an emotional sense. In a practical sense, their lives were becoming more mixed up, too, with the lives of adults. They spent more time with their parents – Stanley's family would enjoy a walk in Epping Forest together on the weekend, or would take a trip to Margate. Somehow, their worlds were not so separate as they had been. They watched the same television programmes as their parents, stayed indoors more, rather than going out with friends. There was a wider sense, too, in which children's lives had been mixed up with those of adults – a phenomenon which had been demonstrated in the reaction to the Bulger murder. Children were now a part of society. Their world was no longer seen as being some separated place, some walled garden or woodland glade where they could frolic, childlike and undisturbed. The adult world was their world, and vice versa: witness, for example, the adult tendency to read *Harry Potter* books, or to visit theme parks unaccompanied by children. Somehow, this left children exposed to all the pressures of the adult world. And at the same time it led to a sense of panic among adults, about where childhood had vanished to. Children were felt to be indulging in adult vices – drink, drugs, violence. And, as ever, there was conflict over who was to blame.

The children themselves, for going off the rails? Their parents, for failing them by being divorced, going out to work (mothers), not going out to work (fathers)? Or society, as a whole, as an entity? Increasingly, the feeling was that society was to blame.

During the mid-1990s, then, the political focus began to turn on children. An education reform act in the late 1980s had begun the process of focusing on what children should be learning at school, and on ensuring they left with the 'right' knowledge, gained under a national curriculum. Now, with the advent of a new Labour government, the drive – in every area of life, it seemed, and children were certainly no exception – was to drive up 'standards'. At school, they must achieve better results. More of them must go to university. Overall, they must be better provided for; they must do more; they must be better; they must improve. A whole range of grand schemes were conceived. By 2008,[40] the targets towards which the government's department for children and schools would be working would include breastfeeding, childhood obesity, bullying, social care assessments, preventable child deaths, exam performance, drug misuse, teenage pregnancy and youth crime, to name but a few. The state now felt the need to measure and improve every aspect of children's lives. Parents, meanwhile, sometimes seemed to be there largely to be blamed when things went wrong. The state, naturally, would take the credit where things went right.

Even before Labour came to power in 1997, John Major's Conservative government had begun the process with a plan to ensure every child received pre-school education. For a while, this particular programme was felt to be a possible panacea for all the perceived ills from which children were suffering. Catch them early, the theory went, and it might be possible to nip all these social ailments in the bud: low standards, delinquency, truancy, unemployment, even crime. But the revelation – hardly new – that educational under-achievement had social causes led to deeper thinking.

Perhaps what was needed was not so much a programme to tackle educational under-achievement as a programme to tackle child poverty. The government set itself a target of cutting relative child poverty by a quarter before 2004 – something which, by and large, it did achieve.[41] The strategy was to try to tackle long-term unemployment on the basis that children born into workless families were very likely to under-achieve themselves.

'Poverty must not be a birthright,' the work and pensions minister, Baroness Hollis, declared in 2000.[42] 'Our strategy is to halt the transmission of low expectations, low aspirations and low outcomes from parent to child.' A 'Sure Start' programme, similar to one already running in the United States, was set up to bring mothers and babies from poor estates into the state's ambit. Five hundred million pounds was spent on setting up centres in the hope people would arrive to ask for developmental advice, health advice, advice on how to stop smoking. Unsurprisingly, the poorest mothers, the teenage mothers and the mothers who coped least well were the least likely to want to go to a centre to be told how to be better, and so the scheme was only a partial success.

Everywhere, though, there was a sense that something big should be done. Children's rights were once again in the ascendancy when Britain ratified the UN Convention on the Rights of the Child in 1991, giving children the legal 'right' to various things – to have special protection, to be able to pursue their talents, to participate in achieving a better future for all children. There was almost nothing, it seemed, that the state could not now promise the child. The British government, underlining an article in the UN convention, even promised its children the right to 'grow up in an environment of happiness, love and understanding',[43] though how this was to be achieved was never made clear. The government did not choose to dwell upon these 'rights' when it made its periodic reports to the United Nations about its progress towards its goals.

And yet the feeling persisted – indeed, continued to grow – that all was not well in the world of the child. Save the Children summed up the situation thus: 'From a very early age, the majority of children's time is taken up by structured activities, leaving very little space for individual choice. Increased perception of danger in public spaces, (adult-centred) consumerism, an achievement-oriented society, child poverty and public prejudice against children on the street are factors contributing to a narrowing of the private space, and hence the liberty, of today's children. Children's wishes often come secondary to what adults deem necessary, safe, educative or more convenient.'[44] Despite this apparent catalogue of complaints, Save the Children was able to conclude that children's lives were getting better. Others begged to differ. Day after day, year after year, the press was full of stories expressing an increased sense of children's vulnerability, of a perceived jeopardy and threat, if not to their present then to their wellbeing at some future, unspecified date. Parents were repeatedly injuncted to take precautions, to protect their young.

In July 2000, just to pick one example, the *Daily Mail* reported that the Imperial Cancer Research Fund had warned that one child in three would grow up to be a 'cancer victim', and had linked this risk with childhood diet. It then featured three families talking about their lifestyles, and accompanied by advice from 'cancer experts': 'WATCH their weight. Obesity has a clear link with bowel and breast cancer. MAKE a point of examining your children's skin, and see your GP about any moles that grow, weep, hurt or appear suddenly. MAKE sure your children eat at least five portions of fruit and vegetables a day. Bowel cancer is less likely to strike if you have a high-fibre diet. LOWER their intake of fats, salt and nitrates. AVOID plastic packaging and cookware. Plastics contain chemicals that may disrupt the fine hormone balance in the body.' The list of injunctions seemed interminable – and this was just what parents were now meant to do to avoid one perceived, far-distant future risk.

The internet, too, had to be policed. 'Popular concerns have been expressed that using a computer is a solitary and potentially addictive activity, provoking fears that some children might become so obsessed with the technology that they will socially withdraw from the off-line world of family and friends,' a report on children's computer use suggested.[45] 'Children, as symbols of the future themselves, are at the heart of debates ... about the "new" dangers that these technologies might bring for the Net generation.'

The potent belief that when we look at our children we look at the future of mankind was at work, and with a new intensity, in the years around the millennium. It was as if the soul of the human race had been taken out of the dark drawer where it had been hidden during the rationalist, thrusting years of the 1980s and 1990s, examined, dusted off and found to have been damaged. Something was going wrong – and the explanations, the exhortations to do better, to do different, were myriad. By 2000, even the Incorporated Association of Preparatory Schools, an organization whose members were largely devoted to getting children into the top public schools and therefore not noted for their lax attitude to educational achievement, was concerned that children were being pushed too hard. At the association's conference that year, the headmaster of Dulwich College Preparatory School worried aloud about the private tuition many children were forced to undergo in order to pass entrance exams: 'They deserve a childhood. They need our protection. There is a need for children to have a life and enjoy it.'[46] The problem, he suggested, was parents', not children's, fear of failure, of the shame they would endure if their offspring failed to win places at the most over-subscribed private schools.

Somehow, the debate was turning in on itself. Increasingly, it was not the fears themselves – delinquency, early pregnancy, abuse, abduction, internet porn – but the fear of the damage the fears were doing, that was exercising public opinion. The panic about children's wellbeing began to give way, in short, to a panic about panic. This took specific forms – the concern that new rules demanding criminal record checks of adults working with children could close sports clubs and bar perfectly blameless people from jobs through technicalities, for example. 'Would You Dare to Help This Child?' the *Daily Telegraph* asked in 2009, its question posed next to a photo of a small boy lying on the floor by an upturned bicycle. 'What sort of society is it where adults suspect other adults, and children are taught to suspect anyone other than their parents, who are often the people who cause them greatest harm?' The article drew ninety-nine comments on the paper's website, almost all of them supportive of the author.

Even terrible crimes against children were now met by the fear that fear itself would be the outcome. After the murder of eight-year-old Sarah Payne in 2000, by a man named Roy Whiting, who had already served a prison sentence for child abduction and indecent assault, a 'but' crept into the comment pages: 'There is not a parent in Britain whose heart does not ache for Sarah Payne's family,' wrote Susan Dalgety in the *Edinburgh Evening News*. But the worst effect of the crime would be its effect on all youngsters: 'Children who would otherwise have been outside in the summer sun, revelling in the glorious freedom of the school holidays, will be trapped indoors because of their parents' fear of evil strangers. And a generation of youngsters, already swaddled in cotton wool, will be warned to treat everyone, even their next door neighbour or local shopkeeper, as a potential abductor.'

The problem went deeper than mere over-protectiveness, though. A 2007 book summed up the state of play. Its title was *Toxic Childhood*. The problem, it suggested, was too much technology, not enough exercise, too much fattening food, all leading to low self-esteem and a risk of developmental disorders such as dyslexia or attention deficit hyperactivity disorder. Too many children were failing to bond with their parents: 'This is the "elephant" standing full square in the living room of every family in the developed world.'

The author described a sulky girl she had once seen, standing on the steps of the Ufizzi gallery in Florence, licking an ice-cream with evident adolescent angst. This poor girl, unaware of the attention she had attracted, became a symbol for all that ailed the Western child: 'Poor child. Poor parents. Poor western civilisation ... How did she get like that? Perhaps she's spent ten years feeding on burgers, pizza and ice cream, washed down with sugary cola. Maybe she spends long hours in a virtual world of her own, absorbing the messages of the marketing men, playing computer games rather than real ones, staring at TV programmes rather than going out to play in the sunshine. Does she lie awake till the early hours, watching unsuitable TV and texting her chums? Has this sedentary, screen-based lifestyle led to problems at school in concentrating, control-ling her temper or relating to other people? And are her parents bewildered that their beloved little girl seems so troubled, when they've provided her with every luxury money could buy?' The answer, in the author's mind at least, was a resounding 'yes'.

The book, alarmist as it was, was backed by an enormous number of child development experts, no fewer than 110 of whom signed a letter its author wrote to the *Daily Telegraph* on the subject. A rise in special educational needs, she said, was particularly worrying: 'Today's special educational needs turn all too often into tomorrow's mental health problems, antisocial behaviour and crime.' The author, along with the experts, had seen the future. And it frightened them.

Conclusion

Children, when seen from a distance by an adult world which fears for its own future, often seem to cause alarm. Look close up and the scene is usually calmer, more reassuring. As the American academic John Sommerville put it in the 1980s: 'Babies are the enemy. Not your baby or mine, of course. Individually they are all cute. But together they are a menace.'[51]

A closer look at one modern childhood, then, might prove reassuring. We might meet Florence Bishop, for instance, born in 2000 into a middle-class family in the south of England, early one weekday evening. Aged seven, Florence was wearing her school uniform on this particular evening and was in the middle of her piano practice. She loved her little magnetic toys, and her hamster.[52] In November, she had already written a list for Father Christmas. She was brimming with health and full of enthusiasm for life. In her no sign whatsoever could be detected of bad diet, poor parenting, incipient delinquency. Hers was the very model of a calm, happy, well-regulated childhood. If anything, Florence's life was possibly *more* regulated than her parents' would have been. She knew exactly what time she must board the school bus each day, and she had always to be sure she had the right books with her. Her mother, unlike her mother's mother in the 1970s, had a full-time job but one or other parent was always at home to greet her when she returned from school; to ensure homework was done and the correct number of vegetables eaten at teatime. Perhaps they worried a little more than their own parents would have done. Florence always had to carry a mobile phone so they could be in touch; she was not yet considered old enough to go out alone. Yet the cadences of Florence's early life carried only a few distant echoes from the heat and the noise and the sense of alarm that were filling up the public arena during those years. And the same, almost certainly, could be said for most children.

Childhood, when dragged into the amphitheatre of public debate, has always been an emotionally charged subject, and increasingly so during the twentieth century. Perhaps, too, it has always been associated with a measure of fear. There is something about childhood that adults find mysterious, unknowable. Maybe it is that feeling that children are not creatures of the past – that is, they can never quite be equated with the children their parents once were; nor the present – their licence to practice in the outside world has strict conditions on it – but of the future. They represent something that is not yet known, something unformed yet precious, something vitally important which could potentially go wrong. They represent, in any age, a huge investment both of money and of time. Sometimes, the return has seemed uncertain. And so that uncertainty has given rise to myths, both great and small, which have persisted, in slightly altered forms, from one generation to the next.

The greatest myths, of course, are the oldest, the most enduring. The myth that children are somehow closer to nature than adults are; and that in being so, they can see and feel truths that adults cannot feel. The child as the seer, as the beating heart of all that is good and pure and honest, has perhaps receded during the twentieth century, but it sang out loud and strong during the eighteenth and nineteenth, through the works of poets such as Blake – 'Sweet babe, in thy face, holy image I can trace'[53] – and Wordsworth:

I cannot paint
What then I was. The sounding cataract
Haunted me like a passion: the tall rock,
The mountain, and the deep and gloomy wood,
Their colours and their forms, were then to me
An appetite; a feeling and a love,
That had no need of a remoter charm.[54]

And, as the flipside of the same coin, the myth that children harbour evil, that, being the germinated seed of the original sin of Adam and Eve, they begin corrupted and must be civilized if they are to become adult humans in a functioning society, has been just as persistent. From the pre-enlightenment version, based on straightforwardly biblical views, to the devil children of twentieth-century fiction – Golding's young savages in *Lord of the Flies*, Damien in *The Omen* – this evil, corrupting child has hung around the edges of society, almost as if there was some need for it. The feeling that there is a dangerous child 'underclass' must surely flow from the same spring: from the street arabs of the nineteenth century to the knife and drug gangs of the early twenty-first, the same fear has hung in the air. Children can be dangerous, they can be corrupting, they can be born of evil.

And again, another facet to the same potent belief: that if there exists a corrupted body of children – never our own, of course – then there must also be a larger, corruptible body which is susceptible to its wiles. The children of nature portrayed by Blake and Wordsworth had a sort of untouchable, homely innocence. But the real myth was never about those children, safe in their cradles before the hearth. The real myth was about other people's children, and the threat they posed. Charles Kingsley's little sweep Tom, emerging blackened from the fireplace in *The Water Babies* into a rich girl's bedroom, and the 'stranger danger' panics of the late twentieth century both pointed in their own ways to this belief – that out there, in the forest, some threat was lurking.

And to these big myths, small myths cling and grow. The vulnerable child can be vulnerable in myriad ways. He can be vulnerable – and the future of the nation with him – because of monsters, bad men, poor nutrition, an unhealthy lifestyle. The early twentieth-century fears about a bread and tea diet breeding a puny urban underclass, and the early twenty-first-century panics about junk food, household chemicals and asthma, all spoke to the same fear. The Edwardians worried about what would become of the Empire, and consequently the nation's prosperity and security when adults in the cities had their children running back and forth to the alehouse for them; a century later, the adults of the early twenty-first century worried about who was going to pay the benefit bills for a generation dragged up in workless homes on sink estates by parents who had barely tried to show them a model of a functioning nuclear family. While parents close to home were doing a good job, were those elsewhere sneaking rotten apples into the barrel? Would the next generation be strong enough to protect and nurture this one in its dotage? In short, if children were the future, what sort of future would they be?

So, there was much that persisted, much that was circular, in the world of the child when viewed from a historical perspective. Perhaps the twentieth-century notion that childhood was something unique and separate and different from adulthood, and that therefore a child should have independent 'rights', began to go into recession at the beginning of the twenty-first. Perhaps, increasingly, the public focus in the new millennium actually – while paying lip service to the notion of rights and individuality – became more fixated on the idea that all children should achieve set goals, that all children should be ready to play their allotted parts in the future of the nation. Perhaps the idea of changing power relations within a family, the

1970s and 1980s feeling that parents were no longer so firmly in the driving seat, was giving way, as the century turned, to a new disciplinarianism, a return to the old notion that actually the key to bringing up a child was not so much freedom as parenting – and the right kind of parenting, at that: 'While establishing a routine is often very hard work and requires a lot of sacrifices on the part of the parents, hundreds of thousands of parents around the world will testify that it is worth it because they quickly learn how to meet the needs of their babies so distress is kept to a minimum,' wrote Gina Ford in her new *Contented Little Baby Book*, considered a major source of advice for twenty-first-century parents.[55]

Yet while some things stayed the same and while some were cyclical, there was much, too, that changed. The story of childhood from the last days of Victoria to the new millennium was the story, if you like, of how the state swallowed its children. Never before had governments had so much to say, so much to do – or indeed, anything much to say or do – about children. Now, in an era when the fingers of the state reached into most walks of human life, the child became a key focus for public policy: a phenomenon which reached a crescendo as the twentieth century came to a close.

If raising children had always been a huge investment for the family, it now became an equally major investment for the state. As the century wore on, a parent's investment in his or her child became increasingly an emotional rather than an economic one – or rather, the desired emotional return grew as the expected economic return dwindled. At the same time, governments took on an ever greater economic, and therefore political, investment in the child. Education, health, criminal justice – all these areas of public policy became battlegrounds over which opposing camps fought over children and their upbringing. Huge sums were spent. And so the collective investment became somehow greater – both personal and political – because every taxpayer – every family – had an ever greater stake in every other taxpayer's children. Naturally, that led to everyone feeling they were entitled to an opinion not just on how to raise their own children, but on how others should raise theirs too. Children, according to modern theorists on the subject, became not just the means of social reproduction – which they had always been – but also the agents of desired social change.[56] And so the perceived consequences of educational failure, emotional disruption or delinquency become more socially pressing; linked both to a feeling that an investment was going to waste, and to a fear that this huge, optimistic social project could be failing.

Investments in health, in housing and in education were all, in effect, investments in the future of the nation. And so it was hardly surprising that a kind of paranoia would continue to grow, even as that investment brought its returns in terms of better health and greater safety for children. As the infant mortality rate plummeted, before and after the war, and as the numbers of child deaths from accidents also fell,[57] the sense that everyone had an interest in the health of other people's children also grew. And the idea took hold that perhaps some people were not tending to their children as they should be doing. And so the notion of bad parenting became an obsession for the media. It fed back, of course, into the deeper notion of the child's vulnerability. And that, too, was fed by the growth of developmental theory during the twentieth century – mainly as a result of Freud's notions about the stages of psychological growth through which a child must pass, and the desperate consequences of a failure to do so. There was a growing sense, then, that a healthy, well-nourished, well-nurtured childhood was essential not just for the future wellbeing of the individual, but for the future wellbeing of the state.

That feeling had always been out there, of course. But now it gained a new intensity. The ideal child of the late Victorian era had been a quiet creature, seen but not heard, obedient and pure. The ideal child of the early twentieth century was elfin, sprite-like, delicate, while the ideal child of the later twentieth century was an increasingly robust, rosy-cheeked creature. All those children, though, had lived an existence centred on the home and on the family. Now, the child became – in theory, if not in practice – a social being even more, inextricably linked to the current and future wellbeing of society itself. When the issue is viewed from this angle, it is clear that social problems were bound to attach themselves to the child. Somehow, the old post-war optimism had completely vanished from the political rhetoric surrounding the life of the child by the end of the century. While a discussion about children in the 1960s would probably have centred on how parents should raise them, what worked and what did not; a discussion about children in the twenty-first century would almost certainly focus at some point on what on earth was going wrong. Old certainties, such as they were, had vanished. Suddenly, children seemed vastly more important than they used to – there were fewer of them – and their emotional stock had risen as their economic stock had fallen since 1945 – although children still worked, fewer were expected to contribute to family budgets. And this, in part, must help to account for the growing sense of unease among parents. Increasingly, children had spending power without earning power. And, increasingly, parents found themselves forking out for the luxuries which their children, cuckoo-like, were demanding from the comfort of their family nest. A parent's investment in a child – both emotional and financial – had grown. And from there arose uncertainty about whether it was all worth it. What was it all for? Children were no longer there to sustain the family, to take over from where their parents left off in the family business or trade. They were no longer there, even, to support their parents in their old age. They were just *there.*

And from *there,* maybe, arose the guilt. In essence, the Western world was becoming an increasingly uncertain place. And the role of the child within it was equally uncertain: if we don't know who we are, who we want to be or how we're meant to get there, then how can we guide our young? Maybe, then, the time has come for retrenchment. Maybe the twentieth century will come to be seen, in terms of children and their history, as the century of choice. The century when thinkers like Freud, with his focus on the individual and his needs, like Neill, with his belief in freedom, and even like Benjamin Spock, who told parents to relax and all would be well, were in the ascendancy. The century in which children became the focus of a great attempted feat of social engineering. In which the child as an individual was asked to assert himself, and in which, sometimes, he even did. Was the experiment a success? The jury is out, but the tone of the debate – more myth than reality, of course – would certainly say no. So perhaps the twenty-first century is bound to be a century of retreat, for a time at least, towards old certainties – more discipline, stricter targets.

The fear and the myths, though, are not just myths and fears about children. They are myths and fears about mankind; ones which have emerged and re-emerged throughout the ages because they have drawn people together as external threats tend to do. Almost as if in uncertain times – and times often have been uncertain – there is a reassurance about it. If the evil, the poison, the violence, is out there, prowling around the dark boundaries of the camp, then those huddled inside nearest to the fire may take comfort in the rhythms of their own lives. Perhaps with retrenchment, with greater cohesion and a clearer sense of common purpose, will come the realization that for the most part there is little out there to fear but the fear itself.

Epilogue

In the Spring of 2011, two Canadian psychologists laid bare a contradiction at the heart of modern family life: that parenting seemed more demanding, more arduous with each passing year, and yet was somehow increasingly idealized in the popular imagination. Their study aimed to find out why.

The academics set up an experiment, with two groups of parents. The first was asked to look at information on both pros and cons – the financial cost of up to £150,000 per child, balanced by the possibility that the child might later provide support to the parent in old age. The second group was given information on the cost, but not the benefits.[1]

So, which group would speak most warmly of the joys of parenthood? The group which had been allowed to contemplate the prospect of a happy old age with its adult offspring at its knee? Or the group which had just realized if it had had one less child, it could have spent the money on a small second home? The result, of course, was that the more parents were asked to confront hard-edged financial reality, the more they in fact focused on the warm, fuzzy feelings parenthood gave them. In short, they were fooling themselves.

In the midst of a recession, as youth unemployment soars and children become ever more costly and burdensome, the question of why parents have them is thrown into ever-sharper relief.[2]

The question has hung around at the margins of public debate for decades. As the American academic John Sommerville put it in 1982: 'At a time when we were confident that our work was making their future brighter, it was easy to think of children as innocent and refreshing . . . Children are more obviously a liability nowadays.'[3] Since then, things have continued to get worse. Children no longer contribute to the family purse as they did in the early years of the twentieth century. Over the past fifty years, traditional industries and the labour market conditions that enabled children to follow their parents into a profession or a trade have all but disappeared. They no longer have a major economic role except as consumers, and they lack a clear economic future as young adults. Yet, as some American academics have put it, children's emotional capital has risen, just as their social and economic capital has fallen.[4] Parents, like the ones in the Canadian study, are upping the ante to justify their unwise investment in child-rearing. As the Canadian psychologists put it: 'The idea that parenthood involves substantial emotional rewards appears to be something of a myth.'[5]

For the most part, the adult world continues to maintain the fiction that everything's fine; that so long as its offspring are safe and warm in the family home, all will be well, which is convenient, since so many of those offspring are finding they can't move on into adulthood.

In March 2012, the *Huffington Post* ran a piece by a recent American college graduate. Its headline, 'Why Generation Y Can't Grow Up – A Recession Tale,'[6] said it all.

The author, Tyler Moss, had a Masters degree, an ocean of debt and 'a barren desert of unemployment opportunities' confronting him. He'd measured his life by milestones – driving test, first legal drink, college – and was left wondering what it had all been for.

He concluded that if the 'Millennials', as he termed his generation of recent graduates, were drifting, they had good reason to do so. In an age of extreme uncertainty, the choices were apparently stark: work incessantly in the hope of clinging to the career ladder in an increasingly precarious climate, or embrace the life of the perpetual adolescent.

Put in those terms, it seemed obvious why so many had plumped for the second option; why so many were, to put it bluntly, choosing not to confront their future, opting instead for a series of coffee-shop jobs – the life of the perpetual backpacker.

'I can guarantee our Depression-era ancestors, living in the cardboard boxes of their Hoovervilles, thought little past the evening's cabbage soup,' Moss wrote. 'We live a blind *carpe diem* that avoids eye contact with tomorrow but with the future so precarious, and with no real choice in the matter, successes and failures are measured by the day.'

Across the Western world – certainly in Britain – young people have been drawing much the same conclusion – although perhaps most of them haven't articulated it with quite the same pristine clarity. This generation is set apart from those who suffered in the recessions of the 1980s, or even of the 1930s, by a major factor: the loss of hope.

This is the generation in which the great twentieth century social project came to an end; the generation for whom, for the first time in well over a century, there is little hope of being better off than the last; it is the generation for whom the likelihood of being better educated, more fruitfully employed, better housed and better provided for in old age than one's parents came to a grinding halt. A child born in 2000 will be more or less as likely as his or her parents to go to university, but much more likely to come out with an enormous debt caused by the payment of higher fees.[7] He or she will have a much-reduced chance of a graduate job, and will struggle to get on to the housing ladder before starting a family. While the next generation will live longer than the last, its chances of having an adequate pension to live on will be much reduced.

However, a historian might say it isn't the lack of opportunity that ails today's youth – in comparison with their forebears of a century earlier, they have ample opportunity – even in the depth of the worst recession for a generation. The real problem is the lack of optimism; the sense of having to work ever-harder yet constantly sliding backwards and that no matter how hard they try, it won't be enough to make them better off than their parents were. It's fundamentally, grindingly alienating and, slowly but surely, it's sucking the motivation out of the young. In a media age success – in the form of money, fame, top-brand stuff – is always near at hand, but it's often just out of reach.

'iPhones! Xboxes! Everything! You can get whatever you want!'[8] read one of the BlackBerry messages directing the rioters to trouble spots in London in the summer of 2011. When the young of Britain's cities went to war, it wasn't the police they were fighting, or the state. Not really; not in any coherent way. They were fighting the Battle of the Bored; the battle of the generation that has lost its reason to defer gratification. For the youth of the eighties there was the hope – borne of generations' worth of positive change – that if you stayed on the right road, you'd get there in the end. For this lot, there isn't much to lose.

In Salford, the local paper suggested the atmosphere during those outbursts was more like the television programme *Shameless* than Spike Lee's *Do The Right Thing*: 'This was more of a party than an angry riot, as youngsters handed old people packs of cigs, and tins of Carlsberg freshly liberated from LIDL... All that was missing was the DJ. This was a very Salford riot.'[9] Of the Tottenham riots a young resident said succinctly: 'It was summer, people had nothing to do.'[10]

Conditions in twenty-first century Britain are still, in absolute terms, fairly good. Indeed, the early twenty-first century might easily be portrayed as a golden age for the youth of the Western world. Whereas a child born in 1910 could expect to live to be fifty, a child born in 2010 will likely reach the age of eighty. Of every thousand born in the UK in 2010, just five will die before their fifth birthdays; of those born a hundred years earlier, 140 will do so. Before World War Two, about three in every hundred children could expect to go to university; by 2010, about half. A child born in 2010 is actually less likely to be in a lone-parent household than he or she would have been in Victorian times – only now family break-up is usually caused by divorce rather than death.

When it comes to employment, however, the situation of the young today is far worse than it was even in the 1930s. Adult unemployment in the thirties stood at about three million, or around fourteen per cent.[11] But youth unemployment was much lower, at around five per cent. In 2012, adult unemployment stands at a little more than eight per cent; youth unemployment at a massive twenty-two per cent.

Perhaps the 2011 riots were born not of poverty, nor of failure, nor even really of anger, but of hopeless aspiration. Of the daily frustration of being able to see a good, prosperous life – on the streets, in shop windows and on the endless stream of girl- or boy-next-door superstar television shows – but of not being able to reach it. Of the feeling that there's nothing doing, that things, when compared to the situation of the preceding generation, can only get worse. And of the perception that if what ails you is the lack of the best clothes, the newest electronic and electrical goods, then you might as well consider a strategy of grab and run, because you haven't got that much to lose. 'This country is quite cold – greed, advertisement, money, adverts on TV, greed, greed, greed. Like the iPhone advert: "If you haven't got it, you haven't got IT"', a Peckham youngster told researchers after the riots.[12] Another described the pervasive sense of excitement: 'It was like a movie.'

Most children still live lives that are safe and emotionally secure, of course. And most still feel hopeful, most of the time, about the future. Take Florence Bishop, aged seven and living in the south of England with two professional parents. She travelled to her private school each morning after a hearty breakfast; she came home each evening to homework and piano practice and expected, quite rightly, that all would be well for her.

Take Stanley Kasumba, aged seventeen and from North London. A little uncertain, perhaps, about the future, but still optimistic. Proud of where he came from. Still hoping his education and maybe a good degree would see him through.[13]

Take the nineteen year-old girl from Tottenham who was interviewed recently by the fashion page of a national newspaper, showing off the high heels and fabulous head tie she wore to church. She was studying health and social care at college, and she worked hard, she said: 'Plan A is to become a doctor. If that doesn't happen, I'd like to be a nurse. If that doesn't happen, I'll be a footballer.' What would become of her, when reality slowly dawned? Disillusionment, a sense of failure?[14]

Sometimes those hopes sound just a little unrealistic. Desperate, even.

There is a grim truth underlying all this youthful optimism: the education system has been forced, in the last forty years, to pick up where the economic system left off. In the early 1960s youth unemployment in Britain stood at around three per cent. Most young people didn't even aspire to a good degree, because they knew they had little chance of it. In any case, their mothers would get them a place at the clothing factory, or their fathers at an engineering works or on the docks. Not any more.

Another convenient fiction has crept in to accompany the one perpetrated by the parents, but this time it's the educationists doing it. If the young don't achieve in the education system these days, they rarely achieve at all. So the professionals in that system find it hard to step on their students' dreams. With good reason, of course: motivation comes with self-belief, with confidence, and the belief that you're going nowhere is quite likely to lead to disaster: 'We were shocked by the number of young people we spoke to who had no hopes or dreams for their future,' the government's riot commission remarked in its interim report.[15] It's imperative that the young are encouraged to believe, even in the face of overwhelming evidence to the contrary, that they can win by sticking to the approved educational route. Their teachers and their advisers often conveniently fail to tell them the truth. Either way, the young seem to have been given the idea that all things are possible, just as the tide has turned; just as that great aspirational post-war project for intergenerational social mobility has ground painfully to a halt.

We live in an age where the messages from the media are all about living the dream. We're told we can all do whatever we want, and that we should. But for many, that can only lead to dashed hopes, alienation and a grinding boredom that – for some – can only be alleviated by thrill-seeking and risk-taking.

If the twentieth century was the time when children were given a sense of self, a sense of entitlement and opportunity, then surely the twenty-first must be one of retrenchment. Yet it is hard to imagine that the future for today's young people will be in effect a return to the black-and-white world of the 1950s. The genies of binge drinking, under-age sex and illegal drug will not go meekly back into their bottles, and nor will the expectation of a comfortable life in which consumer goods are cheap. But likewise it is hard to imagine the young retaining the freedoms they have gained and the spending power they were granted in the post-war years.

Recessions don't last for ever, of course. Economically speaking, there will be better times ahead. But the problems the young face go deeper: even during the boom years of the 1990s, youth unemployment remained stubbornly high – not least because the industrial labour market which used to mop them up in their thousands is gone forever. The truth is that although that the adult world has spent half a century telling the young about their 'rights,' telling them that if they believe in themselves then everything will come good; the young know better. They know their place in the western world is an increasingly tenuous one.

Ask today's parents what their children are for, and they'll talk – as they did to those Canadian researchers – about love and emotional investment. But love isn't enough, and the young of today know that. When we talk about self-worth, surely what we're really talking about is economic worth, a sense of assurance that we are on solid ground in financial terms. Everything else, by and large, stands or falls on that foundation. So when the adult world frets over its children's diets, the discipline in their schools, the clothes they wear and the computer games they play, it protests too much. All the hype, the false expectations and the spin, are about disguising an unpalatable and immutable truth. The one thing we really need to give the young is a clear economic path through life; a path on which they'd be able to give something back to their parents' generation, to make all the hard work and the expense worthwhile. And we've failed. Parents know today's children – *their* children – are facing an uncertain future. And – whisper it – deep down, they know they'd be better off without them.

Notes

Introduction
1   Alice Foley, *A Bolton Childhood*, p.23, Manchester University Extra- Mural Department and the North Western District of the WEA, Manchester 1973.
2   *Daily Mail*, 17 February 1993.
3   http://www.portsmouthhigh.co.uk/general/junior-introduction. Accessed 23 January 2012.
4   Portsmouth High Junior School Prospectus: http://www.child renscommissioner.gov.uk/content/all_you_need_to_know/com missioner. Accessed 23 January 2012.

Chapter 1: Victoria's Children
1   How One Girl's Plight Started the Child-Protection Movement. American Humane Association: http://www.americanhumane. org/about-us/who-we-are/history/mary-ellen-wilson.html. Accessed 5 October 2010.
2   American Humane Association, op. cit. How One Girl's Plight Started the Child-Protection Movement.
3   NSPCC history, http://www.nspcc.org.uk/what-we-do/about-thenspcc/history-of-NSPCC/history-of-the-nspcc_wda72240. html. Accessed 5 October 2010.
4   *The Times* 10 September 1896.
5   Jane Jordan, *Josephine Butler*, p.226, John Murray, London, 2001.
6   Louise A. Jackson, 'Family, community and the regulation of sexual abuse: London 1870–1914', in A. Fletcher and S. Hussey (eds), *Childhood in Question. Children, Parents and the State*, Manchester University Press, Manchester, 1999.
7   Alice Foley, *A Bolton Childhood*.

8   Ibid, p.17.
9   http://www.manfamily.org/PDFs/M%20L%20Man%20Mans %20of%20Kent%20DiaryA.pdf. Accessed 6 October 2010.
10 Andrew Davies, *The Gangs of Manchester: The Story of the Scuttlers – Britain's First Youth Cult,* Milo Books, Preston, 2008.
11 *Hansard,* Nov. 9, 1888, column 830, volume 330. ht tp:hansard. millbanksystems.com/commons/1888/nov/09/#column_830. Accessed 6 October 2010.
12 29 October 1900.
13 *Hansard,* June 19, 1882, Column 1575, volume 270 http:// hansard.millbanksystems.com/commons/1882/jun/19/#column _1575. Accessed 6 October 2010.
14 B. S. Rowntree, *Poverty: A Study of Town Life,* p.314, Macmillan, London, 1901. Reprinted 2000 by the Policy Press, Bristol.
15 John F. Shaw, *Froggy's Little Brother,* by 'Brenda', 1875, London.
16 Diary of Atkinson Skinner zDDX389/1 1 April 1882–26 June 1888, East Riding of Yorkshire archive and local studies service.
17 Rowntree, *Poverty,* p.337.
18 Elizabeth Crawford, *The Women's Suffrage Movement: A Reference Guide 1866–1928,* Routledge, London, 1999, p.444.
19 Elizabeth Crawford, *Enterprising Women: The Garretts and their Circle,* Francis Boutle, London, 2002, Chapter 3.
20 Carol Dyhouse, *Girls Growing up in Late Victorian and Edwardian England,* Routledge & Kegan Paul, London, 1981, p.50
21 The Bryce Commission, 1895.
    Quoted in Dyhouse, op. cit., p. 90.
23 Foley, *A Bolton Childhood,* p. 31.
24 Grahame Allen and Joe Hicks, *A Century of Change: Trends in UK Statistics Since 1900,* House of Commons Library, 1999.
25 Foley, *A Bolton Childhood,* p. 38.
26 Rowntree, *Poverty.*
27 Rowntree, Poverty, p. 210.
28 Rowntree, Poverty, p. 266–294.
29 Lionel Rose, *The Massacre of the Innocents: Infanticide in Great Britain, 1800–1939,* Routledge, London, 1986, p.178–9.
30 Rose, *The Massacre of the Innocents,* Op. Cit.
31 Claire Tomalin, *Jane Austen: A Life,* Penguin Celebrations, London, 2000.
32 *Hansard,* 25 March 1897, column 1532, volume 47. h t t p : / / hans a r d . m i l l b a n k s y s t e m s . c o m /lords/1897/mar/29/#column _1532. Accessed 7 October 2010.

Chapter 2: Cosseted Edwardians

1   Sonia Keppel, *Edwardian Daughter*, Hamish Hamilton, London, 1958, p.3.
2   *The Times*, 15 February, 1909.
3   Ibid.
4   See 'Worlds Enough and Time: The cult of childhood in Edwardian fiction', by Adrienne E. Gavin and Andrew F. Humphries, (eds.) *Childhood in Edwardian Fiction Worlds Enough and Time*, by Adrienne E. Gavin and Andrew F. Humphries, (eds.), Palgrave Macmillan, London, 2009.
5   See Rosemary Hill, 'Wild waters are upon us', *Guardian*, 13 June 2009.East Riding of Yorkshire archives, file numbers DDX/381/17 onwards.
6   Keppel, *Edwardian Daughter*, p. 23.
7   H. D. C. Pepler, *His Majesty*. Headley Bros, London, 1905. p.35.
8   Ellen Key, *The Renaissance of Motherhood*, translated from the Swedish by Anna E. B. Fries. New York and London, G. P. Putnam's Sons, Knickerbocker Press, 1914, p.134–5.
9   H. D. C. Pepler, *His Majesty*. Headley Bros, London, 1905. p.35.
10 Quoted in H. D. C. Pepler, *His Majesty*. Headley Bros, London, 1905, p. 14.
11 Keppel, *Edwardian Daughter*, p. 34.
12 Ibid.
13 Ibid, p.31.
14 Quoted in Hardyment, *Dream Babies*, p.103.
15 Olive Everson, *Mrs Parsley Remembers – In the Shadow of the Big House. Recollections of a Suffolk Life*, Robert Blake, Lavenham, Suffolk, 1991.
16 Helen Campbell, *Practical Motherhood*, Longman, London, 1910. Quoted in Hardyment, *Dream Babies*, p.103, Sept. 1952.
17 Christina Hardyment, *Dream Babies: Childcare from Locke to Spock*, Jonathan Cape, London, 1983.
18 Lizzie Allen Harker, *Parallels: From A Romance of the Nursery*, John Lane, London and New York, 1903.
19 Quoted in Hardyment, *Dream Babies*, p.155.
20 *The Times*, February 1909, op. cit.

Chapter 3: Scout's Honour

1   Quoted in Tim Jeal, *Baden-Powell: Founder of the Boy Scouts*, Hutchinson, London, 1989, p.359..
2   Anne Colquhoun, Phil Lyon & Emily Alexander, 'Feeding minds and bodies: The Edwardian context of school meals', *Nutrition*

and Food Science, 2001, vol. 31, issue 3, pp. 117–25.

3   Miss E. F. M. Sowerbutts, file number 89/6/1, Imperial War Museum.

4   Quoted in Donald Read (ed.), *Documents from Edwardian England*, George Harrap, London, 1973, p.22.

5   Ibid. p.24.

6   *Report of the Inter-Departmental Committee on Physical Deterioration*, 1904, quoted in Read (ed.), *Documents from Edwardian England*, p.213.

7   S. C. Johnson, *A History of Emigration*, Routledge, London, 1913, quoted in Read (ed.), *Documents from Edwardian England*, pp.18–19.

8   Hardyment, *Dream Babies*, p.113.

9   Hodgson, Helen, *Mrs Blossom on Babies,* Scientific Press: London, 1909.

10 Quoted in Hardyment, *Dream Babies*, op. cit., p.97.

11 Quoted in Read (ed.), *Documents from Edwardian England*, p.220.

12 Everson, *Mrs Parsley Remembers*, p.19.

13 George Perry and Alan Aldridge, *The Penguin Book of Comics*, Penguin, London, 1989, p.54.

14 Simon Popple and Joe Kember, *Early Cinema: From Factory Gate to Dream Factory*, Wallflower Press, London, 2004, p.18.

15 Elsie Oman, *Salford Stepping Stones*, Neil Richardson, Manchester, 1983, p.11.

16 Quoted in Popple and Kember, *Early Cinema*, p.149.

17 Keppel, *Edwardian Daughter*, p.27.

18 http://www.bbc.co.uk/radio4/history/longview/longview_20030408.shtml. Accessed 13 October 2010.

19 Keppel, *Edwardian Daughter*, p.31.

20 Everson, *Mrs Parsley Remembers*, p.10.

21 Nordau, Max, *Degeneration,* D. Appleton, London: 1895.

22 Keppel, *Edwardian Daughter*, p. 90.

23 Keppel, *Edwardian Daughter*, p. 103.

24 Oman, *Salford Stepping Stones*, p. 19.

25 Quoted in Justine Picardie, 'How bad was J. M. Barrie?', *Telegraph*, 13 July 2008.

26 Hermione, Countess of Ranfurly, *The Ugly One: The Childhood Memoirs of Hermione, Countess of Ranfurly, 1913–1939*, Penguin, London, 1998, p.33.

27 Ranfurly, *The Ugly One*, p. 36.

28 Private papers of A. F. Uncle, Item 89/7/1, Imperial War Museum.

29 Oman, *Salford Stepping Stones*, p.19.

30 *Mrs Parsley Remembers*, p.37.

31 E. Sylvia Pankhurst, *The Home Front*, Century Hutchinson, London, 1987, p.20

32 Pankhurst, *The Home Front*, p. 248.

33 Pankhurst, *The Home Front*, p. 21.

34 Ranfurly, *The Ugly One*, p.83.

35 Ranfurly, *The Ugly One*, p.37–40.

36 Harry Watkin, *From Hulme All Blessings Flow – A Collection of Manchester Memories*, Neil Richardson, Manchester, 1985, p.20.

37 Quoted in Jeal, *Baden-Powell*, p.470.

38 *From Hulme All Blessings Flow*, p. 21.

39 *Headquarters Gazette*. November 1914.

40 Michael Rosenthal, *The Character Factory*, HarperCollins, London, 1986.

41 Jeal, *Baden-Powell*, p.471.

42 Speech by the Director General of the Security Service, Jonathan Evans, at Bristol University, 15 October 2009, https://www.mi5.gov.uk/output/mi5_defending_the_realm.html. Accessed 15 October 2010.

43 Jeal, *Baden-Powell*, p.471.

44 Private papers of W. H. Williams, documents 4045. Imperial War Museum.

45 Richard Van Emden, *Boy Soldiers of the Great War*, Headline, London, 2006.

46 Pankhurst, *The Home Front*, p. 275

47 See http://www.seayourhistory.org.uk/content/view/708/921. Accessed 15 October 2010.

48 See http://www.firstworldwar.com/diaries/aboysexperiences.htm. Accessed 15 October 2010.

49 Committee of Inquiry into Breaches of the Laws of War, First Interim Report January 1919.

50 Steve Humphries and Richard Van Emden, *All Quiet on the Home Front*: A Oral History of Life in Britain during the First World War, Headline, London, 2004, p. 180.

51 Day, *London Born*, p. 6.

52 Oman, *Salford Stepping Stones*, p. 125.

53 Watkin, *From Hulme All Blessings Flow*, p.23.

54 Ranfurly, *The Ugly One*, p.48.

Chapter 4: Between the Wars

1 Day, *London Born*.

2 Day, *London Born*, p. 28.

3   Martin Pugh, *We Danced All Night, A Social History of Britain Between the Wars*, Vintage, London, 2009.

4   Richard Overy, *The Morbid Age: Britain Between the Wars*, Allen Lane, London, 2009.

5   Emma Smith, *The Great Western Beach: A Memoir of a Cornish Childhood Between the Wars*, Bloomsbury, London, 2008, p. 17.

6   Smith, *The Great Western Beach* p. 8.

7   Ranfurly, *The Ugly One*, p. 122.

8   Ranfurly, *The Ugly One*, p. 130.

9   Ranfurly, *The Ugly One*, p. 103.

10 Frederick Truby King, *Feeding and Care of Baby*, Whitcombe and Tombs, Christchurch, New Zealand, 1907, OUP, 1945, p. 1.

11 King, *Feeding and Care of Baby*, p. 9.

12 See Overy, *The Morbid Age*, pp. 94–102.

13 Day, *London Born*, p. 17.

14 *Report of the Departmental Committee on Sterilisation*, HMSO, 1934.

15 Kenneth Wills, *What fathers should tell their sons*; Mary Schwarlieb, *What mothers must tell their children*: British Social Hygiene Council, London, 1925.

16 'Experimental tests of general intelligence,' quoted in Brian Evans and Bernard Waites, *IQ and Mental Testing: An Unnatural Science and its Social History*, Humanities Press, New Jersey, 1981, p. 55.

17 Cyril Burt, *The Young Delinquent*, University of London Press, London, 1925.

18 Pugh, *We Danced All Night*, p. 200.

19 Cyril Burt papers, University of Liverpool Special Collections andArchives. D191 26/3 Material relating to the Board of Education Consultative Committee

20 http://www.nationalarchives.gov.uk/podcasts/emigration-tocanada.htm. Accessed July 8, 2012.

21 Hickson, *Child Migrant From Liverpool*, p. 4.

22 Hickson, *Child Migrant From Liverpool*, p. 7.

23 Hickson, *Child Migrant From Liverpool*, p. 13.

24 Hickson, *Child Migrant From Liverpool*, p. 51.

25 Note by Anne Bott in Flo Hickson, *Flo: Child Migrant from Liverpool*, Plowright Press, Warwick, 1998, p. i.

26 John Lane, *Fairbridge Kid*, Fremantle Arts Centre, Fairbridge, Western Australia, 1990.

27 Speech to the Imperial Education Conference, copy in University of Liverpool Special Collections and Archives, File D191 26/3.

28 W. D. Wills, *Homer Lane. A Biography*, George Allen & Unwin, London, 1964, pp. 156–195.

29 Lane, Homer, *Talks to Parents and Teachers*, George Allen and Unwin, London, 1928, pp 188–193.
30 Interview with the author, April 2010.
31 National Archives, HO 144/21511.
32 Interview with the author, April 2010.
33 Also detailed in Bernard Kops, *The World is a Wedding*, first published by MacGibbon & Kee, London, 1963. This edition Five Leaves, Nottingham, 2008, p. 35.

Chapter 5: War Babies
1 Mass Observation, Diarist number 5223, Diary of K. Watts, Boy aged 15 years, 2 Frederick Street, Aldershot, Hampshire, 29 August–4 September 1939. Mass Observation Reports, University of Sussex Library Special Collections, ICHAP 5, p. 120.
2 London Metropolitan Archives, information leaflet no.32: http://217.154.230.218/NR/rdonlyres/96DAF40C-91DD-4E AA-A79F54D83E80F154/0/32THEEVACUATIONOFCHILDREN FROMTHECOUNTYOFLONDONDURINGTHESECONWO RLDWAR19391945.pdf. Accessed 16 December 2011.
3 Kops, *The World is a Wedding*, p. 50.
4 Ibid, p. 54.
5 http://www.bbc.co.uk/my-story/stories/sadness/171219/. Accessed 18 October 2010. Archive since removed.
6 Quoted in Martin Parsons, *War Child: Children Caught in Conflict*, Tempus Publishing, Stroud, Gloucestershire, 2008.
7 National Federation of Women's Institutes, *Town Children Through Country Eyes: A Survey on Evacuation, 1940*, Abinger, Surrey, 1943.
8 *Manchester Guardian*, 5 November 1939.
9 Anon, *Our Towns: A Close-Up*, Oxford University Press, London, 1943, p. iii.
10 Mass Observation File report 299, June 1940, University of Sussex Library Special Collections.
11 Kops, *The World is a Wedding*, p. 52.
12 6 August 1940.
13 Interview with the author, 6 April 2010.
14 http://www.historylearningsite.co.uk/blitz_and_world_war_ two.htm, http://www.historylearningsite.co.uk/children_and_ world_war_two.htm. Accessed 19 October 2010.
15 Kops, *The World is a Wedding*.
16 Professor Mary Davis, Centre for Trade Union Studies, London Metropolitan University, http://www.unionhistory.info/time-

line/1939_1945.php. Accessed 18 October 2010.

17 *Nursery World*, 26 August 2004, http://www.nurseryworld. co.uk/news/712786/Battling/. Accessed 18 October 2010.

18 HO/144/21511/National Archives: London.

19 Interview with the author, 2 June 2010.

20 Ibid.

21 Ibid.

22 Refugee Voices project, Association of Jewish Refugees in Great Britain. Accessed at the Weiner Library, London. Copyright of the Association of Jewish Refugees.

23 Mass Observation Report 299, June 1940, University of Sussex Library Special Collections.

24 http://www.wartimememories.co.uk/evacuation.html. Accessed July 8 2012.

25 Ibid.

26 *Guardian*, 17 February 1943.

27 Quoted in the *Guardian*, February 17 1943.

28 Richard M. Titmuss, *Problems of Social Policy*, HMSO, London, 1950, pp. 324–326 and 524–526.

29 Quoted by James Griffiths, *Hansard*, 16 July 1943, column 566, volume 391.

30 *Hansard*, 19 January 1944, column 207 volume 396.

Chapter 6: Born in the Ruins

1 Refugee Voices project, Association of Jewish Refugees in Great Britain.

2 Terence O'Neill, *Someone to Love Us*, HarperCollins, London, 2010.

3 For a more detailed account, see http://www.familylawweek. co.uk/site.aspx?i=ed70624. Accessed July 8, 2012.

4 Interview with the author, 24 June 2010.

5 Quoted in David Kynaston, *Family Britain 1951–57*, Bloomsbury, London, 2009, p. 570.

6 Andrew Holden, *Makers and Manners: Politics and Morality in Postwar Britain*, Politico's, London, 2004, p. 43.

7 *The Times*, June 19, 1953.

8 Interview with the author, 5 June 2010.

9 Interview with the author, 2 June 2010.

10 Michael Foreman, *After the War Was Over*, first published Pavilion Books, London, 1995. This edition Puffin Books, London, 1997, p. 59.

11 Ibid.

12 Ibid, p. 28.

13 Ibid, p. 40.
14 David Docherty, David Morrison and Michael Tracey, 'The last picture show?', 1987, quoted in *A Century of Change: Trends in UK Statistics Since 1900*, House of Commons Library.
15 Kathleen Box, *The Cinema and the Public*, Mass Observation Archive, University of Sussex
16 Foreman, *After the War Was Over*, p. 32.
17 Steve Holland, *The Mushroom Jungle: A History of Postwar Paperback Publishing*, Zeon Books, Wiltshire, 1993, p. 182.
18 Ibid.
19 Interview with the author, 2 June 2010.
20 Interview with the author, op. cit.
21 Ibid.
22 David Kynaston, *Austerity Britain, 1945–51*, Bloomsbury, London, 2007, p. 368
23 Ibid, p. 364–365.

Chapter 7: Children of the Social Revolution
1   See, for example, Tak Wing Chan and Brendan Halpin, *The Instability of Divorce Risk Factors in the UK*, 13 April 2008. users. ox.ac.uk/~sfos0006/papers/change8.pdf, accessed July 8, 2012.
2   Interview with the author, 26 August 2010.
3   Conservative Political Centre, *Unhappy families*, London, 1971.
4   *Guardian*, 5 and 17 September 1969.
5   Interview with the author, 20 August, 2010.
6   Interview with the author, 20 August 2010.
7   www.ncds.info. Accessed July 8, 2012.
8   3 June 1972.
9   Interview with the author, 5 June 2010.
10 John Barron Mays, *Education and the Urban Child*, Liverpool University Press, Liverpool, 1962.
11 Derek Gillard, *The Plowden Report*', www.infed.org/schooling/plowden_report.htm.
12 Ibid.
13 Interview with the author, 20 August 2010.
14 *Guardian*, 28 June 1971.
15 'Good children or happy ones?', *Observer*, 5 January 1964.
16 'British mums in arms', *Observer*, 12 January 1964.
17 'The private world of children's games', *Observer*, 6 August 1961.
18 Maureen Oswin, *The Empty Hours*, Allen Lane, London, 1971.
19 'Empty life in a full ward', *Guardian*, 5 August 1971.
20 Interview with the author, 20 August 2010.

21 1988 film in which Dustin Hoffman plays an autistic savant.

22 20 April 1968.

23 James Obelkevich and Peter Catterall (eds), *Understanding Post-War British Society*, Routledge, London, 1994, p. 147.

24 Birth Statistics Series. FM1, Office for National Statistics, London.

25 'The teenage adults', *Guardian*, 30 January 1970.

26 Sutherland, John, *Offensive Literature*, London, Junction Books, pp. 111–113.

27 6 July 1971.

28 1 April 1971.

29 'Children's rights and violence', 11 December 1971.

30 M. D. Phillips, 29 April 1971.

31 Interview with the author, 26 August 2010.

32 The Oz Trial: John Mortimer's Finest Moment, in *The First Post*, January 2009.

33 Martin Hoyles (ed.), *Changing Childhood*, Writers and Readers Publishing Co-operative, London, 1979.

34 Quoted in ibid.

35 John Holt, *Escape from Childhood*, Dutton, New York, 1974, p. 12.

36 Quoted in Sandra Robinson, *Children's Rights – Historic Developments*, Cumberland Lodge, Windsor, 2007, http://www.cumberlandlodge.ac.uk. Accessed 13 December 2010.

37 *Hansard*, 7 February 1979, column 712, volume 962.

38 Gitta Sereny, *Cries Unheard: The Story of Mary Bell*, Macmillan, London, 1998.

39 Ibid, p. 86.

64 Ibid, p. 124.

40 Ibid, p.19.

41 http://www.communitycare.co.uk/Articles/20/10/2005/51331/Knock-it-down-and-start-again.htm. Accessed 6 January 2012.

42 *Report of the Committee of Inquiry into the Care and Supervision Provided in Relation to Maria Colwell*, HMSO, London, 1974.

43 Ibid.

44 'Increase in violence against children', *Guardian*, 21 November 1969.

Chapter 8: Eighties to ASBOS
1 Interview with the author, 24 June 2010.

2 Colin Pritchard and Richard Williams, 'Comparing possible child abuse related deaths in England and Wales with the major developed countries, 1974–2006', *British Journal of Social Work*, 2009, PP. 1–19.

3   Interview with the author, op. cit.
4   See Marcus Crouch, *The Nesbitt Tradition: The Children's Novel 1945–1970*, Ernest Benn, London, 1972.
5   Interview with the author, 21 September 2010.
6   *Economist*, 12 December 1981.
7   Ibid., 1 May 1982.
8   Interview with the author, op. cit.
9   November 1981, http://www.amielandmelburn.org.uk/collections/mt/pdf/81_11_12.pdf. Accessed 14 December 2010.
10 Neil Postman, *The Disappearance of Childhood*, W. H. Allen, London, 1983, p. 77. John Sommerville, *The Rise and Fall of Childhood*, Sage, London, 1982, p. 29.
11 *Guardian*, 15 December 1987.
12 13 August 1974.
13 Sommerville *The Rise and Fall of Childhood*, p. 13.
14 *Hansard*, 10 March 1986, vol. 472, column 473–97.
15 *Guardian*, 21 December 1984.
16 20 October 1985.
17 Gitta Sereny, *The Invisible Children*, Pan, London, 1986, p. 217.
18 Jean Renvoize, *Incest – A Family Pattern*, Routledge & Kegan Paul, London, 1985. Reported in the *Guardian*, 27 November 1984. *Hansard*, 29 November 1985, vol. 87, columns 1117–34.
19 *Hansard*, 29 June 1987, vol. 118, columns 255–9.
20 http://www.bbc.co.uk/tees/content/articles/2007/05/29/cleveland_child_abuse_2_feature.shtml. Accessed 14 December 2010.
21 Bryan Appleyard, 'Children speared on the horns of a demonic dilemma', *Sunday Times*, 30 September 1990.
22 'Satanic ritual forces families to suffer from a hell on earth', *Sunday Times*, 1 April 1990.
23 'Satanic Verses', *Guardian*, 10 September 1994.
24 *Daily Mail*, 20 February 1993.
25 Wellingborough, 19 February 1993.
26 6 February 1994.
27 *Hansard*, 30 November 1995, column 716, volume 267.
28 'How we make demons of children', 28 November 1993.
29 'Time to let the children play (and live)', 9 April 1994.
30 C. Pritchard and T. Sayers, 'Exploring potential "extra-familial" child homicide assailants in the UK and estimating their homicide rate: perception of risk – the need for debate', *British Journal of Social Work*, vol. 2008, issue 2, pp. 38, 290–307.
31 'We did not want to tempt fate', *Daily Mail*, 15 March 1994.
32 *Hansard*, 6 February 1990, vol. 515, column 782–827.

33 *Daily Mail,* 17 February, 1993.
34 Nan Spowart, 'The death of innocence', 3 September 1998.
35 'Battery children', *Independent,* 2 September 1999.
36 Interview with the author, 16 November 2007, published in *The Times,* 22 January 2008.
37 Department of Children, Schools and Families, Children's Plan, 2008, https:www.education.gov.uk/publications/eOrderingDownload/Children's_plan_summary.pdf. Accessed 20 December 2010.
38 'Policies towards poverty, inequality and exclusion since 1997', Joseph Rowntree Foundation, York, 2005, http://www.jrf.org.uk/sites/files/jrf/0015.pdf. Accessed 20 December 2010.
39 *Hansard,* 16 February 2000, columns 233–305.
40 http://www.education.gov.uk/childrenandyoungpeople/neathandwellbeing/60074766/uncrc, accessed 12.7.12.
41 Jonathan Bradshaw and Emese Mayhew (eds.), *The Well-Being of Children in the UK,* second edition, Save the Children, London, 2005. First published 2002, http://www.york.ac.uk/inst/spru/wellbeingsummary.pdf. Accessed 20 December 2010.
42 Sarah L. Holloway and Gill Valentine, *Cyberkids – Children in the Information Age,* Routledge Falmer, London, 2003, pp. 1–2. 'Extra tuition damaging children', *Scotsman,* 26 September 2000.
43 20 October 2009.
44 'No child must suffer from overprotection', 19 July 2000.
45 'Children Are At Risk – From Their Terrified Parents', 7 February 1999.
46 Sue Palmer, *Toxic Childhood,* Orion, London, 2007.

Conclusion
1 Somerville, *The Rise and Fall of Childhood.*
2 Interview with the author, 13 November 2007
3 William Blake, *A Cradle Song, Songs of Innocence and Experience, The Illuminated Books,* William Blake Trust/Princeton University Press, Princeton, New Jersey, 1998. First Published 1974.
4 'Tintern Abbey', http://www.blupete.com/Literature/Poetry/WordsworthTinternAbbey.htm. Accessed 21 December 2010.
5 Gina Ford, *The New Contented Little Baby Book: The Secret to Calm and Confident Parenting,* Vermilion, London, 2006, p. 29.
6 See, for example, Allison James, Chris Jenks and Alan Prout, *Theorising Childhood,* Polity, Cambridge, 1998.
7 http://www.ons.gov.uk/ons/rel/social_trends_rd/social_trends/-no__30__2000_edition/index.html. Accessed 12.07.12.

Epilogue

1   *Idealizing Parenthood to Rationalize Parental Investments*, Richard P. Eibach and Steven E. Mock, Psychological Science *February* 2011 vol. 22 no. 2 203 – 208.

2   ONS labour market statistics, table A06. Educational status, economic activity and inactivity of young people. http://www.ons.gov.uk/ons/rel/lms/labour-market-statistics/march-2012/table-a06.xls

3   John Sommerville, p. 9, op cit.

4   See Zelizer, Viviana A., *Pricing the Priceless Child: The changing social value of children*, New York: Basic Books, 1985.

5   *Idealizing Parenthood to Rationalize Parental Investments*, Richard P. Eibach and Steven E. Mock, Op Cit.

6   http://www.huffingtonpost.com/tyler-moss/generationy_b_1354104.html, accessed 6 July, 2012.

7   *Demand for Higher Education to 2020 and Beyond*, Bahram Bekhradnia, www.hepi.ac.uk/files/31HEDemandto2020andb8yondsummary.doc, accessed July 6, 2012.

8   From 'Reading The Riots', published by the *Guardian* in conjunction with the London School of Economics, December 12, 2011. Quoted by Theresa May in the *Mail on Sunday*, December 18, 2011.

9   *Salford Star*, 9/8/11.

10 *Riots, Communities and Victims Panel, 5 Days in August: An interim report on the 2011 English Riots*. http://riotspanel.independent.gov.uk/wp-content/uploads/2012/04/Interim-report-5-Days-in-August.pdf. Accessed 13 July, 2012.

11 *Unemployment in Interwar Britain*, Professor Barry Eichengreen, *ReFresh*, Volume 8, Spring 1989. http://www.ehs.org.uk/ehs/refresh/assets/Eichengreen8a.pdf. Accessed July 6, 2012.

12 Ibid.

13 Interviews with the author.

14 Interview with the *Guardian*: http://www.guardian.co.uk/fashion/2012/jan/20/weekender-francesca-omojudi.

15 Riots, communities and victims panel, op. cit.

Bibliography

BOOKS

Allen Harker, Lizzie, 1903. *Parallels: From A Romance of the Nursery*. London: John Lane.

Anon, 1912. *The Cruelty Man: Actual Experiences of an Inspector of the NSPCC Graphically Told by Himself.* London: NSPCC.

Aries, Philippe, 1962. *Centuries of Childhood*. New York: Vintage.

Blake, William, 1794. *Songs of Innocence and Experience*. The Illuminated Books edition, 1998. New Jersey: The William Blake Trust/Princeton University Press.

Burt, Cyril, 1925. *The Young Delinquent*. London: University of London Press.

Campbell, Beatrix, 1997. *Unofficial Secrets: Child Sexual Abuse: The Cleveland Case*. London: Virago.

Campbell, Helen, 1910. *Practical Motherhood,* London: Longman.

Cohen, Phil, 1997. *Children of the Revolution*. London: Lawrence & Wishart.

Conway, Ambrose, 2007. *The Reso*. Oxford: Kings Hart Books.

Crawford, Elizabeth, 1999. *The Women's Suffrage Movement: A Reference Guide 1866–1928*. London: Routledge.

Crawford, Elizabeth, 2002. *Enterprising Women: The Garretts and their Circle*. London: Francis Boutle.

Crouch, Marcus, 1972. *The Nesbitt Tradition: The Children's Novel 1945–1970,* London: Ernest Benn.

Darnton, Robert, 1984. *The Great Cat Massacre and Other Episodes in French Cultural History*. London: Allen Lane.

Davies, Andrew, 2008. *The Gangs of Manchester: The Story of the Scuttlers – Britain's First Youth Cult*. Preston: Milo Books.

Day, Sidney, 2004. *London Born*. Compiled and edited by Helen Day. London: Fourth Estate.

Dorling, Daniel, 2010. *Injustice: Why Inequality Persists*. Bristol: Policy Press.

Dyhouse, Carol, 1981. *Girls Growing up in Late Victorian and Edwardian England*. London: Routledge & Kegan Paul.

Evans, Brian and Waites, Bernard, 1981. *IQ and Mental Testing: An Unnatural Science and its Social History*. New Jersey: Humanities Press.

Everson, Olive, 1991. *Mrs Parsley Remembers – In the Shadow of the Big House. Recollections of a Suffolk Life*. Lavenham, Suffolk: Robert Blake.

Foley, Alice, 1973. *A Bolton Childhood*. Manchester: University of Manchester Extra-Mural Department and the North Western District of the WEA.

Ford, Gina, 2006. *The New Contented Little Baby Book: The Secret to Calm and Confident Parenting*. London: Vermilion.

Foreman, Michael, 1989. *War Boy: A Wartime Childhood*. London: Pavilion.

Foreman, Michael, 1995. *After the War Was Over*. London: Pavilion Books. This edition London: Puffin Books, 1997.

Gavin, Adrienne E., and Humphries, Andrew F. (eds.), 2009. *Childhood in Edwardian Fiction*. London: Palgrave Macmillan.

Gribble, David (ed.) 1987, *That's All Folks: Dartington Hall School Remembered: Reminiscences and Reflections of Former Pupils*. Crediton, Devon: West Aish Publishing.

Hardyment, Christina, 1983. *Dream Babies: Childcare from Locke to Spock*. London: Jonathan Cape.

Hickson, Flo, 1998. *Flo: Child Migrant from Liverpool*. Warwick: Plowright Press.

Holden, Andrew, 2004. *Makers and Manners: Politics and Morality in Postwar Britain*. London: Politico's.

Holland, Steve, 1993. *The Mushroom Jungle: A History of Postwar Paperback Publishing*. Wiltshire: Zeon Books.

Holloway, Sarah L. and Valentine, Gill, 2003. *Cyberkids – Children in the Information Age*. London: RoutledgeFalmer.

Holt, John C. *Escape From Childhood*. New York: Dutton.

Hoyles, Martin (ed.), 1979. *Changing Childhood*. London: Writers and Readers Publishing Co-operative.

Humphries, Steve, and Van Emden, Richard, 2003. *All Quiet on the Home Front: An Oral History of Life in Britain during the First World War*. London: Headline.

Jackson, Louise A. Family, community and the regulation of sexual abuse: London 1870–1914. In: Fletcher, A. and Hussey, S., eds, 1999. *Childhood in Question. Children, Parents and the State*. Manchester: Manchester University Press.

James, Allison, Jenks, Chris and Prout, Alan, 1998. *Theorising Childhood*. Cambridge: Polity.

Jeal, Tim, 1989. *Baden-Powell: Founder of the Boy Scouts*. London: Hutchinson.

Jordan, Jane, 2001. *Josephine Butler*. London: John Murray.

Keppel, Sonia, 1958. *Edwardian Daughter*. London: Hamish Hamilton.

Key, Ellen, 1914. *The Renaissance of Motherhood*. Translated from Swedish by Anna E. B. Fries. New York, London: G.P. Putnam's Sons.

Kops, Bernard, 1963. *The World is a Wedding, From East End to Soho*. London: MacGibbon and Kee. This edition Nottingham: Five Leaves, 2008.

Kynaston, David, 2007. *Austerity Britain, 1945–51*. London: Bloomsbury.

Kynaston, David, 2009. *Family Britain 1951–57*. London: Bloomsbury.

Lane, John, 1990. *Fairbridge Kid*. Fairbridge, Western Australia: Fremantle Arts Centre.

Masefield, John, 1911. *The Street of Today*. London: Dent.

Mayall, Berry and Morrow, Virginia, 2011. *You Can Help Your Country: English Children's Work during the Second World War*. London: Institute of Education.

Mays, John Barron, 1962. *Education and the Urban Child*. Liverpool: Liverpool University Press.

Neill, Alexander Sutherland, 1972. *Neill! Neill! Orange Peel!* New York: Hart.

Nowell-Smith, Simon. (ed.), 1964. *Edwardian England, 1901–1914*. Oxford: Oxford University Press.

Obelkevich, James and Catterall, Peter (eds.), 1994. *Understanding Post-War British Society*. London: Routledge.

Oman, Elsie, 1983. *Salford Stepping Stones*. Manchester: Neil Richardson.

O'Neill, Terence, 2010. *Someone to Love Us*. London: HarperCollins.

Oswin, Maureen, 1971. *The Empty Hours*. London: Allen Cape.

Overy, Richard, 2009. *The Morbid Age: Britain Between the Wars*. London: Allen Lane.

Palmer, Sue, 2007. *Toxic Childhood*. London: Orion.

Pankhurst, E. Sylvia, 1932. *The Home Front.*, London: Century Hutchinson.

Parsons, Martin, 2008. *War Child: Children Caught in Conflict*. Stroud, Gloucestershire: Tempus Publishing.

Pepler, Douglas, 1915. *Justice and the Child*. London: Constable.

Pepler, H. D. C., 1905. *His Majesty*. London: Headley Bros.

Perry, George, and Aldridge, Alan, 1989. *The Penguin Book Of Comics*. London: Penguin.

Popple, Simon and Kember, Joe. 2004. *Early Cinema: From Factory Gate to Dream Factory*. London: Wallflower Press.

Postman, Neil, 1983. *The Disappearance of Childhood*: London, W. H. Allen.

Pugh, Martin, 2008. *We Danced All Night: A Social History of Britain Between the Wars*. London: Bodley Head.

Ranfurly, Hermione, Countess of, 1998. *The Ugly One: The Childhood Memoirs of Hermione, Countess of Ranfurly, 1913–1939*. London: Penguin.

Read, Donald, 1973. *Documents from Edwardian England*. London: George Harrap.

Renvoize, Jean, 1985. *Incest – A Family Pattern*. London: Routledge & Kegan Paul.

Rose, Lionel, 1986. *Massacre of the Innocents: Infanticide in Great Britain, 1800–1939*. London: Routledge.

Rose, Lionel, 1991. *The Erosion of Childhood: Child Oppression in Britain 1860–1918*. London: Routledge.

Rose, Nikolas, 1985. *The Psychological Complex: Psychology, Politics and Society in England 1869–1939* . London: Routledge Kegan Paul.

Rosenthal, Michael, 1986. *The Character Factory*. London: HarperCollins.

Rowntree, B. S., 1901. *Poverty: A study of Town Life*. London: Macmillan. Reprinted. Bristol: The Policy Press, 2000.

Schaffer, H. Rudolph, 2004. *Introducing Child Psychology*. Oxford: Blackwell.

Sereny, Gitta, 1986. *The Invisible Children*, London: Pan.

Sereny, Gitta, 1998. *Cries Unheard: The Story of Mary Bell*. London: Macmillan.

Skidelsky, Robert , 1969. *English Progressive Schools*. Harmondsworth, Middlesex: Penguin Books.

Slater, Nigel, 2003. *Toast*. London: Fourth Estate.

Smith, Emma, 2008. *The Great Western Beach: A Memoir of a Cornish Childhood Between the Wars*. London: Bloomsbury.

Sommerville, John, 1982. *The Rise and Fall of Childhood*. London: Sage.

Summerfield, Penny, 'Women, war and social change: women in Britain in World War Two'. In: Marwick, Arthur, 1988. *Total War and Social Change*. London: Macmillan.

Sutherland, John, 1982. *Offensive Literature*: London, Junction Books.

Titmuss, Richard M., 1950. *Problems of Social Policy*, London: HMSO/Longmans.

Tomalin, Claire, 2000. *Jane Austen: A Life*. London: Penguin Celebrations.

Truby King, Frederick, 1907. *Feeding and Care of Baby*. Christchurch, New Zealand: The Royal New Zealand Society for the Health of Women and Children, distributed by OUP, 1945.

Van Emden, Richard, 2006. *Boy Soldiers of the Great War*. London: Headline.

Wagner, Gillian, 1982. *Children of the Empire*. London: Weidenfeld and Nicolson.

Watkin, Harry, 1985. *From Hulme All Blessings Flow – A Collection of Manchester Memories*. Manchester: Neil Richardson.

Wills, W. D, 1964. *Homer Lane. A Biography*. London: George Allen & Unwin.

Yorke, Katherine, 1998. *The Strange Family at Yorke's Hill*. Norfolk: Lark's Press.

Zelizer, Viviana, 1985. *Pricing the Priceless Child*. New York: Basic Books.

JOURNALS

Colquhoun, Anne, Lyon, Phil and Alexander, Emily, 2001. 'Feeding minds and bodies: The Edwardian context of school meals'. Nutrition and Food Science, 31(3), pp. 117–125

Pritchard, C., and Sayers, T., 2008. 'Exploring potential "extra-familial" child homicide assailants in the UK and estimating their homicide rate: perception of risk – the need for debate'. *British Journal of Social Work*, 36, p290–307.

Pritchard, Colin and Williams, Richard, 2009. 'Comparing possible child abuse related deaths in England and Wales with the major developed countries, 1974–2006'. *British Journal of Social Work*, 2009, pp. 1–19

Rapp, Dean, 1990. 'The early discovery of Freud by the British general reading Public', 1912–1919. *Social History of Medicine*, 3, pp. 217–45.

Soloway, Richard, 1982. 'Counting the degenerates: The statistics of race deterioration in Edwardian England'. *Journal of Contemporary History*, 17, pp. 137–64.

OTHER PRINTED PUBLICATIONS

Anon, 1943. *Our Towns: A Close-Up*. Oxford: Oxford University Press.

Allen, Grahame, and Hicks, Joe, 1999. *A Century of Change: Trends in UK Statistics since 1900*. House of Commons Library.

Barlow, Sir Thomas, 1917. *The Incidence of Venereal Diseases and its Relation to School Life and School Teaching*. (An address delivered at the AGM of the Incorporated Association of Head Masters, January 1917) National Council for Combating Venereal Diseases.

Birth Statistics. Series FM1. London: Office For National Statistics.

Bradshaw, Jonathan and Mayhew, Emese, (eds.), 2002. *The Well-Being of Children in the UK*. London: Save the Children.

Committee of Inquiry into Breaches of the Laws of War, 1919. First Interim Report.

Conservative Political Centre, 1971. *Unhappy Families*. London.

Department of Children, Schools and Families, 2008. *Children's Plan*.

Great Britain Committee of Inquiry into the Care and Supervision Provided in Relation to Maria Colwell, *Report of the Committee of Inquiry into the Care and Supervision Provided in Relation to Maria Colwell*, 1974. London: HMSO.

Great Britain Departmental Committee on Sterilisation, *Report of the Departmental Committee on Sterilisation*, 1934. London: HMSO.

Joseph Rowntree Foundation, 2005. *Policies Towards Poverty, Inequality and Exclusion since 1997*. York.

National Federation of Women's Institutes, 1943. *Town Children Through Country Eyes: A Survey on Evacuation*, 1940. Abinger, Surrey.

Scharblieb, Mary, 1925. *What Mothers Must Tell Their Children*. London: British Social Hygiene Council. 12th edition, 1931.

Webb, Martha Beatrice, 1917. *The Teaching of Children as to the Reproduction of Life*. London: National Council for Combating Venereal Diseases. 6th edition, 1922.

Wills, Kenneth, 1925. *What Fathers Should Tell Their Sons*. London: British Social Hygiene Council.

ARCHIVE MATERIALS

Child Migration. DO 35 686/7. London: National Archives.

Cyril Burt papers, University of Liverpool Special Collections and Archives.

Dartington Hall School and other 'disturbances'. HO 144/21511. London: National Archives.

Diary of Atkinson Skinner zDDX389/1 1 Apr 1882–26 Jun 1888. Beverley: East Riding of Yorkshire Archive and Local Studies Service

Mass Observation Reports, University of Sussex library Special Collections.

Private papers of Miss E. F. M. Sowerbutts, file no. 89/6/1. London: Imperial War Museum.

Private papers of A. F. Uncle. Documents 120. London: Imperial War Museum.

Private papers of W. H. Williams. Documents.4045. London: Imperial War Museum.

Refugee Voices project, Association of Jewish Refugees in Great Britain. Accessed at the Weiner Library, London. Copyright of the Association of Jewish Refugees.

Index

Boy Scouts (*cont.*)
World War I casualties 79, 83
World War I service 77–80, 85
boys, leisure 62
Boys' Brigade 61–2
Brady, Ian 190–1
Brameld, William 33–4
bread 56–7
breast-feeding 48, 60, 150
Briddock, Alan 152–4, 172–3
British Communist Party 158
British Hygiene Council 98
British Paediatric Association 181
British Trust for Ornithology 112
British Union of Fascists 117–18
Brookes, George 33
Brown, Dorothy 130
Brown, Edward Vipont 48
Brown, Flo 107–8
Brown, Gwynneth 107, 108
Brown, Martin 192–3, 220
Buckmaster, Viscount 210
Bulger, James, murder of 3, 220–3, 225, 233
Burgess, George 194
Burt, Cyril 98, 99–105, 110
Bury and Norwich Post 32, 36
Butler, Josephine 14–15
Butler, 'Rab' 140–1

Cable Street, Battle of 117–18
Campbell, Helen 51
Campbell, Janet 29
Camps, Francis 198
Canada, child migration to 106, 109, 135–6
cancer, and diet 235
cannabis 182
Cannell, Phillis 140
Cannon, Richard 148–9, 159
care, freedom from 201–2
Care and Feeding of Children (Holt) 61
career options 203, 205, 248
Carlile, Kimberley 198
Carrington, C. A. 130–1
Chelsea Babies Club 94
Chelsea Boys 19–20
Chester, HMS 83
Chesterton, G. K. 98
child abuse 144–7, 202
battered child syndrome 198
missed warnings 195, 196, 197, 199
recognition of problem 194–9

sexual 215–19
child consumerism 227, 248
child development 244
Bowlby's theory of attachment 150
stages 93–4, 174
child development movement 52
child indoctrination, inter-war years 113–17
child migration
inter-war years 105–9
World War II 135
child murderers 101–5, 192–4, 220–3
child murders 190–4, 202, 224, 237
child neglect 12–13
child prostitution 14–15, 212
child psychology 48, 94
child rearing
Edwardian approach 48–52
natural approach 48
child sex-trafficking 14
child sexual abuse 15, 215–19
child starvation 12–13
child wellbeing 230–8, 244
childcare experts
Edwardian 48–52
inter-war years 95, 96
childcare manuals 60
childhood, changing attitudes to 1–8, 187–90
childishness, importance of 42–3
children
added value 228–9
as burden 209–10
financial liability of 247–8
investment in 245
as investment in the future 240
as lifestyle choice 225
myths about 240–2
parental fears about 223–5, 228
purpose of 208
put first 195, 223–5
role of 246
state investment in 243–4
Children Act 1948 146–7
Children and Young Persons (Harmful Publications) Act, 1955 158
children first 195, 223–5
Children's Act 1908 104
Children's Angry Brigade 185
Children's Charter 9–15
Children's Commissioner for England 5–6
Children's Express 229
children's homes, sexual

abuse accusations 216
Children's Legal Centre 213
children's literature
career novels 204–5
Edwardian 44–5
girls 204–5
inter-war years 95–6
children's mental health system 181
Children's Overseas Reception Board 135–6
children's rights 5, 185–6, 189–90, 199, 213, 214–15, 234, 242
Children's Rights (magazine) 185
Child's Play 3 (film) 221
Christian Action Research Education Campaigns 212
Churchill, Winston 139
cigarettes 56
cinema 63–4, 156–7
City of Benares, SS, sinking of 135–6
Clark, Gill and Neil 225
class divide, the 66–9
Cleveland child sexual abuse case 216–18
Clinton, Hillary Rodham 189
Cold War, the 155–9, 203–4
collective investment 243–4
Colwell, Maria 194–9
Colwell, Pauline 194–5, 195–7
Colwell, Raymond 195–6
Comăneci, Nadia 203–4
Comic Cuts 63
comics and comic strips 62–3, 157–8
communism 115–17
Communist Sunday Schools 115–16
comprehensive schools 175–6
computers 236
Condon, John 82–3
confidence 253
conformity, post-war 149–50
Connor, John 20
consent, age of 15
Conservative Political Centre 168–9
Contented Little Baby Book (Ford) 243
contraception 59, 184, 212–13
Coon, Caroline 215
Cooper, Bob and Doris 195, 196
Copsey, Emma 32
Cornwell, Jack 83
corruption, fear of 241–2
Court, David 181
crime 100
Criminal Law Amendment Act 15
criminal punishment 104

criminality, and childhood
   experience 193–4
Crompton, Richmal 96
Croydon High School 28
cruelty 3
Cuban Missile Crisis 159
Curry, Bill 113, 118, 131

Daily Mail 22, 59, 63, 115, 221–2,
   225, 235
Daily News 104
Daily Telegraph 116, 238
Daily Worker 116
Dalgety, Susan 237
dangers 32–3, 219–20
Dartington Hall School 111–13,
   118, 130–2
Darwin, Charles 51, 98, 105
Darwinism 51
Davies, Maureen 219
Dawson, Judith 218
Day, Sidney 75–6, 86, 89–92,
   97
de Vere Stacpoole, Henry 45
de Witt, Dorothy 131
death, attitude to 33–4
defective children 100
Degeneration (Nordau) 55–6,
   71
Denham, Buckinghamshire
   122–3, 128–9
Dennis, Felix 187
dependency 189
Derwent, Lord 170
deserting fathers 167–9
Devine, Alexander 20–1
Dewar, Dora 81
Dick Barton (radio crime
   series) 163–4
Dickens, Charles 12, 19
diet 4, 34, 56–7, 74, 140, 227,
   235, 242
disabled children
   changing attitudes to
      178–81
   special schools advocated
      100
*Disappearance of Childhood,
The* (Postman) 207–8
discipline, Locke on 2
disease
   danger of 32–3
   evacuees 125
   World War II deaths 139
disposable income 182, 245
disturbed children 169–70
divorce 167–9, 211, 223, 225, 251
doing nothing 163
Downey, Lesley Ann 191
Dowse, Natalie 201–4
Dr.Barnardo's homes 46–7
dress

Edwardian 47–8
   Scuttlers 21
   and youth culture 160–1
drinking 24, 98, 233, 242
drugs and drug abuse 182–3,
   184, 233
Dulwich College Preparatory
   School 236
dummies 60
Dundee 57, 60
Dyer, Amelia 37–8

Eagle (comic) 157
Economist, the 206
Edinburgh Evening News 237
education
   driving up standards 233
   elementary 29–30
   European refugee presence
      130–1
   evacuees and 124
   free secondary 153
   girls 28–9, 203, 205
   grammar school applica-
      tions 154–5
   inter-war years 109–17, 118
   investment in 244
   late-Victorian 25–30
   liberal 174–5
   mixed sex classes 22–3
   national curriculum 233
   and the Plowden Report
      174–5
   pre-school 233–4
   private 27–8
   private lessons 173–4
   progressive 109–17, 118
   reform 140–1, 172–6
   religious 26
   state role 6
   during World War I 81
   and youth violence 22–4
Education Act 1944 140–1, 153
educational under-achievement 234, 236, 252–3
Edward VII, King 41, 47, 68
Elementary Education Act
   1870 25–6, 28, 39
eleven plus exam 100, 153, 154,
   155, 173–4
Elizabeth II, Queen, marriage
   147–8
Ella from the West Country
   229
Elton, Lord 27
emboldenment, children's
   181–2
emigration 60
Émile, Ou de l'éducationi
   (Rousseau) 2
emotional capital 248
emotional investment 17

Empire Settlement Act 1923
   106
Englishness 53
Enlightenment, the 2, 92–3
errands 77
Estonia, refugees from 155–6
eugenics 97–9
evacuees 106, 121–9
   sent overseas 135–7
Evans, Edward 190–1
Everson, Olive 50, 57, 62, 66–7,
   69, 74
evil 3, 193, 220, 241, 246
evolution 51

Factory Acts 13
Fairbridge, Kingsley 106, 108
false expectations 254
family
   breakdown 223
   Edwardian 47
   importance as social unit
      15–16
   late-Victorian times 15–19
   loss of power 6
   post-war 148–51
   power relations 242–3
   sanctity of 225
Family Allowances 127, 140, 151
Family and Youth Concern 212
family size
   decline in 5, 58–9, 94–5,
      147, 245
   need for large 139
Farley, Albert 82–3
fathers
   deserting 167–9
   post-war 149
Fawcett, Millicent Garrett 28
feelings, expression of 230–3
Feldman, Marty 187
femininity, Edwardian 47
films, featuring Satanic
   children 220
Firestone, Shulamith 187–8,
   202
Firth Park Grammar School
   153–4
Fisher Boys 160
flogging 20
Foley, Alice 1–2, 16–17, 24,
   29–30, 33–4
food additives 227
Ford, Gina 243
Foreman, Michael 132–3, 141,
   154, 155, 155–6, 157, 158–9,
   160–1
Forster, William 25, 28, 39
Foucault, Michel 188–9
Fox, Penny 224
freedom 42, 213–14, 246
fresh air, benefits of 95